Lonely planet

Offbeat

100 AMAZING PLACES AWAY FROM THE TOURIST TRAIL

Intro

Long waits for the vaporetto in Venice. Fighting for space to snap Angkor Wat's famous sunrise. Congested trails in the USA's most beloved national parks. And annoyed (and outnumbered) locals wondering what has happened to their homes and backyards amid the crowds. If this sounds familiar, you've probably seen overtourism in action.

The number of people travelling internationally has grown steadily since the 1950s, an era that was widely regarded as the 'golden age of air travel' in the West – despite the fact that air fares in that decade were extortionate compared with what they are today. Intense airline competition, falling fares and increases in disposable incomes are just some of the key reasons why travel has boomed in the past few decades: pre-pandemic, the United Nations World Tourism Organization recorded around 1.5 billion annual international tourist arrivals globally. But where do 1.5 billion people go?

The problem is, not all destinations are created equal in the eyes of tourists. In recent years we have cultivated homogenous travel desires whereby, often, we're all striving towards the same experiences. We collectively dream of seeing the Eiffel Tower in Paris (check), the USA's Grand Canyon (check) or the Hong Kong skyline from Victoria Peak (check). I, like many others, have been guilty of gathering these travel adventures like a kid hoarding sweets.

In the past five years or so, the rise of the term 'overtourism' — the problem of having too many tourists in a destination — has come to represent our increasing acknowledgement of how intense tourism can take its toll on environments and communities

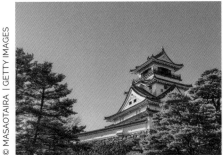

© MASAOTAIRA | GETTY IMAGES

© EKKACHAI PHOLROJPANYA | GETTY IMAGES

around the globe. With this in mind, *Offbeat* was born out of a desire to spotlight alternatives to the world's well-trammelled travel highlights.

Between these pages, the term 'offbeat' encompasses everything from overlooked second cities in Europe to remote islands off Africa and off-the-beaten track ruins in Asia. Some of the places covered here are more well known than others, reflecting the diversity in our readers' own experiences. You'll find direct alternatives to popular destinations that have become uncomfortably crowded, but there are also many inclusions that stand alone as unique destinations you just might not have thought of visiting before.

Travelling beyond the classic honeypot destinations is a terrific way to spread your money to corners of the globe where local people desperately need it. Lonely Planet has always been a passionate advocate of travel as a force for good. Even in the busiest of destinations, you can have a positive impact by spending money with local businesses and supporting those that give back to the places they operate in. But travel further afield to places where tourists are few and far between and your visit has the potential to make a real difference to people's lives, creating incomes and opportunities that can empower entire communities.

The COVID-19 pandemic gave us the opportunity to reset our travel patterns and make tourism more sustainable for the future. Dispersing travellers more equally across the globe is key. The tantalising question now is: where do you want to go? Hopefully this book can provide some new answers.

Lorna Parkes, Editor

Palm Island, Australia **p296**

Sunshine Coast Trail, Canada **p120**

Eastern Cape, South Africa

Contents

100 AMAZING PLACES AWAY FROM THE TOURIST TRAIL

Tatra Mountains, Poland **p258**

Yogyakarta's temples, Indonesia **p70**

Africa
& the Middle East

The 18th-century
Agha Bozorg Mosque
in Kashan, Iran

Algeria

THE SLUMBERING NORTH AFRICAN GIANT WITH A LEGENDARY SAHARAN HEART

Africa's largest country lies just a short hop from Europe. The north, with its snow-flecked mountains and stunning coastline, is home to cosmopolitan and charismatic cities such as Algiers and Constantine, as well as some of the most magnificent Roman sites in existence – Timgad and Djemila are both vast, perfectly preserved Roman towns with barely another tourist in sight. Algeria's other big draw is

its extraordinary Saharan region. Whether it's a glimpse of the sand seas that surround Timimoun, or the burnt-red mountains of the far south, these are the desert landscapes of legend.

Yet for all Algeria's peach-coloured dunes and grand ruins, the country only receives around 30,000 tourists a year, the vast majority of which are people coming from France to visit family members. A complex recent history and perceptions of safety in the country are the most likely reasons for the lack of visitors, yet Algeria has improved security immensely in recent years and for much of the country there are no significant issues for travellers.

GO IF YOU LIKE…

- 🤍 *pyramids of Giza, Egypt*
- 🤍 *Morocco*
- 🤍 *temples of Angkor, Cambodia*
- 🤍 *ancient sites*
- 🤍 *epic desert landscapes*
- 🤍 *welcoming people*

Why go to Algeria?

Since the horrors of the *décennie noir*, the civil war of the 1990s, the country has enjoyed a period of peace. Algerians are slowly rebuilding their country, often in the face of crushing bureaucratic inertia. Cultural festivals are springing up and chic shops and restaurants are common on the bustling streets of Algiers, Oran and Constantine. The government has loosened restrictions on private ownership of hotels, something that would have been unthinkable 20 years ago.

There is no doubt that visiting here is a challenge. But Algeria has never lost its mystique and you'll quickly discover that there are so many world-class places to visit. Almost all of them are not only safe, but crying out for the visitors they so richly deserve.

GETTING THERE

Assuming your visa is in order, getting in and out of Algeria is normally a fast and pain-free affair. The vast majority of visitors arrive in Algeria by air. In general, there's not much of a public transport network between airports and ferry ports and city centres, but there are always plenty of taxis, and they don't tend to charge new arrivals much over the odds.

WHEN TO GO

Mar–Jul

The north literally blossoms in the spring; warm, dry days are perfect for exploring sprawling Roman sites.

AMAZING CROWD-FREE EXPERIENCES

 Savour the rare beauty of Algiers, a city that never fails to make an impression. Climb to the hillside Casbah and enjoy seafood fresh from the Bay of Algiers.

 See Roman history come alive in Djemila, one of North Africa's most spectacular ancient cities. Linger in the temples and markets, and stroll the bath chambers.

 Spend time in the lovely old city of Constantine, set in a natural gorge with a rich architectural legacy of magnificent bridges.

 Strike out into the dunes of the Grand Erg Occidental from the red oasis town of Timimoun, one of the most beautiful of the Sahara.

 Drink in the glorious vision of Timgad, one of the finest Roman sites in existence.

 Bargain for a boldy patterned carpet in the main square of Ghardaïa, peeking at a pristine medieval town and then swimming in the shade of date palms.

Above: Founded around 100 CE, Timgad has ancient ruins that are among Africa's finest Roman remains

Sinai Trail

HIKE WITH BEDOUIN INTO THE WILD ON EGYPT'S FIRST LONG-DISTANCE PATH

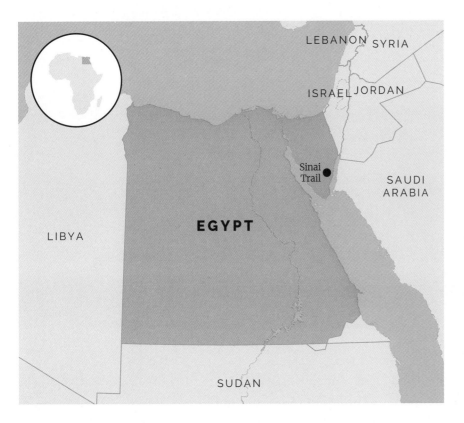

Most visitors to Egypt's Sinai peninsula only view the jagged peaks of the region's mountains as a dusky backdrop to the beach and Red Sea resorts, but the country's first long-distance trekking route is now making it easier than ever to strike out into the peninsula's desert heartland to explore. The Sinai Trail winds for 550km (342 miles) through some of the country's most wild and stark landscapes. Operated by eight of the peninsula's Bedouin tribes, this community-based tourism project reveals the raw beauty of the Sinai's interior while also benefitting the region's Bedouin communities, who have long been shut out of the coastal tourism development in South Sinai.

For hikers, the Sinai Trail offers access into parts of the region most people don't see: one of the greatest wilderness areas in the Middle East. More importantly, it creates fairly paid employment opportunities for Bedouin guides while also providing a focus for both intertribal cooperation and preserving Bedouin heritage. If you really want to get off the beaten track, this is as far from it as you can be.

GO IF YOU LIKE...

- 💙 *trekking*
- 💙 *mountain-≠≠peak vistas*
- 💙 *Bedouin culture*
- 💙 *the Jordan Trail*
- 💙 *desert landscapes*
- 💙 *ancient history*

Why go to the Sinai Trail?

The Bedouin cooperative in charge of the trail is bringing tourism into the Sinai on its own terms, via this mammoth trekking challenge encompassing both visceral desert scenery and the Sinai's deep history. Follow ancient Bedouin routes from sweeps of rock-pitted desert plateau through sinewy orange-hued canyons. Climb up to Bedouin gardens secreted in the valleys of Sinai's High Mountains, before hiking up the craggy peaks themselves. Or trek through wide *wadis* (valleys) and over high passes to isolated, spring-fed oases and out to the pharaonic temple of Serabit El Khadim.

The entire Sinai Trail circuit takes around 55 days to trek in full, but most hikers opt to walk a trail section rather than the whole route. All treks through this vast, remote wilderness are accompanied by trained Bedouin guides and support staff (such as cameleers to carry water and camping equipment) from the tribe whose territory you're trekking through.

Right: The Sinai Trail passes through rock-pitted desert, canyons and valleys of the Sinai's High Mountains

Below: St Katherine's Monastery, overlooked by Jebel Katarina, Egypt's highest peak

© SHUTTERSTOCK | ALEXANDREE

FIRST-TIME TIPS

The Sinai Trail organises group thru-treks and shorter group hikes of trail sections at regular intervals on their website (sinaitrail.net) and Facebook page (facebook.com/sinaitrail) — great for solo travellers who want to hike with other people.

Begin or end your Sinai Trail trip with a few days by the sea, staying in a hoosha (palm-thatch) hut on the sand at one of the basic beach camps strung out along the shore between Nuweiba and Taba.

You need to be geared up to hike the Sinai Trail. Bring a tent, sleeping bag, sleeping mat, personal first-aid kit and really good hiking shoes.

GETTING THERE

The Sinai Trail's most popular trailheads from which to begin a trek are just north of Nuweiba on Sinai's east coast and at St Katherine in the High Mountains of South Sinai. Sharm El Sheikh is South Sinai's international flight hub. From Sharm there's a daily bus to Nuweiba. To get to St Katherine from the South Sinai resort towns, you'll need to take a taxi.

WHEN TO GO

Mar–May

In spring, the temperatures are ideal for hiking and the desert is at its most colourful. Alternatively, aim for Egypt's autumn months of October and November.

AMAZING CROWD-FREE EXPERIENCES

 Climb Jebel Katarina, Egypt's highest summit. Rising to 2629m (8625ft), Mt Katherine offers sunset views of peaks that stretch down to the coastline.

 Explore the yawning *wadis* and sand seas of remote west Sinai on the Serabit El Khadim circuit, with ancient rock inscriptions and old British mining settlements.

 Visit the 12th-dynasty pharaonic temple of Serabit El Khadim. Dedicated to Hathor, it's surrounded by the pharaohs' ancient turquoise mines.

 Discover the lush, hidden Bedouin gardens and orchards of the High Mountains area.

 Hike Jebel Musa, the Sinai's holiest pilgrimage site, using the Wadi Al Arbain Trail. It winds past the sixth-century Monastery of the Forty Martyrs, several hermit cells and the Rock of Moses along its way up Mt Sinai.

 Bag the High Mountains peak of Jebel Abbas Basha. The remnants of Khedive Abbas I's never-finished palace are a reward at the summit.

Left: Giraffes are a highlight of Naboisho, as are lions, cheetahs, elephants and hippos

Naboisho Conservancy

THE SAME CULTURE AND WILDLIFE AS THE MAASAI MARA, BUT FEWER JEEP CROWDS

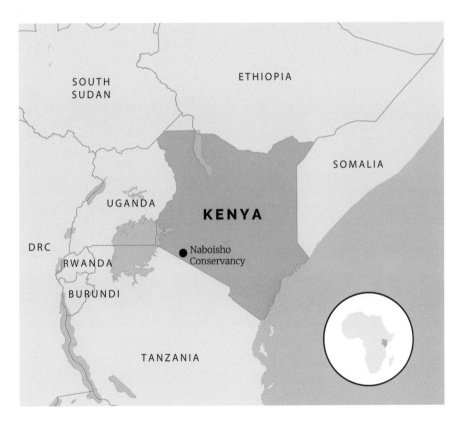

Kenya's Naboisho Conservancy is just as rich in wildlife as the more famous Maasai Mara National Reserve it borders, but strict limits on tourist numbers make for a much more authentic safari experience. Created in 2010, this private conservation area offers 350 acres of acacia-dotted wilderness for every visitor bed. There are also rules on the number of cars that can attend a sighting, so you won't find dozens of 4WDs crowding around animals. Instead, you'll have Naboisho's large population of lions almost to yourself – plus cheetahs, elephants, buffaloes, giraffes, wildebeest, hippos and more.

Big game isn't the only draw — Naboisho's landscapes are a knock-out, the Africa of your imagination. And visitors have a direct, positive impact on preserving them for the local community — travel companies lease the land from Maasai people, who earn an income from conservancy fees and their employment at Naboisho's nine camps. Each camp has a distinct identity and all provide a high standard of accommodation, with stylish tents and alluring social spaces for sundowners.

GO IF YOU LIKE...

- 💜 *Maasai Mara National Reserve*
- 💜 *unforgettable wildlife*
- 💜 *nights under canvas*
- 💜 *local encounters*
- 💜 *walking safaris*
- 💜 *dazzling savannah-scapes*

Why go to Naboisho?

For many, an African safari is a once-in-a-lifetime trip, and the Naboisho Conservancy does not disappoint. Visitors are often amazed by their proximity to the animals, reporting elephants brushing past their jeep and being close enough to a lion to hear her yawn. Not subject to the same restrictions as state-run national parks, conservancy guides are able to work more flexibly and offer experiences that the neighbouring Maasai Mara National Reserve can't – such as night game drives.

Exceptionally knowledgeable about their homeland, most of the area's guides are trained at the Conservancy's Koiyaki Guiding School, just one of the community initiatives making a real difference to the lives of local people. Naboisho means 'coming together' in the Maasai language, and the conservancy was founded on the principle that if the land was managed for the benefit of both humans and animals, the two could thrive side by side. And by all accounts it's working.

GETTING THERE

Kenya's main international gateway is capital Nairobi's Jomo Kenyatta Airport. From there, it's a four-hour drive to Naboisho Conservancy – camps inside the conservancy can arrange a driver pick-up. It's also possible to make the journey by one-hour internal flight from Nairobi's Wilson Airport. Book with companies such as Kenya Airways, AirKenya and Safarilink.

WHEN TO GO

Late Jun–Oct

Although there are good wildlife-viewing opportunities year-round, the driest months are best – vegetation is thinner and animals gather at rivers and water holes to drink. The wildebeest migration, nature's greatest spectacle, runs August to October.

FIRST-TIME TIPS

Most visitors require an e-visa to enter Kenya (evisa.go.ke), which usually takes around 48 hours to process.

....

Temperatures range from a daytime max of 30°C (86°F) to around 10°C (50°F) at night, so pack both a warm jacket and a pair of shorts, a cosy beanie and a sun hat. You don't need to buy specialist safari clothing: muted colours that blend in with the landscape are fine.

....

Safari lodges are careful about safety. Vehicles are open-sided, but guides are experienced so you never feel at risk. Camps are unfenced but tents are often fitted with panic buttons and staff add another layer of security, chaperoning guests between different areas of the camps during twilight hours.

AMAZING CROWD-FREE EXPERIENCES

 Step out on a guided bush walk. You'll learn how plant life is used by locals – and more than you ever thought possible about animal dung.

 Visit a Maasai village. Camps work closely with their local communities, who are happy to receive their guests and offer colourful beadwork and carvings for sale.

 Get out early. Animals are most active just before dusk and after dawn – morning game drives tend to be quieter and sunrise over the savannah is magical.

 Allow time for experiences to unfold, instead of fixating on seeing certain animals. Predators go a long time between kills, but witnessing one can be pure drama.

 Take a hot air balloon tour over the Mara Reserve. Kenya's premiere natural attraction is incomparably peaceful from an aerial perspective.

 Eat al fresco – savannah style. Most camps offer a 'bush breakfast' or a hamper to take out on a game drive. Picnics don't get more exciting than this.

Clockwise from top left: A family of African elephants; leopards are among the big cats in Naboisho; a lone safari jeep instead of touring traffic

Left: Maletsunyane River leads to a waterfall that's home to the world's longest commerical abseil

Lesotho

THE TINY MOUNTAIN KINGDOM WHERE COMMUNITIES ARE INVESTING IN TOURISM

which encircles Lesotho. In 2019, just 800,000 international tourists explored its exhilarating 3000m-plus passes, compared with the 15.8 million who visited South African highlights such as Table Mountain and the Blyde River Canyon.

The former British protectorate's community-run backpacker lodges, often occupying the mountaintop trading posts that once served the remote villages of thatched *rondavel* (roundhouse) huts, remain a travel secret. Even Prince Harry's connection to the country, where he worked with AIDS orphans on his gap year and co-founded the charity Sentebale, has yet to put this rugged country on typical sub-Saharan travel itineraries.

Dominated by the Drakensberg and Maluti mountain ranges, tiny Lesotho can claim to be the world's highest country – even its lowest point, in the so-called Lowlands, stands at around 1400m (4593ft) high. While hiking or trekking on a sturdy Basotho pony through this sparsely populated mountain kingdom, you're more likely to meet a shepherd clad in a traditional Basotho blanket than the tourist crowds of South Africa,

GO IF YOU LIKE...

- ♥ *Morocco's High Atlas*
- ♥ *Blyde River Canyon*
- ♥ *mountain hiking*
- ♥ *horse riding*
- ♥ *African culture*
- ♥ *challenging drives*

Why go to Lesotho?

Lesotho's chief draw is its seemingly endless mountain landscapes, sprinkled with snow in winter, coloured pink by sunsets, crisscrossed by epic passes, riven by waterfalls, and offering a range of altitudinous adventures. Remote southern Sehlabathebe National Park and relatively accessible Ts'ehlanyane National Park protect vast swaths of wilderness, and a 40km (25 mile) hike or pony trek connects the latter to the yawning valleys and highland meadows of Bokong Nature Reserve.

Thanks to years of upgrades by Chinese road engineers, experiencing the mountain kingdom is as easy as jumping in a hire car to the cloud-scraping passes, although knuckles still whiten on the likes of God Help Me Pass (2281m/7484ft). At journey's end is a handful of community-run backpacker lodges in former trading posts, where mountain explorations, village visits, cold Maluti lager and campfire camaraderie await. Traverse the peaks on a guided hike or pony trek between lodges, and don't miss Semonkong Lodge's novel pub crawl by donkey.

GETTING THERE

Fly to Johannesburg or Durban, then hire a car and overnight in Clarens or the South African Drakensberg en route to Lesotho. Maseru Bridge, near Lesotho's capital Maseru, is the main border crossing; some of the roads bordering South Africa's Eastern Cape and KwaZulu-Natal provinces require a 4WD. Buy a good road map, rather than relying on Google Maps.

WHEN TO GO

Sep–Apr

Skiers may prefer the winter, but spring, summer and autumn are more practical for travelling in Lesotho. Summer temperatures can exceed 30°C (86°F) in the valleys, but you'll still have cool conditions in the mountains, sometimes below freezing.

FIRST-TIME TIPS

If you plan to stop for lunch, phone ahead as staff in remote restaurants will have to fire up the kitchen and find the cook.

4WD is best, but touring in 2WD is possible with judicious enquiries about road conditions. If driving from South Africa, request a letter of permission from the rental outfit to drive over the border.

If you're visiting South Africa after Lesotho, stock up on South African rand, which is universally accepted in Lesotho; Maloti (Lesotho's currency) aren't in South Africa.

Lesotho has some of the world's highest rates of violence against women. Women are advised not to travel alone here.

AMAZING CROWD-FREE EXPERIENCES

 Cross the Gates of Paradise Pass to Malealea Lodge, a converted trading post offering community-guided trekking, mountain biking and village choir sessions.

 Plunge 204m (670ft) down Maletsunyane Falls on the world's longest commercial single-drop abseil, and recover in the Duck & Donkey Tavern at Semonkong Lodge.

 Find timid antelopes, dramatic rock formations and indigenous 'che-che' forest in Ts'ehlanyane National Park, where Maliba Lodge gazes up a mountain valley.

 Cross from South Africa on the epic Sani Pass and toast the Drakensberg at Sani Top, home to Africa's highest pub, cosy *rondavel* accommodation and challenging hikes.

 Stay a night at the serene Katse Dam and tour this 36-sq-km (14 sq mile) engineering marvel, which supplies Johannesburg with water and generates hydroelectric power.

 Carve fresh powder on the slopes and snow park of Afriski Mountain Resort, followed by a pizza in Sky Restaurant, Africa's highest restaurant at 3010m (9875ft).

Above: Pony trekking is a highlight in Lesotho, where rough trails allow tourists to pass through sparsley populated terrain

Tetouan

MOROCCO'S OVERLOOKED WHITE CITY IS AN ARTISTIC HAVEN STEEPED IN HISTORY

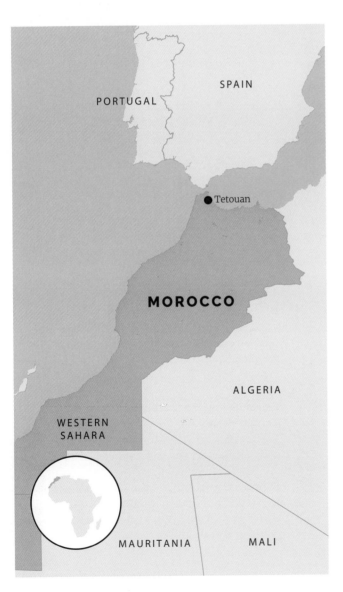

There's something immensely appealing about the small city of Tetouan, where white buildings cling to the Rif mountainsides. While so many head for the blue-washed streets of nearby Chefchaouen, those in the know travel slightly further north to Tetouan to avoid the crowds. Phoenicians established a port here and third-century Roman remains dot the hillsides. The city has a cosmopolitan air thanks to centuries of immigrants. Jews and Moors escaping 15th-century Spain settled here, as did later Ottoman-era Algerians fleeing the French. Then between 1912 and 1956, Tetouan was capital of northern Morocco's Spanish Protectorate.

Art Nouveau buildings still grace the Spanish part of town, while the Arab-influenced medina lures you into its tiny streets. There's an important school of fine art, one of Morocco's best museums of contemporary art, and at the Royal Artisan School young people learn ancient crafts like leatherwork and zellij mosaic. Despite all this, Tetouan welcomed just 40,000 foreign tourists in 2019 – half the number of busy Chefchaouen.

GO IF YOU LIKE...

- ♥ *Chefchaouen*
- ♥ *Al-Andalus history*
- ♥ *arts and crafts*
- ♥ *medina alleys and riads*
- ♥ *mountain walks*
- ♥ *Art Nouveau architecture*

Why go to Tetouan?

Tetouan's medina is a World Heritage Site and a member of Unesco's Creative Cities Network. Dip into all this artiness with a visit to the Archaeological Museum for its pre-Islamic pottery and fabulous Roman mosaic floors from Lixus. Old photographs of Tetouan can be found at the remarkable Dar El Oddi. In the Spanish district of Ensanche, all roads lead to the graceful, fountain-filled Plaza Moulay El Medhi surrounded by cafes, restaurants and the pretty yellow church, Iglesia Bacturia.

The Ensanche is also where you'll find fine examples of Hispano-Moorish Art Nouveau architecture. Music can be enjoyed at the Andalusian Music Festival in April and August's Festival of Women's Voices. The medina has a handful of lovely riads to stay in, full of Moorish arches and decorative tiles. This old quarter is still a thriving community centred around everyday life with markets, hammams and mosques — and not a pushy carpet seller in sight.

GETTING THERE

Tetouan can be reached in just over an hour by bus from Tangier, travelling through the majestic Rif Mountains. From the bus station, it's a quick taxi ride into the medina. Tangier is connected to Spain by ferry, by air from Marrakesh or by train on the high-speed Al Boraq trainline from Casablanca.

WHEN TO GO

May–Oct

Tetouan's sunny, Mediterranean climate avoids the brutal heat of Morocco's interior, making spring, summer and autumn all good times to visit. July and August are very busy with Moroccans holidaying on the nearby coast.

FIRST-TIME TIPS

Learn a little Moroccan Arabic, and brush up on your Spanish. While French is spoken in most of Morocco, it won't help you much up here. <u>Spanish is the lingua franca</u> in this former capital of the Spanish Protectorate.

. . . .

Don't miss the opportunity to <u>stay at a riad guesthouse</u> in the medina. The architecture and decoration are unlike those found in any other city in Morocco.

. . . .

<u>Dress conservatively</u>: both men and women should cover knees and shoulders. Save your skimpy clothes for the beach resorts on the Mediterranean, just a 20-minute drive away.

AMAZING CROWD-FREE EXPERIENCES

 Soak up the atmosphere of the hassle-free medina, stopping off at Dar El Oddi to gawp at a fine example of a family home.

 Explore quirky Place Hassan II, flanked by the Royal Palace, a wall studded with Hands of Fatima, and four street lamps designed by Gaudí pupil, Enrique Nieto.

 Join an Artisans of Tetouan Visit run by Green Olive Arts for an up-close-and-personal dive into the intricate crafts of the city.

 Dine on superb Moroccan cuisine with a Spanish twist at Blanco Riad or El Reducto in the medina.

 Be wowed by the Museum of Contemporary Art — as much for the spectacular old Spanish station housing it as for the exciting art inside.

 Spend a day walking in the Rif Mountains with a guide, stopping for lunch in a village home and spotting ancient water mills for grinding wheat.

Above: Like many hill towns in Andalucia, the former capital of Morocco's Spanish Protectorate is full of whitewashed buildings

Hassan Echair
*fine artist &
professor, Institut
National des
Beaux-Arts Tetouan*

WHY I LOVE TETOUAN

Tetouan's culture is enriched by its Arab-Andalus and Amazigh history. It's calm and peaceful, the pace of life is slow and it's well-located between mountains and sea, not far from the deep countryside.

Must-have local experience?
Go time-travelling! The medina and the Ensanche, panoramic mountain views, footpaths along the river and proximity to the sea provide both an ancient and a modern dimension, as if visitors find themselves in a time machine.

Favourite season?
I like spring for the mountain landscapes gently bathed in this special Mediterranean light. Also autumn, when the mild, pleasant climate is perfect for hikes.

Ibo Island

LOW-KEY INDIAN OCEAN LODGES GIVE AN OLD PORTUGUESE PORT NEW LIFE

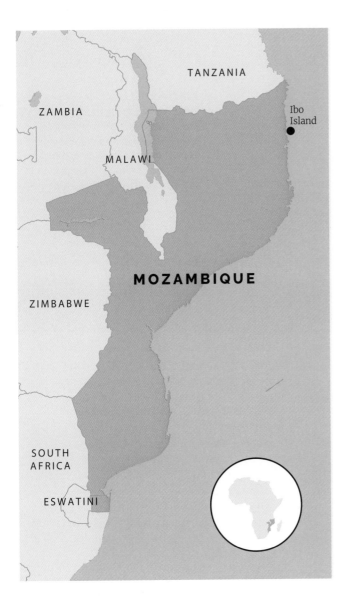

Amid the placid waters of Mozambique's Quirimbas archipelago, Ibo is an island of mystical allure. Wooden dhows with distinctive triangular sails converge on its quiet shores, dilapidated villas and crumbling, moss-covered buildings line its car-free streets, and a crossroads of cultures – Arabic, Swahili, Indian and Portuguese – reflect a long, tempestuous, history.

Framed by mangroves and coral reefs, the island remains unspoiled. Less known than fabled Mozambique Island further south, its subtle grandeur has yet to be marked by large-scale tourism. Access is challenging, unless you charter a plane, and on-island tourist facilities, bar a handful of excellent lodges, are scant. A village of around 4000 people hugs the northwest coast, while impenetrable mangroves and scattered smallholdings cultivating a unique wild coffee plant fan out further south. In the old colonial 'stone town', rows of Pompeii-like ruins are interspersed with restored mansions and forts – the legacy of Ibo's history as a Portuguese port where enslaved Africans were traded.

GO IF YOU LIKE...

- 💙 *Mozambique Island*
- 💙 *Zanzibar*
- 💙 *Lamu Island*
- 💙 *Portuguese history*
- 💙 *fresh seafood*
- 💙 *boat journeys*

Why go to Ibo Island?

Covering just 15 sq km, Ibo is a diminutive island with a potent atmosphere that mirrors its rich melange of Muslim and Christian heritage. An ideal way to experience it is on a clear, moonlit night, when the old colonial edifices of the once handsome stone town take on a haunting, almost surreal aspect. Bereft of paved roads, commercial shops, or even a bank, the historic settlement is akin to a ghost town. Yet, despite its somnolence and lack of infrastructure, the island – once you get there – is a comfortable place to bed down courtesy of its handful of well-appointed lodges.

At these establishments you can relax in elegant digs that reflect Ibo's diverse mix of cultures and organise a number of interesting diversions, many of them water-based. Go crab catching with local fishermen, snorkel in waters harbouring dolphins, or sail around the farther flung parts of the archipelago in a traditional wind-powered dhow.

GETTING THERE

Boats to Ibo (45 mins) leave from Tandanhangue in the remote north of mainland Mozambique, a bumpy 6-7 hour drive from the larger city of Pemba. Alternatively, direct charter flights from Pemba take 20 minutes and land at Ibo's tiny airstrip about 15 minutes' walk from the town.

WHEN TO GO

May–Oct

The rainy season ends around May and dry weather persists until October. July and August are peak season. The island celebrates its 250-year-old Kueto Siriwala festival in late June.

AMAZING CROWD-FREE EXPERIENCES

 Walk to neighbouring Quirimba Island. At low tide the two islands are effectively joined by a series of sandbars.

 Sample Ibo Island's low-caffeine coffee at Casa das Conchas in the old town. The house is covered in an attractive mosaic of local shells.

 Keep your eyes peeled on a birdwatching stroll around the island. Around 250 species can be spotted from a small network of paths that head south from the town through patches of woodland.

 Glide out on a boat to the São Gonzalo sandbank between Ibo and Matemo island, for a lazy afternoon on Ibo's nearest beach.

 Marvel at the mildewed magnificence of Stone Town with its silversmiths, mansions and three surviving forts — hire a guide to help navigate.

 Join locals for dinner in a village house, arranged through the lodges, to see local people do amazing things with fresh fish, vegetables and Ibo's unusual wild coffee.

Clockwise from top left: Ibo has a handful of excellent lodges; its village has an unmanicured charm; aerial view of Ibo's shallow shores

__Jörg Salzer__
owner, Miti Miwiri
Boutique Hotel

WHY I LOVE IBO ISLAND

The people, the remoteness, the quietness and the colours. Even after many years on Ibo Island, it feels like a massive privilege to live in such a magical place.

__Must-have local experience?__
Seek out local dances and traditions such as the musiro mask [a wood powder traditionally worn by Ibo's Mwani women]. Explore the historical old stone town with its three fortresses; and try Ibo's super-fresh and great seafood.

__Favourite season?__
Mid-April to June and September to November, due to the pleasant climate – plus, the wind is not too strong, which is important for any boat activities.

Eastern Cape

ECO-HOSTELS AND GRASSROOTS ART ON A JOURNEY THROUGH EPIC LANDSCAPES

The Eastern Cape is South Africa's second-largest province and one of the nation's most traditionally African regions. But its location between the well-trodden Garden Route and Durban's famous beaches means many travellers pass straight through, missing out on the wonderful Wild Coast (as the former Xhosa homeland of the Transkei is known) and the Karoo semi-desert. Those who linger, however, find epic adventures.

The province is where, in 1820, UK settlers docked in Algoa Bay, giving a British character to Gqeberha (Port Elizabeth) and the university town of Makhanda (Grahamstown). It's also where Nelson Mandela was born, and where he and Oliver Tambo met at Fort Hare University in 1939. The Eastern Cape's undeveloped infrastructure makes it challenging yet hugely rewarding to visit. Brave the potholes for community-run hostels in the Wild Coast's remote Xhosa villages, and artsy towns in the Karoo and Drakensberg. The area is also full of natural spectacles, from sunset in the rocky Valley of Desolation to the annual Sardine Run.

GO IF YOU LIKE...

- 💚 *the Garden Route*
- 💚 *Durban's beaches*
- 💚 *Southern African culture*
- 💚 *long-distance hikes*
- 💚 *quirky small towns*
- 💚 *hiking and activities*

Why go to the Eastern Cape?

Here there's the sense of freedom that many travellers hope to find in Africa. The string of community-run eco-hostels between East London and Port St Johns, and around the alternatively minded mountain village of Hogsback, have developed a cult following among those in search of South African culture. Hillside Bulungula Lodge, also home to Bulungula Incubator NGO, is one of the best, with thatched *rondavel* huts, a shipping-container reception and a scenic location overlooking a sandy beach on one of the Wild Coast's many river mouths.

One of the Karoo's big attractions is its grassroots art. Amid the vast Karoo landscapes, the towns of Nieu Bethesda, Graaff-Reinet and Cradock are home to galleries and museums. One of the former's cultural highlights is the Owl House, an 'outsider art' museum holding 300 statues that inspired Athol Fugard's play *The Road to Mecca*. You can also hike the forested Tsitsikamma section of the Garden Route National Park.

Right: The Eastern Cape is a hotbed for community-run tourism projects

Below: A trunk-off around a waterhole in Addo Elephant National Park

© MICHAEL HEFFERNAN | LONELY PLANET

Siseko Yelani
owner & guide,
Uncuthu Tours,
East London

WHY I LOVE THE EASTERN CAPE

Nature and ubuntu *(friendliness) – and the fact that it's still very cultural. It's undeveloped in many parts, so there's an authentic South African feel that you don't get in some areas.*

Must-have local experience?
A multiday hike to unlock the area's nature and culture, whether from Coffee Bay to Mdumbi and on to Port St Johns, or from Morgan Bay down to Chintsa.

Favourite season?
Come between late May and July to see marine life up close during the Sardine Run, and for temperatures that are ideal for hiking.

FIRST-TIME TIPS

It's possible to tour the province in a 2WD vehicle, as long as you <u>check on backroad conditions</u> and forgo remoter spots.

....

Phone ahead to <u>check that Wild Coast lodges have space,</u> or risk having to backtrack down a pothole-ridden road to find alternative accommodation.

....

Stay the night in one of the <u>private wildlife reserves</u> east of Addo Elephant National Park, such as Shamwari Private Game Reserve or Amakhala Game Reserve.

....

If you visit in June/July, catch the lively <u>National Arts Festival</u> in Makhanda (Grahamstown).

GETTING THERE

The Baz Bus, a hop-on, hop-off backpacker shuttle, makes several stops along the N2 on its run between Cape Town and Durban via Gqeberha (Port Elizabeth). The Wild Coast and Hogsback backpacker lodges can pick you up from Mthatha and East London respectively, but you'll need your own wheels to explore the Karoo and the Drakensberg.

WHEN TO GO

Jan–Apr

After the Christmas holidays you'll enjoy quiet beaches, readily available accommodation and relatively good roads. The rains around March give the landscape a lush green tint. Visit the Karoo in the mid-year winter months, for cooler temperatures.

AMAZING CROWD-FREE EXPERIENCES

 Experience one of the Karoo's most enchanting oases in the artistic village of Nieu Bethesda, paired with the grand Victorian houses of Graaff-Reinet.

 Explore arid mountain landscapes in the Karoo's Camdeboo and Mountain Zebra national parks, respectively home to the Valley of Desolation's dolerite columns and more than 1000 rare Cape mountain zebras.

 Hiking and tubing through the Tsitsikamma forest at the raging Storms River Mouth, and surfing the legendary waves of Jeffreys Bay.

 Make friends in a Xhosa village community while staying in a *rondavel* at eco-lodges and off-grid hostels like Bulungula, Mdumbi, Buccaneers, Terra-Khaya and Elundini.

 Head to the mountains and forest trails at Hogsback and the Drakensberg eyrie of Rhodes. Locals claims the rock formations influenced JRR Tolkien, born in Bloemfontein.

 See the Big Seven – the Big Five plus great white sharks and southern right whales – in Addo Elephant National Park, South Africa's third-largest national park.

Iran

PERSIAN HOSPITALITY STILL DEFINES THE ERSTWHILE LAND OF SHAHS

While life in Iran has fundamentally changed from the glamorous era of the shahs, it remains a country rich in cultural and natural attractions, from Roman ruins and resplendent mosques to vast deserts and dramatic mountains.

Since the mid-1990s, a steadily increasing number of tourists have come to explore its charms. Yet Iran remains something of an off-the-beaten-track destination, side-stepped by many travellers put off by the nation's political volatility, or the visa and travel insurance logistics impacted by it. Intrepid travellers who have made the effort, however, will tell you that you won't regret following in their footsteps for a second.

Iran was a popular destination for European jetsetters in the mid-20th century, before being claimed by the 'hippie trail' backpackers of the 1970s. Then came the Iranian Revolution of 1978-79, which changed the former heart of the Persian Empire forever. Crackdowns on social freedoms introduced by the new Islamic Republic dimmed Iran's appeal among many would-be tourists, exacerbated by the Iran—Iraq War of the 1980s.

GO IF YOU LIKE...

- 💜 *mosaic-covered mosques*
- 💜 *Persian food and hospitality*
- 💜 *wild landscapes*
- 💜 *ancient ruins*
- 💜 *bustling souks*
- 💜 *tea culture*

Why go to Iran?

From ancient ruins to grand former palaces, intricately tiled mosques to spice-scented souks – you could spend months touring Iran's cultural attractions alone. Then there's the nation's vast desert landscapes dotted with historic *caravanserais* (roadside inns), snow-capped peaks home to some of the world's least crowded ski slopes, and a gorgeous Gulf coast just waiting to be explored. But for many visitors, the highlight of visiting Iran is experiencing the hospitality this corner of the Middle East has been famed for since ancient times.

An increasing number of organised tour options have made it easier than ever to visit the country, but budget travellers will find that a cheaper – and often more enriching – way to visit is with an independent local guide, which costs around US$10hr/$75 per day. Travelling this way offers more flexibility with your itinerary, a deeper connection with your host, and ensures your tourism dollars directly support locals.

GETTING THERE

Most travellers fly into Tehran or Shiraz international airports. It's also possible to enter Iran by road from Armenia, Azerbaijan, Turkey, Pakistan and Turkmenistan; check visa requirements in advance to ensure you can enter overland.

WHEN TO GO

Mar–Nov

While some travellers may wish to avoid the sultry mid-summer months of July and August, the warmer months are generally ideal for visiting – unless you're coming to ski, then aim for January to March.

AMAZING CROWD-FREE EXPERIENCES

Head to Miankaleh Wildlife Sanctuary and Wetland in the southwestern corner of the Caspian Sea from October to March, where the only crowds are hundreds of pink flamingos.

Go hiking in summer, or skiing in winter, in the Alborz mountains, which dramatically rise up from the northern fringe of Tehran.

Step back into the time of the shahs at the historic house museums and the tranquil Fin Garden in Kashan, roughly half way between the cities of Tehran and Esfahan.

Wander the beautifully preserved streets of the 'red village' of Abyaneh, just over an hour's drive south of Kashan, where locals continue to embrace age-old traditions.

Explore the ancient Persian city of Bishapur. While the ruins of Persepolis are an unmissable Iran sight, these lesser known ruins also make a terrific day trip from Shiraz.

Cool off in the idyllic turquoise pools and waterfalls of Raghaz Canyon, a three-hour drive southeast of Shiraz.

Clockwise from top left: Sheikh Lotfollah Mosque, Isfahan; locals communing in a city square; the ancient city of Persepolis

Sufi Tavafi
_independent
tour guide_

WHY I LOVE IRAN

I love Iran most for its people, who can be so kind. When I'm travelling abroad, it's Iran's Persian hospitality that I miss the most.

Must-have local experience?
There are some beautiful islands to explore in the Persian Gulf. Qeshm, the largest, is known for its geological sites, but I love to go there for the excellent

snorkelling around Hengam Island, just off the south coast of Qeshm.

Favourite season?
I love being in Shiraz in spring, when the air is perfumed with the scent of orange blossoms blooming in the city's many gardens.

Northwestern Jordan

A QUIET NATURE HAVEN WHERE TOURISM IS DOMINATED BY SOCIAL ENTERPRISES

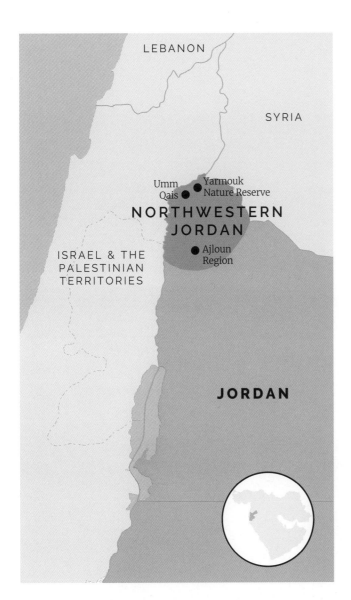

LEBANON

SYRIA

Umm Qais

Yarmouk Nature Reserve

NORTHWESTERN JORDAN

ISRAEL & THE PALESTINIAN TERRITORIES

Ajloun Region

JORDAN

Home to the World Heritage-listed rock-cut city of Petra and the otherworldly desertscapes of Wadi Rum, not to mention the famously salty Dead Sea, it's easy to see how the Kingdom of Jordan has become one of the most popular travel destinations in the Middle East. With so many big-hitters to choose from, however, many of the nation's lesser known but similarly wonderful draws are often missed by travellers following the typical bucketlist.

One area of the country rich in attractions yet light on visitors is the northwestern corner. While the sprawling ruins of the Hellenistic city of Jerash at the gateway to the region are commonly visited on a day trip from the capital Amman, the lush nature reserves, fascinating ancient ruins, gloriously slower pace and wealth of community-based tourism initiatives in Northwestern Jordan offer plenty of reasons to stay longer. Take time to soak up the scenery, explore little visited historic sites and connect with nature and Jordanian culture on a deeper level.

GO IF YOU LIKE...

- ♥ *ancient ruins*
- ♥ *community-based tourism*
- ♥ *homestays*
- ♥ *hiking*
- ♥ *Middle Eastern cuisine*
- ♥ *spectacular views*

Why go to Northwestern Jordan?

The Greco-Roman ruins of Gadara draw intrepid travellers (albeit mostly day trippers) to the village of Umm Qais in Jordan's northwestern corner. Along with the ruins, the site also has one of the country's most incredible vistas, stretching across the Jordan Valley towards Israel and the Sea of Galilee. On a clear day you may even be able to spot the snow-capped mountains of Lebanon beyond. But it's not just about ruins and views here. Umm Qais is also at the forefront of Jordan's community-tourism scene, with everything from cooking classes to beekeeping and hiking to tempt visitors to linger.

Further south, the lush Ajloun region offers an excellent array of homestay options. There's a splendid historic castle here and hiking trails in Ajloun Forest Reserve, along with some innovative social development initiatives. In between, seek out the ruins of Pella. Like Gadara, it's one of the 10 cities of the fabled Roman Decapolis.

Right: The Greco-Roman ruins of Gadara fall quiet at sunset when day trippers leave

Below: The Ajloun region offers homestays and hiking trails

© KATHRYN SULLIVAN | SHUTTERSTOCK

FIRST-TIME TIPS

Wear loose-fitting clothing covering shoulders and knees. Women travellers aren't required to wear a headscarf except in mosques, but it's wise to have one handy.

When dining with a host family, it's polite to leave a little bit of food on your plate.

Don't hike too close to Northwestern Jordan's borders with Israel, the Palestinian Territories and Syria, nor take photographs of border checkpoints.

Show respect to local hosts by learning a few common Arabic words before your trip such as marharba *(hello) and* shukran *(thank you).*

GETTING THERE

Compared with other parts of Jordan, the north is well served by public transport. Minibuses link most towns and villages (and the main city of Irbid, from where buses run to Amman). A bit of patience is required as you wait for buses to fill up, but no journey in the north is likely to cost more than JD1.

WHEN TO GO

Mar–May

The region is particularly scenic during the spring months, when the hills of Northwest Jordan are ablaze with wildflowers. Evenings can be chilly, even in summer.

AMAZING CROWD-FREE EXPERIENCES

 Conquer the 675km (420 mile) Jordan Trail (or just a section of it) – this ultimate slow adventure begins in Umm Qais.

 Stay with a local family in the Ajloun area, arranged through the community-run Al Ayoun Society (facebook.com/alayounsociety), among other operators.

 Explore the well preserved 12th-century Ajloun Castle, built atop Mt 'Auf (1250m /4100ft) as part of the defensive chain to keep out the Crusaders — it receives only a fraction of Petra's crowds.

 Watch the sunset from the ruins of Gadara after the day-trippers have left. Designed to connect travellers to memorable, sustainability driven community-run experiences, Beit Al Baraka (barakadestinations.com) offers a memorable guesthouse stay nearby.

 Explore the Ajloun Forest Reserve and surrounding social development projects, including the Soap House, the Biscuit House and the House of Calligraphy. Arrange visits via local operator Wild Jordan (wildjordan.com).

Bursa

ISTANBUL'S ALTER EGO – THE FORGOTTEN CRADLE OF THE OTTOMAN EMPIRE

I stanbul gets all the glory in Turkey, but it's not the only old Ottoman capital. Just across the Sea of Marmara, sprawling out at the foot of Uludağ (Mt Ulu), Bursa is ground zero for the Ottoman Empire; the city where Osman Gazi founded the dynasty around 1300. This is where the early sultans first flexed their muscles. When they weren't too busy swallowing territory, consolidating power and eyeing up Constantinople as the ultimate prize, they stamped Bursa with what would become the Ottoman Empire's distinctive architectural style.

Bursting with cultural heritage, from whirling dervish ceremonies to traditional shadow-puppetry, you'd think more of İstanbul's 15 million annual foreign visitors would hop across the Marmara for a look. But Bursa receives only a tenth of that figure as travellers swerve past to skip down the coast. For those that do make the trip, the city's masterpiece multidomed mosques, tile-clad mausoleums and vaulted *bedestens* (market halls) come without İstanbul's entry-queue crowds and Instagramming-gaggles hogging all the photo ops.

GO IF YOU LIKE...

- 🩶 *Istanbul*
- 🩶 *the Grand Bazaar*
- 🩶 *Ottoman architecture*
- 🩶 *whirling dervishes*
- 🩶 *historic cities*
- 🩶 *local food culture*

Why go to Bursa?

Bursa has always been a dynamic city. When it got dumped as Ottoman capital, it simply shrugged its shoulders and reinvented itself as the empire's powerful silk-trading hub. Steeped in history, traditions remain strong in Bursa, making it easy for visitors to explore Turkish culture. The Kapalı Çarşı, Bursa's sprawling bazaar district, is still studded with grand *hans* (roadside inns) built during its silk-trade heyday. This is also the home of Karagöz shadow-puppet theatre and one of the best places in Turkey to watch a genuine whirling dervish ceremony – one that isn't just being performed for tourists. Plus, Bursa is the birthplace of the country's famed dish of İskender kebap, a dish of sliced döner meat, piled high on pide bread, doused in a rich tomato sauce and drizzled with browned butter. Bursa isn't just about ancient traditions, though. Enjoy some of the city's modern attractions by joining the locals for weekend brunch at İnkaya neighbourhood's leafy breakfast-restaurants, then board the Bursa Teleferik for a scenic, 9km (5.5 mile) cable-car ride up Uludağ's slopes.

Right: Find Bursa's silk-trading heritage in the Koza Han silk bazaar and its tea gardens

Below: Bursa's 14-century, 20-domed Grand Mosque is an exquisite example of Ottoman architecture

© NEJDET DUZEN | SHUTTERSTOCK

FIRST-TIME TIPS

Kebapçı İskender, on Ünlü Caddesi, claims to have invented <u>Turkey's famous İskender kebap dish</u>. Don't leave town without eating it at this restaurant, where it reaches perfection.

To use Bursa's public transport <u>buy a Bursakart</u> (the city's rechargeable travel card). They can be purchased and topped up from machines at metro and some tram stations, and at Mudanya port if arriving by ferry.

Bursa's hamams (Turkish baths) are a cheaper and less made-for-the-tourists alternative to those in İstanbul.

To enter mosques or attend the dervish ceremony, wear clothes covering arms and legs; women should <u>don a headscarf</u>.

GETTING THERE

From İstanbul, the easiest and quickest way to get to Bursa is to cross the Sea of Marmara by ferry. BUDO ferries run between Eminönü in central İstanbul to Mudanya on the Sea of Marmara's southern shore, with a journey time of two hours. From Mudanya, regular buses and *dolmuşes* (minibuses) zip the last 25 minutes to Bursa.

WHEN TO GO

May & Sep–Oct

Late spring or autumn, when the temperatures are mild, is the perfect time for pounding the city's pavements as you explore.

AMAZING CROWD-FREE EXPERIENCES

 Watch the dervishes whirl at Karabaş-i Veli Kültür Merkezi, which hosts nightly *sema* (whirling dervish ceremonies) that visitors are welcome to attend for free.

 Gaze at the Muradiye Complex's finery. A roll-call of early sultans and their family members are buried within intricately painted and tiled mausoleums here.

 Explore Bursa's shadow-puppetry heritage at Karagöz Museum, which also hosts a weekly show. Or head to Karagöz Antique Shop for an impromptu performance.

 Admire the exquisitely tiled Yeşil Cami (Green Mosque) and Yeşil Türbe (Green Tomb), built for Mehmed I.

 Taste *dondurmalı irmik helvası* (ice cream with warm semolina halva). This local delicacy is served up in the courtyard cafe of the bazaar's Fidan Han.

 Visit the 20-domed Ulu Cami (Grand Mosque), which Beyazıt I built in 1399 when he realised he wasn't going to make good on his pledge to build 20 mosques.

Left: Mleiha's Umm Al Nar tombs date back to the Bronze Age

Mleiha Archaeological Site

PALEOLITHIC HISTORY LAID BARE IN THE ARABIAN DESERT DUNES OF SHARJAH

Tourism in the UAE is all about opulent hotels, influencers posing by resort pools, theme parks and vast shopping malls – right? While UAE tourism campaigns do seem determined to focus on 21st-century flash, out amid the Emirate of Sharjah's desert expanse is one of the most significant archaeological sites in the region. Excavations at Mleiha have revealed a human history that rolls back to the

Paleolithic era (around 130,000 years ago), proving the Arabian Peninsula as the jumping-off point for early humans as they migrated out from Africa and spread into Asia and Europe.

While Mleiha's surrounding landscape of rolling orange-hued sand dunes and jagged mountain peaks offer up desert distractions within easy driving distance of Dubai, its wadis (valleys), caves and rock-strewn plateaus are home to ancient tombs, settlement remains and flint-knapping (stone-tool making) sites that weave the story of Mleiha's long and layered occupation. If you assumed the UAE's pre-oil boom history was insignificant, think again.

GO IF YOU LIKE…

- 💜 *Abu Dhabi Louvre*
- 💜 *Al Ain, Abu Dhabi*
- 🤍 *early-human history*
- 💜 *epic desert landscapes*
- 🤍 *hiking*
- 🤍 *astronomy*

Why go to Mleiha?

If you're at all interested in the Arabian Peninsula's history, Mleiha is profoundly important. While most significant for its early-human Paleolithic era finds, Mleiha has proven a popular spot for human habitation throughout history. Excavations here uncovered a Neolithic settlement, cemetery and flint-knapping site (11,000 years old), Umm Al Nar tombs from the Bronze Age and the remains of a fortified pre-Islamic-era settlement that had thriving trade connections with the coast.

Mleiha's mind-boggling history has been made easily accessible, too. The on-site museum walks visitors through the different layers of civilisation, while the variety of guided tours on offer range from 4WD trips around the main archaeological sites to hikes focused on specific areas. Surrounded by a sweeping desertscape, this is also one of the easiest places in the UAE to head out into the dunes with horse rides, dune-buggy trips, overnight camping and astronomy activities all organised at Mleiha's visitor centre.

GETTING THERE

Mleiha is within day-tripping distance of Dubai, 76km (47 miles) east from the city and 61km (38 miles) east from Sharjah city. The site is just on the outskirts of the small settlement of Maleha in the Emirate of Sharjah. No public transport runs to the site, but non-drivers can book private transport from any of the UAE's coastal cities directly through Mleiha Archaeological Centre.

WHEN TO GO

Nov–Mar

Winter is the best time to be striking out into the UAE's desert heartland to Mleiha, both for your own comfort while visiting and for softer light for photography.

AMAZING CROWD-FREE EXPERIENCES

 Hike Jebel Buhais on a guided archaeology-focused walk up to the remnants of an Iron Age fort. Panoramic views of the rugged desert mountain scenery around Mleiha await at the top.

 Take a dune-buggy or 4WD tour up to Fossil Rock. The undulating Faya sand dunes surrounding the archaeological site are one of the UAE's stark desert landscapes.

 Bed down for the night at Mleiha's camp to experience a star-strewn desert sky and sunrise over the dunes.

 Soak up the scenery on horseback, exploring the rolling dunes that ring the Mleiha area. Desert hacks head out in the hour before sunset, when the landscape looks its most dramatic.

 Take in the history of Mleiha's Faya Caves on a guided archaeology walk through the Valley of the Caves.

 Watch sunset and then join a stargazing tour — the perfect way to extend your Mleiha adventures into the evening.

Above: Beyond the archaeology, Mleiha is a desert landscape of stark beauty, with dunes and rock formations

Ajmal Hasan
*head of operations
& tourism
development*

WHY I LOVE MLEIHA

Mleiha is a treasure trove of archaeological and natural history wonders. What I love about it the most is the fact that early humans lived in this area more than 130,000 years ago, and the amazing wildlife, including rare animals and plants, found here.

Must-have local experience?
The overnight camping experience offered by Mleiha Archaeological Centre is a must, combining archaeology and education with tourism.

Favourite season?
Winter (late October to April) is the best time to visit, as days and nights are cooler and outdoor activities can be enjoyed to the max.

Prambanan temple
complex on Java,
Indonesia

Asia

Banteay Chhmar

TOPPLED KHMER TEMPLES AND SLEEPY VILLAGE HOMESTAYS

Jayavarman VII, the 12th-century ruler of the Khmer Empire. But unlike Angkor, Banteay Chhmar was left untouched when the collapsing Khmer kingdom reverted to Hinduism, preserving a snapshot of Cambodian Buddhism's golden age.

Time has toppled many of Banteay Chhmar's towering temples, but the ruins are still wonderfully evocative. You can wander around the vine-strangled remains of ancient shrines and intricate bas reliefs recalling the great deeds of Jayavarman VII with only birdsong for company, staying overnight in rustic village homestays where hearty home-cooking is part of the magic.

Angkor may be one of the wonders of the world, but on a busy day it can feel like the whole world has come to visit Angkor Wat. Northwest of Angkor, Banteay Chhmar provides a more peaceful 'lost city' experience with its collection of sublime Buddhist ruins tumbling from a quadrangle of jungle, unseen by all but a hardy few. Like some of the principal structures at Angkor, the temples at Banteay Chhmar were constructed by King

GO IF YOU LIKE...

♥ *Angkor*
♥ *Sukhothai, India*
♥ *Sapa homestays, Vietnam*
♥ *Hampi, India*
♥ *ruined temples*
♥ *dangling vines*

Why go to Banteay Chhmar?

The principal allure of a trip to Banteay Chhmar is the serenity. It's quite possible to be the only person standing in awe of the enormous faces of Avalokiteshvara that crown the towers of the main temple, or creeping like a latter-day Indiana Jones between jungle vines to view carved friezes that vividly recall the victories of King Jayavarman VII.

The other perk is that this definitely isn't the Disneyfied, exclusively-for-tourists version of Cambodia that sometimes surfaces in Angkor's tourist hub, Siem Reap. Accommodation is not in boutique spa hotels but in simple village homestays, and meals consist of whatever the host family is having for dinner – not pizzas, pastries and espresso coffee.

Coming here means going without some of Angkor's creature comforts, but for photographers looking to slowly compose art-piece shots of empty, awesome ruins and explorers looking to connect with a Cambodia that exists for locals first and tourists second, there's nowhere better.

GETTING THERE

The gateway to Banteay Chhmar is the rough-and-ready town of Sisophon, on the highway running between Siem Reap and Poipet on the Thai border. Siem Reap has the nearest airport, but you can also get here from Bangkok, crossing the border at Aranya Prathet/Poipet. To reach Banteay Chhmar from Sisophon, charter a taxi or *moto* (motorcycle taxi).

WHEN TO GO

Nov–Mar

The best time to visit Cambodia is the dry season, from November to March, avoiding the deluges of the southwest monsoon. If visiting off-season, aim for October, when the skies are clearing but the rains have taken some of the sting out of the heat.

© KARIN DE MAMIEL | GETTY IMAGES, © JORGEN UDVANG / ALAMY STOCK PHOTO, © SAILINGSTONE TRAVEL / ALAMY STOCK PHOTO

FIRST-TIME TIPS

If you're crossing into Cambodia by land, visas are available on arrival – bring passport photos and US dollars; if you have everything ready there's less chance you'll be stung for unofficial 'fees' when you cross.

Be careful wandering off the beaten track without a guide – some six million unexploded landmines are still scattered in the Cambodian countryside.

Keep an eye on your valuables – Cambodia is notorious for drive-by bag snatchings and phone-grabbing gangs.

Watch out for flooding from May to September when Cambodian rivers often burst their banks, causing widespread disruption.

AMAZING CROWD-FREE EXPERIENCES

Wander the timeless cloisters of Banteay Chhmar's main temple, and goggle at car-sized carvings depicting Avalokiteshvara, the Buddhist god of compassion.

Get your Indiana Jones on at nine satellite temples, crumbling into picturesque ruin. Prasat Ta Prohm is topped by a fine four-faced statue of Avalokiteshvara.

Commune with nature in the jungle – wildlife populations are dwindling around Angkor, but you'll see more tropical birds than people at Banteay Chhmar.

Stay with a family in a village homestay for a fascinating insight into local life and tasty home-cooked Khmer food. Banteay Chhmar's Community-Based Tourism (CBT) project offers several options.

Explore on two wheels. The roads are worn and rutted, but there's plenty to see by bike – like Prasat Mebon, a ruined temple set in a bird-filled reservoir.

Take a guided walk with villagers through sprawling farmland, and see what life is really like in this quiet corner of Cambodia.

Clockwise from top left: Banteay Chhmar's 12th-century ruins; the main temple is surrounded by a moat; a statue of nāga king Vasuki

Con Son

NEW TRAILS AND MARINE CONSERVATION PUT THIS TROPICAL DOT ON THE MAP

The mountains crash into the sea in Con Son, a coral-fringed island off the coast of southern Vietnam. One of 16 volcanic islands and islets of the Con Dao archipelago, Con Son feels like a world removed from the bustling market towns of the Mekong Delta across the water. The 52-sq-km (20 sq mile) island has a population of around 7000 inhabitants and contains large swaths of untouched forests, lotus flower-covered lakes and deserted beaches fringed by casuarina trees.

Wildlife emphasises nature's starring role. Endangered sea turtles nest on the sands, while abundant marine life (and several wrecks) lie just offshore. The island is also home to more than 80 bird species, and the endemic long-tailed macaque, which can be spotted on island treks. Yet the air of tropical paradise belies a dark past. Con Son was once hell on earth for the thousands of prisoners who languished in island jails during French rule and the American-backed regime. Former prisons and cemeteries serve as powerful memorials to those who suffered and perished here.

GO IF YOU LIKE...

- 💜 *tropical islands*
- 💜 *Phuket, Thailand*
- 💜 *uncrowded beaches*
- 💜 *authentic markets*
- 💜 *diving & snorkelling*
- 💜 *wildlife watching*

CHINA

LAOS

THAILAND

VIETNAM

CAMBODIA

● Con Son Island

Why go to Con Son Island?

Vietnam created the Con Dao National Park as part of a marine and land reserve in 1993. Only recently, however, has conservation become a top priority in the archipelago. New partnerships with the private sector and an ambitious volunteer programme have helped protect one of Vietnam's most important sea turtle nesting sites. In 2020, the park saw the hatching and release of more than 170,000 baby turtles.

Sustainable travel is a big part of the draw of Con Son and a new network of well-marked trails sets the stage for DIY walking adventures. If you've been to popular destinations elsewhere in Southeast Asia, like Phuket or Koh Samui, you'll be pleasantly surprised by the lack of crowds and absence of package tourism on Con Son. The island's serene tropical landscape makes an ideal setting to reconnect with the natural world — both on land and in the sea.

GETTING THERE

Con Son is linked to Tran De in the Mekong region by fast ferry, but be aware that crossings can be rough and services can be cancelled during bad weather. Another option is to fly direct from Ho Chi Minh City's Tan Son Nhat International Airport (SGN) to Con Dao Airport (VCS). The one-hour flight runs several times a day and is operated by Vietnam Airlines.

WHEN TO GO

Mar–Sep

Although the driest time to visit Con Son is from November to February, if you want to observe nesting sea turtles, plan a trip between June and September. For diving, visibility is best from March to July.

FIRST-TIME TIPS

Check well in advance for the latest entrance requirements into Vietnam, and apply for your e-visa (https://evisa. xuatnhapcanh.gov.vn) at least one week before your arrival. Print out and bring your approved e-visa with you, whether arriving via air, sea or overland.

....

You can arrange turtle-watching excursions through the national park headquarters (condaopark. com.vn), located in the hills above Con Son town. Pick up a map and pay the park admission fee here.

....

With little traffic on the roads, Con Son is ideal for exploring by motorbike or bicycle, either of which can be hired at most hotels.

AMAZING CROWD-FREE EXPERIENCES

 Dig your heels in the golden sand at Bai Nhat, one of Con Son's loveliest beaches. The views across the waves to the nearby island of Hon Ba are mesmerising.

 Look for macaques and black squirrels on the forest-lined walk from Vong Beach to Dam Tre Lagoon. Bring snorkelling gear for a refreshing swim at the end of the trail.

 Start the day with a delicious plate of noodles at lively Con Son market. It's also a good spot to pick up fresh tropical fruits and other snacks.

 Learn about the past on a visit to harrowing Phu Hai, the largest of 11 prisons scattered around the island.

 Watch nesting sea turtles lumber in from the ocean to lay their eggs on the beach during a guided overnight turtle-watching tour.

 Swim over colourful coral reefs while spying rays, parrotfish, hawksbill turtles and other marine life on a diving or snorkelling excursion.

Clockwise from top left: Con Son Prison Museum; 11 notorious former prisons exist on the island; deserted sands fringing Con Son

Daniel Coldrey
master scuba diver & manager, Con Dao Dive Centre

WHY I LOVE CON SON

Con Son is, at the moment, still untouched and has a great biodiversity of fauna and flora, both on land and below the water. It also has the best scuba diving and snorkelling in Vietnam, with spectacular coral reefs and marine life.

Must-have local experience?
Con Son is the resting place of heroine Vo Thi Sau [a guerrilla fighter executed by the French at Con Son Prison in 1952]. People in Vietnam come to pray at her tomb and visit the many other memorials around the island for prisoners who tragically died here.

Favourite season?
Although it's the rainy season, I love March to October, when diving is best and nesting sea turtles come ashore.

Kaziranga National Park

SWAP THE SAFARI CROWDS FOR RHINOS AND TIGERS AT THIS ASSAM HIDEAWAY

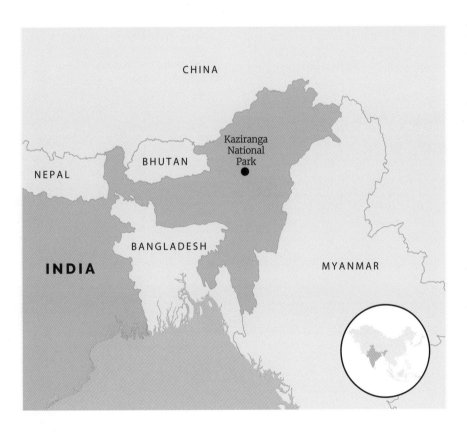

highway. In the park's more remote ranges, you can go all day without seeing another safari group.

This provides an amazing opportunity to get close to one-horned rhinos, as well as elephants, tigers, wild buffaloes and a noisy throng of northeast Indian birdlife. Around two thirds of the world's surviving one-horned rhinos live inside the reserve, hidden by dense elephant grasses but easily spotted near the reserve's silent, sky-reflecting waterholes. Visiting Kaziranga is also an excuse to see underexplored Assam, with its fascinating sacred cities, ancient Shaivite temples, tea plantations and inundated river islands.

India's big national parks may be full of tigers and wild elephants, but they're also full of people trying to spot them. Not so Kaziranga National Park in Assam, the last major refuge for the one-horned Indian rhinoceros. While Bandipur National Park sees upwards of 200,000 wildlife-spotters a year, Kaziranga sees around 70,000 visitors, mostly local spotters who stick to the accessible Kohora range, close to Assam's main east-west

GO IF YOU LIKE...

- *Bandipur NP, India*
- *Chitwan NP, Nepal*
- *Khao Sok NP, Thailand*
- *Sinharaja Forest Reserve, Sri Lanka*
- *African wildlife safaris*
- *Chilika Lake, India*

Why go to Kaziranga NP?

Visitors once entered Kaziranga on elephant back, with elephant guns in hand. But hunting was banned in 1908 and today there's growing awareness of the harm that riding elephants can do to these giant, gentle mammals. Modern-day visitors do their stalking with cameras and long lenses from the back of safari jeeps. In fact, a normal lens will do just fine, as you can get astonishingly close to one-horned rhinos at the many waterholes, and stand a chance of spotting tigers, gaur (wild water buffalo), wild elephants and abundant birdlife, including hornbills, pelicans and rare fish eagles. International visitors are rare, especially away from the main Kohora range. The quieter Bagori range has rhinos by the dozen, and the empty, eastern Agoratoli range has the most spectacular birdlife.

GETTING THERE

These days, getting to Assam is easy, thanks to regular flights and overnight trains to Guwahati, the Assamese state capital. Buses run regularly from Guwahati to near the park gate at Kohora, which has the biggest selection of lodges. Alternatively, book a car transfer; lodges on the edge of the national park can arrange driver pick ups from Guwahati.

WHEN TO GO

Jan–Mar

The rains turn the tracks through Kaziranga to mires during the monsoon; visit from January to March, when the tall elephant grass is stripped back, making it easier to spot rhinos.

FIRST-TIME TIPS

Pick your range: Kaziranga has four zones, but rhino sightings are easiest in the Kohora and Bagori ranges, while the Agoratoli range is best for birdlife.

Pay for a whole jeep; vehicles can fit six people, but if you share with a noisy group, wildlife may make itself scarce.

Book safaris through accommodation — lodges can make all the arrangements, including sorting out a pick up and drop off at the end of the day.

AMAZING CROWD-FREE EXPERIENCES

 Start a safari day early, with mists clearing over the elephant grass, and spot a one-horned Indian rhino emerging from the undergrowth just metres away.

 Stake out a spot by a waterhole at dawn to watch adjutants, storks, fish eagles, kingfishers and pelicans swooping low over the waters.

 Relax on the balcony at a Kaziranga eco-lodge at sunset, watching tropical birds come in to roost. The thatched stilt houses of Diphlu River Lodge (diphluriverlodge.com) and the elegant cottages at Infinity Resorts (infinityresorts.com/infinity-resorts-kaziranga) are highlights.

 Make a detour to view the mighty Brahmaputra – Assam's vast, mud-brown river – from Majuli Island, an ancient centre for Hindu *satras* (Vaishnavite monasteries).

 Add bonus national park experiences across the river at Orang National Park, a little-visited reserve that is home to India's densest population of tigers.

Above: Thick forests harbour lots of wildlife at Kaziranga **Below:** the park is the last major refuge for the one-horned Indian rhinoceros

Nagaland

AN IMMERSIVE TRIBAL ADVENTURE IN INDIA'S LAST FRONTIER

with a staggering 1.6 million to Rajasthan. If you want to experience India as it was before mass tourism, look no further.

Once known as headhunters (though thankfully no more), the assorted tribes of Nagaland hold onto many of their fascinating pre-colonial traditions. Most groups have nominally converted to Christianity, but animist traditions such as decorating homes with buffalo skulls still endure. It's possible to spend weeks in Nagaland without seeing a single fellow traveller; travel is slow and discomfort levels can be high, but staying in village homestays will immerse you deeply in the life of this fascinating Indian outpost.

For decades, Nagaland was the edge of the known world in India – a mesmerising last frontier, bound by misty mountains, studded with tribal villages and tantalisingly off-limits to travellers thanks to lingering red tape from colonial times. The last decade has seen the obstacles to travel slowly whittled away, but the message has been slow getting out: fewer than 6000 foreign visitors made it to Nagaland in 2019, compared

GO IF YOU LIKE...

- 🤍 *Northern Thailand*
- 🤍 *the Vietnam Hills*
- 🤍 *Myanmar*
- 🤍 *Borneo*
- 🤍 *tribal encounters*
- 🤍 *pushing back frontiers*

Why go to Nagaland?

While the bureaucracy that used to impede travel to Nagaland is fading away, this is still a destination for proper adventurers. Transport is provided by rattletrap buses and ageing jeeps that creep at a snail's pace along rutted mountain roads. But that's a small price to pay for the reward of staying in a rustic homestay within a tribal village for a deep dive into Naga life. In villages such as Shiyong and Longwa around Mon in central Nagaland, you can stay with the descendants of headhunters, in homes full of heirloom tribal artefacts. Guests get to sample never-tasted-before Naga cooking (including dishes prepared with fiery Naga ghost chillies) and enjoy balcony views over mist-cloaked valleys.

The area is changing rapidly as the modern world finds its way into the hills, but in off-the-map locations, villages of buffalo-skull-adorned thatched huts cling on. And they're still occupied by villagers who walk around with ever-useful, hand-forged machetes.

GETTING THERE

The easiest way to reach Nagaland is to fly to Guwahati in Assam, then travel overland by bus or jeep to Mokokchung and on to the villages around Mon. The state capital, Kohima, is in the far south of the state, a gruelling 18 hours by bus from Mon. Consider chartering a jeep and driver for the whole trip rather than relying on public transport.

WHEN TO GO

Oct–Apr

The monsoon drenches the hills, so stick to the dry winter months. The Hornbill Festival in Kohima in December is the biggest event in the Naga calendar, drawing people from across the country in traditional tribal finery.

AMAZING CROWD-FREE EXPERIENCES

Explore Kohima's fascinating markets. Outside the Hornbill Festival, you may not see another traveller around stalls piled with frogs, hornet grubs and ghost chillies.

Pay your respects at Kohima's War Cemetery. This lonely graveyard is a moving memorial to some of the deadliest battles of WWII.

Bed down in a village homestay in the hills around Mon, admiring the boar-tusk and hornbill skull adornments worn by the owners' ancestors.

Take a walk in the Naga hills, where local guides can lead you through the bamboo groves to tea plantations, thatched villages and viewpoints.

Eat a traditional Naga meal at a guesthouse or village market. Naga cooking is full of foods you've probably never tried, like mushroom chutney.

Visit a *morung*, a communal longhouse in more traditional Naga villages where young men live before marriage; *morung* are often adorned with ancient animist totems.

Clockwise from left: A local woman serves up hornet stew; Naga ghost chillies; sunset over misty Nagaland hills

Yogyakarta's temples

BOROBUDUR AND PRAMBANAN ARE JAVA'S GREATEST ANCIENT TREASURES

Set along the plains of Central Java, beneath the shadow of volatile Mt Merapi, lie Indonesia's two most stunning temple complexes: Borobudur and Prambanan. Sitting either side of the city of Yogyakarta – a cradle of Javanese culture and a popular destination in itself – these two World Heritage-listed temples date to a similar era (8th to 10th century), but they're very distinct from one another. Borobudur's celestial stupa is the world's largest Buddhist temple, while Prambanan's ancient complex of 240 temples is mostly Hindu.

Just like Cambodia's Angkor Wat, which also incorporates elements of Buddhism and Hinduism, both were abandoned and lost to the jungle for almost 800 years before being unearthed by European explorers.

And while Borobudur and Prambanan are equal to Cambodia's Angkor in grandeur and mystique, somehow Java's extraordinary temples haven't managed to evoke the same level of romance and adventure. Whether that's because they've never had Lara Croft to boost their appeal is a matter open to conjecture.

GO IF YOU LIKE...

♥ *Angkor Wat, Cambodia*
♥ *Bagan temples, Myanmar*
♥ *Hampi, India*
♥ *Persepolis, Iran*
♥ *Karnak, Egypt*
♥ *Palenque, Mexico*

Why go to Yogyakarta's temples?

Predating Angkor Wat by 400 years, Borobudur is one of the world's great Buddhist monuments. Lauded as an architectural masterpiece, its imposing circular pyramidal-shaped stupa is designed as a spiritual path to guide visitors through the three levels of Buddhist cosmology. Take your time to admire its 2672 exquisite relief panels, each depicting Buddhist and Javanese folklore. At the top, transcendental views unfold over jungle and hills amid evocative bell-shaped stupas and statues.

To the east of Yogyakarta lies its other blockbuster attraction: Prambanan. Indonesia's (and one of the world's) largest Hindu complexes features 240 temples scattered across vast plains, but the highlight is undoubtedly the main cluster of intricate 10th-century temples. Sitting within its inner zone, each is dedicated to Hindu deities including Brahma, Vishnu and Shiva; Shiva's temple rises 47m (154ft) and features outstanding reliefs depicting scenes from the epic Hindu poem *Ramayana*.

Right: Prambanan is one of the world's largest Hindu complexes, with 240 temples

Below: The volcanic peak of Mt Merapi provides an irresistible backdrop to the ruins of Borobudur

© ALEXANDER MAZURKEVICH | SHUTTERSTOCK

© PPHILIP LEE HARVEY | LONELY PLANET

FIRST-TIME TIPS

For <u>optimal photography</u>, visit Borobudur at sunrise, and Prambanan at sunset. The ticket price is higher, but it's worth it.

....

The combined Prambanan/ Borobudur ticket <u>makes admission to both sites cheaper</u>, but doesn't include visits for sunrise or sunset.

....

In a nation of more than 270 million people, attractions can get busy. <u>Avoid weekends and holidays</u> at Yogyakarta's temples, if you can.

....

<u>Dress respectfully</u> with clothing that covers shoulders and knees.

GETTING THERE

Both domestic and international flights arrive at Yogyakarta's new airport, 45km (28 miles) outside the city. Many tourists use the city of Yogyakarta as a base to visit both temples, with Borobudur positioned 41km (25 miles) northwest of the city and Prambanan 16km (10 miles) to the east. Plenty of local buses ply the route, or otherwise join a local tour.

WHEN TO GO

Apr–Dec

April to December is the best time to visit weather-wise. For atmosphere, time your visit with the full moon in May when Borobudur celebrates the Vesak festival, commemorating the birth, enlightenment and death of the Buddha.

AMAZING CROWD-FREE EXPERIENCES

Learn about the ancient Javanese religion of Kejawan. Kaleidoscope of Java's (kaleidoscopeofjavatour.com) peaceful tours explain how it applies to Borobudur.

Soak up traditional Javanese culture while experiencing relaxed Borobudur's village life at a *kampung* homestay. Search at kampunghomestayborobudur.com.

Find enlightenment over sunset meditation beneath a Bodhi tree at Candi Mendut – a magical, less-visited temple where you can contemplate Borobudur's 1200-year history.

Swap sunrise for sunset at Borobudur to experience its tranquility and spirituality without the crowds. Vice versa, come to Prambanan at 6am to be alone.

Jump on a bicycle to explore Prambanan's outlying temples at a leisurely pace. Beyond the complex itself, other area highlights include the hilltop palace of Kraton Ratu Boko and Buddhist-inspired Candi Plaosan.

Bag tickets for Prambanan's spectacular Ramayana Ballet, a unique telling of the Hindu epic against a backdrop of its temples.

Left: The otherwordly
rope bridges of Oku Iya
Ni-jū Kazura-bashi
in the Iya Valley

Shikoku

JAPAN'S OUTDOORSY PILGRIMAGE ISLAND THAT CHAMPIONS ZERO-WASTE LIVING

Shikoku seldom makes it onto most international visitors' travel itineraries of Japan, even though the island has much to offer. Major events such as Tokushima city's annual Awa Odori Matsuri, Japan's equivalent of the Rio Carnival, bring in local crowds in August. Matsuyama's venerable Dōgo Onsen is a magnet for hot spring fans. And every three years Shikoku's Kagawa Prefecture co-hosts the Setouchi Triennale, a superb contemporary arts festival covering nearby islands such as Naoshima and Shōdo-shima.

But beyond the headline attractions there are also many under-the-radar experiences and destinations. Search out the sustainability projects in the zero-waste village of Kamikatsu. Head to the remote Iya Valley to stay in an 18th-century thatched farmhouse and to raft the upper reaches of the Yoshino River. Hike part, or all, of the island's 88 temple pilgrimage route. Or join surfers along the rugged southern Pacific coast, between the two spectacular capes of Muroto-misaki and Ashizuri-misaki. This is Japan far from the madding crowds.

GO IF YOU LIKE…

- ♥ *Honshū*
- ♥ *outdoor adventures*
- ♥ *temple pilgrimages*
- ♥ *nature*
- ♥ *artistic discoveries*
- ♥ *timeless traditions*

Why go to Shikoku?

Shikoku is famous for its religious pilgrimage around 88 temples connected with the venerable Buddhist monk Kōbō Daishi. Most of the pilgrims complete the route by motorised transport, rather than on foot. If you take up the challenge to walk or cycle the 1400km (870 mile) route you'll end up bedding down in some very off-radar Shikoku locations. Venture deeper into Shikoku's interior to find Chiori, a beautifully restored traditional thatched house and atmospheric base for exploring the Iya Valley. The staggeringly steep gorges here are spanned by wisteria vine bridges, amazing feats of ancient engineering: the least visited bridges are in Higashi-Iya.

Shikoku is also a sustainability pioneer of Japan. A 45-minute drive southwest of Tokushima City is Kamikatsu, a village which has been aiming to generate zero waste since 2003. Visitors can see its efforts in action at the microbrewery, restaurant and general store Rise & Win Co, occupying a building made from totally recycled elements, and Hotel WHY, which is part of the village's innovative zero waste centre.

GETTING THERE

For over 1300 years, pilgrims have arrived in Shikoku by boat. That leisurely method of reaching the island is still possible with ferry routes from several ports on Honshū and Kyūshū. Alternatively, there's the train from Okayama via the one rail link over the Seto Ōhashi bridge, plus highway buses from the mainland, and flights to one of the four prefectures' major airports.

WHEN TO GO

Apr & Nov

Summer can be stiflingly hot, while winter sees snow on the higher peaks. April is the best month for cherry blossoms, November for autumn colours.

FIRST-TIME TIPS

Buy the All Shikoku Rail Pass (shikoku-railwaytrip.com) for travel around the island by JR trains. The pass can be purchased for three to seven days, and also offers discounts on some ferry and bus lines.

....

If you are planning on attending Tokushima's famous dance festival, Awa Odori Matsuri, in August, book well in advance for accommodation in and around the city.

....

Though the train is good for general island travel, several highlights – including the Iya Valley, the two southern capes of Muroto-misaki and Ashizuri-misaki, and many of the 88 Temples – have no nearby train stations and tricky bus connections. Consider hiring a car to reach them.

AMAZING CROWD-FREE EXPERIENCES

 Take the 2.7km (1.7 mile) cable car to mountain-top Tairyū-ji in Tokushima Prefecture – the longest ropeway in Western Japan.

 Search out the secluded Oku Iya Ni-jū Kazura-bashi vine bridges, hanging side by side over the Iya Valley.

 Explore the fascinating interior of Ōzu-jō, in Ehime Prefecture – one of Japan's most authentically reconstructed castles, an original survivor from the Edo period.

 Swim or surf in the warm waters off Ōkinohama, Shikoku's most magnificent sandy beach, on the road to the southern cape of Ashizuri-misaki.

 Climb the gently rounded, 1955m (6414ft) peak Tsurugi-san. This is Shikoku's second-highest mountain and one of Japan's 100 Famous Mountains.

 Rent a bicycle in Shimanto City to explore the beautiful valley of the Shimanto-gawa, Japan's last remaining undammed river.

Clockwise from top left: Ryozenji temple on Shikoku's pilgrimage trail; the zero-waste village of Kamikatsu; Yosakoi Festival in Kōchi

Linda Ding
co-ordinator,
INOW Homestay,
Kamikatsu

WHY I LOVE
SHIKOKU

Shikoku is nature in all her glory – from the mountain ranges covered in evergreen cedar, to the shock of cherry blossoms hanging over clean, gurgling streams.

Must-have local experience?
Join us at INOW homestay in Kamikatsu (inowkamikatsu.com) to experience organic rice farming. A lot of the old traditions in farming are still alive in the countryside, though quickly disappearing with the onset of depopulation. For anyone who loves to eat rice, this is an opportunity to try growing it for themselves.

Favourite season?
I love autumn. Seeing the changing leaves falling softly into clear rivers below is poetry in motion.

Tōhoku

CHANGE IS AFOOT IN HONSHŪ'S UNDERDEVELOPED NORTHERN QUARTER

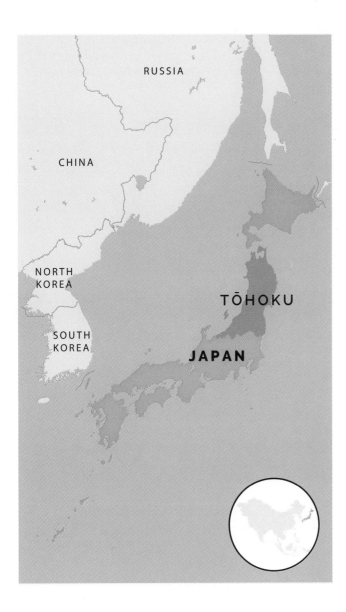

Tōhoku has long been considered remote. This region in the northeast of Japan's main island, Honshū, has a mountainous spine running north to south, rocky coastlines on the Pacific side and intensely snowy winters on the Sea of Japan side. Its historic isolation has bred traditions unique to the region, like spectacular festivals and mystical religious practices. It also means that Tōhoku remains less developed than most other parts of the country. Nature looms large — hulking volcanoes, alpine meadows, shockingly blue caldera lakes, virgin beech forests and dramatic ria coasts are all here. Oh, and onsen – Tōhoku has some of the best hot springs in all of Japan, the kind with rustic wooden bathhouses, milky white waters and outdoor baths under the stars.

Tōhoku is no longer hard to reach: the Tōhoku Shinkansen (bullet train), completed in 2010, connects the region with the capital, Tokyo, in a matter of hours. And yet, the six prefectures that make up the region remain among the least visited in the country.

GO IF YOU LIKE...

- ♥ *Japanese Alps*
- ♥ *Swiss Alps*
- ♥ *Kyoto*
- ♥ *hot springs*
- ♥ *ski holidays*
- ♥ *myths & legends*

Why go to Tōhoku?

Parts of Tōhoku were heavily damaged by a devastating earthquake and tsunami in 2011. In addition to restoring infrastructure to the region, the ongoing recovery effort has resulted in the opening of some noteworthy new attractions. Chief among these is the Michinoku Coastal Trail, a walking path hugging the Pacific from Aomori in the north to Fukushima in the south for around 1000km (620 miles), passing through small fishing towns and taking in some spectacular vistas. New boutique hotels and gourmet spots – coastal Tōhoku is famous for its seafood – are appearing up and down the coast in an effort to draw visitors to the region. At a time when many destinations have become ambivalent (or worse) towards travellers, Tōhoku is eager to welcome them. Visitors here are met with Japan's famous hospitality while largely being spared the country's often vexing crowds – so far.

GETTING THERE

Most visitors fly into Narita International Airport, just outside Tokyo. It's then easy to reach the region via the Tōhoku Shinkansen, which travels north from Tokyo to key cities, including Sendai (2hr) and Aomori (Shin-Aomori Station; 3hr 15 min). If needed, Tōhoku also has a number of regional airports, the largest of which is Sendai International Airport.

WHEN TO GO

May–Nov

The peak travel period in Tōhoku is during the summer – for hiking and traditional festivals – and the late fall, when the leaves change colour. Winter is cold and snowy, which is great for snow sports, though some remote destinations all but shut down.

AMAZING CROWD-FREE EXPERIENCES

Hike Dewa Sanzan's trails, with mysterious shrines and a magnificent wooden pagoda. The 'three mountains of Dewa' is one of the most spiritual places in Japan, where religious ascetics have trained for centuries.

Soak in hot springs at Nyūtō Onsen, home to seven secluded inns and their bathhouses, ranging from rustic to luxurious.

Shop for traditional crafts in Morioka. This small northern city is known for its ironware, textiles and lacquerware, and has several venerable old shops.

Admire Hirosaki-jō, one of Japan's few remaining original castles and now the centrepiece of a large public park. It's really only crowded when the cherry blossoms bloom in late April.

Make an early morning trip to Aomori's fish market to sample some of the prefecture's outstanding seafood.

Explore the charming rural hamlet of Tōno, famous for its folk legends. Rent a bicycle and peddle past rice paddies, wooden farmhouses and bucolic streams.

Clockwise from top left: Autumn colours at Nyūtō Onsen; Dewa's sacred Mt Haguro; the spiritual forests of Dewa Sanzan

Kyrgyzstan

WHERE YURT LIFE, WARM HOSPITALITY AND BIG LANDSCAPES COME CALLING

Landing on the outskirts of Bishkek, the sharp snowy ridges of the Tien Shan stretch to the southern horizon. Though only four or five hours by plane from major travel hubs, Kyrgyzstan seems to stand a world apart. Without the trailhead and transportation infrastructure of Switzerland or the teahouse trekking convenience of Nepal, visitors come to Kyrgyzstan to experience open wilderness and glimpses of traditional semi-nomadic lifestyles. In most of the country – more than 90% of which is mountainous – travellers are far more likely to meet a shepherd on horseback or a free-ranging herd of horses than to cross paths with another tourist.

Tempted by the horse-trekking and hiking, biking and climbing, even backcountry heli-skiing and freeriding, the primary draw for first-time visitors is adventure. What keeps them coming back, however, is more often the local culture: inviting hospitality in regions where many locals still live a seasonal semi-nomadic lifestyle; good community-based tourism infrastructure; and a disposition even sunnier than the *tunduk* (yurt roof) on the national flag.

GO IF YOU LIKE…

- ♥ *epic mountain adventures*
- ♥ *traditional nomadic culture*
- ♥ *sleeping in yurts*
- ♥ *mountain-backed beaches*
- ♥ *endless pots of tea*

Why go to Kyrgyzstan?

With a small but active community tourism network and a wealth of under-explored mountain valleys, options for travel in Kyrgyzstan are expanding all the time. The multiday hike to incredible Ala-Köl lake and horse-trekking over the Kyzart Pass to wide Son-Köl lake remain ever popular, but there's even more potential for travellers with a keen sense of adventure, and are looking to head off into the unknown.

Along the way, stay in local guesthouses and family-run yurt camps – many of which are affiliated with regional community-based tourism organisations that can arrange guides, transportation or elusive bookings where host families might only have phone signal when they climb the nearest mountainside. Among the younger generations of locals, a growing interest in the outdoors corresponds to a huge rise in the number of trekking and ski guides offering their services to tourists (including a growing cadre of English-speaking guides as well).

GETTING THERE

Primary flight hubs for departures to Bishkek are Istanbul, Dubai and Moscow. Alternatively, overland travel across Central Asia is still the best way to experience the geographic and cultural transitions that once defined the routes of the ancient Silk Road caravans through the region.

WHEN TO GO

Jun–Sep

Summer opens up endless possibilities in the mountains of the country, from yurt stays at high-altitude lakes to climbs atop icy peaks, as well as perfect beach weather on the shores of Issyk-Köl lake.

AMAZING CROWD-FREE EXPERIENCES

 Puff up the 4105m (13,468ft) Sary-Mogul Pass, from which rugged glacial valleys fall towards the Alay Valley and Peak Lenin (7134m/23,406ft) in the far distance.

 Reach the end of the road at the abandoned Soviet mining town of Engilchek, and then continue through the mountains up the 60km-long (37 mile) Engilchek Glacier.

 Step into the cool darkness of a shepherd family's yurt along a remote mountain trail, invited in from a hike for tea and bread.

 Decipher more than 10,000 petroglyph carvings high in the mountains of Saimaluu Tash Valley, accessible only in mid-summer after the snows melt.

 Stargaze beneath an endless panorama of the cosmos from your tent door, yurt roof or one of countless spots far from any light pollution.

 Stare up from the foot of the thundering 300m (984ft) Shar Waterfall, a surprisingly accessible but little-known day hike near Tash Rabat Caravanserai.

Clockwise from top left: Statue of Lenin in Kochkor; village life in rural Kyrgyzstan; horses are a vital part of Kyrgyz culture

Maksim Anosov
co-owner,
FeelNomad Travel

WHY I LOVE KYRGYZSTAN

Travelling here, the landscape rapidly changes from day to day. Snow peaks transition to deserts, lakes, beaches, forest and back to snowy peaks again.

Must-have local experience?
A yurt stay and the hospitality of local people. The places and scenery where yurt camps are located are just amazing.

Favourite season?
Each season is an unbelievable experience, whether that's a beautiful high waterfall in summer or the same one frozen in winter. I love the transition. Since I love skiing I enjoy winter, with its perfect sunny days and fresh air around high peaks.

Ipoh

THIS FORMER FRONTIER TOWNSHIP IS MALAYSIA IN MICROCOSM

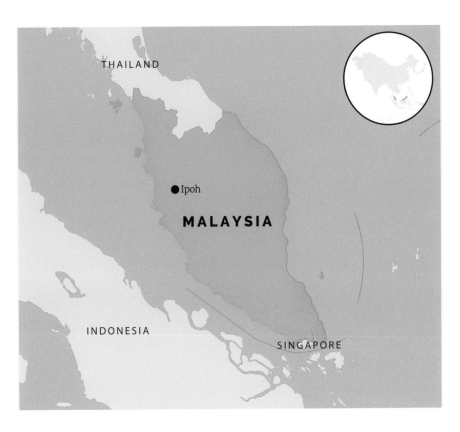

THAILAND

●Ipoh

MALAYSIA

INDONESIA

SINGAPORE

En route between the Cameron
Highlands and Penang, but rarely
the destination in itself, savvy
travellers who head to Ipoh can
feast on some of Malaysia's best
food and wander neat streets of
colonial-era shophouses that
once buzzed with the intrigue
of organised crime during
Ipoh's heyday. Tin miners were
instrumental in forging the identity
of this former frontier township,
filling the surrounding karst
outcrops with ornate cave temples
and the back-lanes with clubhouses
that once doubled as opium dens,
brothels and gang headquarters.
Ipoh is a snapshot of Malaysia's
layered heritage that's deliciously
unsullied by package tourism,
tourist bars and souvenir shops.

Kuala Lumpur, Melaka and Penang steal the thunder
in Peninsular Malaysia, but that's no bad thing
as it leaves lovely Ipoh charmingly unadulterated by
mass tourism. This laid-back country capital made its
fortunes from 19th-century tin-mining before slipping
into peaceful obscurity. Today, Ipoh is Malaysia in
microcosm, with a captivating potpourri of Chinese,
Indian and Malay culture.

GO IF YOU LIKE...

- 🤍 *Penang, Malaysia*
- 🤍 *Hoi An, Vietnam*
- 🤍 *Kuching, Malaysia*
- 🤍 *Chinese–Malay food*
- 🤍 *coffee culture*
- 🤍 *cave temples*

Why go to Ipoh?

You'll notice something different about Ipoh as soon as you arrive. The streets overflow with things to see – historic alleyways, intriguing clan-houses and vividly colourful temples squeezed into limestone caverns – but tourism here plays second fiddle to local life. You can wander the backstreets in blissful peace, feeling like the only tourist in town, and dive deep into Malaysia's rich cultural melange.

Bring an appetite – Ipoh's culinary traditions place the city right up there on the top podium with Kuala Lumpur, Melaka and Penang. Rise early to fit in a double breakfast – *dosas* (rice and lentil pancakes) at dawn in Ipoh's Indian quarter, then a mid-morning pick-me-up at a nostalgic Malay *ko pi* (coffee) house. After dark, it's all about Chinese-influenced *tauge ayam* – fragrant soy-seasoned steamed chicken served over beansprouts, the definition of perfection in simplicity.

GETTING THERE
Ipoh has a tiny airstrip served by local shuttles, but the nearest major airports are in Penang and Kuala Lumpur. You can reach Ipoh easily by bus or train from either hub (journey time is 2hr-3hr 30min); air-con buses arrive at Terminal Amanjaya, 8km (5 miles) north of town, while trains rumble into the handsome Taj Mahal-like train station on the edge of Ipoh's old town.

WHEN TO GO

Jun–Aug

The Malay peninsula is well watered year-round, but the months from June to August are generally the driest time to visit, with plenty of sunshine for sightseeing.

FIRST-TIME TIPS

Dress modestly – Ipoh is a very relaxed Malay town, but this is still a Muslim country so follow the lead of locals when it comes to exposing skin. Mid-length shorts and t-shirts are fine; anything shorter may raise eyebrows.

....

Be weather-ready as rain can come at any time in humid Malaysia. October and April are particularly soggy months in Ipoh, and the rain can put a dampener on sightseeing.

....

Call ahead to arrange a car and driver – *reaching Ipoh's cave temples and other sights outside the centre is vastly easier if you have a vehicle and a well-informed local guide.*

AMAZING CROWD-FREE EXPERIENCES

 Delve into Ipoh's clan history at the charming Han Chin Pet Soo museum, where you'll discover the city's surprising history as a hotbed of organised crime and racketeering.

 Explore Kellie's Castle, crumbling quietly by the Raya River. This flamboyant mansion was constructed by a Scottish planter who employed Tamil builders from India.

 Go cave-temple hopping among the karst cliffs around Ipoh, pockmarked by Buddhist shrines full of fantastical statuary.

 Wander the Jalan Dato Tahwil Azar night market – every night, locals take to the streets to haggle for clothes, shoes, electronics and, curiously, pomade.

 Track down Ipoh's signature dish, fragrant *tauge ayam* (chicken and beansprouts). After dark, find it around the junction of Jalan Yau Tet Shin and Jalan Dato Tahwil Azar.

 Seek out sweet Ipoh treats such as egg custard tarts, white *ko pi* (coffee made with palm margarine and condensed milk) and *tau fu fah* (warm silken tofu pudding).

Clockwise from top left: Ipoh's speciality 'white' coffee; the karst cliffs around town are full of cave temples; a relic from Ipoh's past

Kanchenjunga Region

WELCOME TO THE UNSPOILT HIMALAYA IN NEPAL'S SILENT CORNER

While more than 57,000 trekkers and mountaineers tackle Everest Base Camp every year, the Kanchenjunga Conservation Area sees just 900 visitors annually. Don't expect apple pie (Everest's traveller comfort food) at every stop – you'll need backing from a trekking agency to follow the rough trails that climb to the base camps above Pang Pema and Ramche.

To soften the blow, remote farming villages provide welcome hot meals for the adventurous who make it out to this remote corner. And in exchange for the effort and expense, you'll get a truly unspoilt vision of the Himalaya, passing through some of the most dramatic terrain on the planet.

The trek to Everest Base Camp may transport hikers two-thirds of the way up the world's highest mountain, but the trails can often feel mobbed. Walkers who crave equally spectacular vistas with bonus silence trade the crowded paths of the Everest region for the empty wilds of far eastern Nepal, where Kanchenjunga – the third highest mountain on Earth at 8586m (28,169ft) tall – rises amid a glacial garden of snow peaks.

GO IF YOU LIKE...

- Everest Base Camp
- Sikkim, India
- Patagonia, Chile/Argentina
- mountains
- serious hiking holidays
- silence

Why go to Kanchenjunga Region?

The hike to Everest Base Camp is probably the world's most famous trek, so why make things harder by heading off the beaten path to Kanchenjunga? The answer is: for the peace and quiet. On the trails around EBC, overnight stops come with wi-fi, apple pie and constant company. In the Kanchenjunga Region, you can walk for days without seeing another trekking group – or another living soul, on more remote stretches of the trail.

So you won't have the distraction of a polyglot chorus of hikers discussing the view while you ponder your own insignificance in the face of the tallest mountains on the planet. The other perk of trekking in the Kanchenjunga Region is cultural immersion; assisting walkers is just a sideline for the Buddhist villagers who live here year-round, offering a window onto a way of life dictated by the rugged rhythms of the mountains themselves.

GETTING THERE

Kanchenjunga treks start from either Basantpur near Hile, or Taplejung near Ilam. Eco-minded travellers can cut out the air-miles by taking buses and jeeps to the trailheads from Kathmandu – a gruelling journey of at least 24 hours. Alternatively, small planes buzz into the miniature airstrip at Suketar near Taplejung, via the plains town of Biratnagar.

WHEN TO GO

Mar–May & Oct–Nov

Savvy trekkers avoid the bitter cold of winter and the view-obliterating rainclouds of the summer monsoon. The months immediately before and after the monsoon are best, offering warm, clear days and not too chilly nights.

FIRST-TIME TIPS

Make arrangements for Kanchenjunga treks before you set off – you'll need a permit (US$10 per week), which must be obtained through a trekking agency.

....

Get your TIMS (Trekking Information Management System) card from Kathmandu's Tourist Service Centre – you can't walk Nepal's main trekking routes without it.

....

Pay the Rs 2000 fee to enter the Kanchenjunga Conservation Area at Kathmandu's Tourist Service Centre or at the reserve entrance.

....

Ascend slowly. Acute Mountain Sickness is a serious danger here, so limit your rate of ascent and take a rest day every three days or so, or after any large gain in elevation.

AMAZING CROWD-FREE EXPERIENCES

 See Kanchenjunga face to face. The best, so-close-you-can-almost-touch-it views of the world's third-highest mountain are saved for those who make it to base camp.

 Tie Buddhist prayer flags on a mountain pass – your prayers for a successful trek will then be carried to heaven on the breeze.

 Follow the icy tongues of glaciers in the final stages of treks to Kanchenjunga, edging along the flanking moraines.

 Bathe in glacial meltwater; washing on Kanchenjunga treks is done in rustic camp showers (or not at all). Make time for at least one invigorating dip in a glacial stream.

 Have a night out on the tongba, the favoured tipple of the eastern Himalaya – a warm millet beer, best sampled in cook-pot-filled village kitchens.

 Take a tea tour in Ilam, where local tea plantations welcome visitors and you'll probably be the only tea-tourist in town.

Above: You'll need a permit to trek in the Kanchenjunga Region, but the rewards are huge

__Abhi Shrestha__
Rural Heritage
Nepal & Snow
Cat Travel

WHY I LOVE KANCHENJUNGA

Annapurna is enchanting, Everest is stunning, Kanchenjunga is rough! That's what defines Kanchenjunga. It's more remote, the wilderness is unadulterated and its people live in their own untouched world.

__Must-have local experience?__
Talking to locals. You won't forget times shared with yak herder families at 5000m!

__Favourite season?__
The best time to come is dictated by the weather. This is a tough place and it's best to visit when the weather is at its best, which means peak season (April to May and October to November). Kanchenjunga doesn't attract hordes of trekkers like some other trekking regions in Nepal, so it's never busy.

North Luzon

HEADHUNTERS AND SPANISH HISTORY IN THE JUNGLE HIGHLANDS ABOVE MANILA

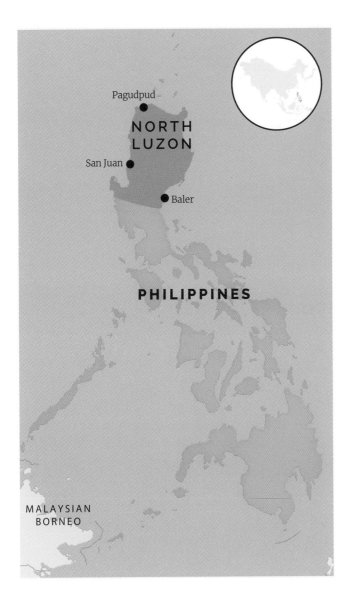

While the sugar-white beaches and world-class dive sites around Boracay, Cebu and El Nido are renowned worldwide, North Luzon – the 'head' of the 'old lady' that is the Philippines archipelago – is often overlooked. Yet it encapsulates the essence of the country better than any other island. Along the sea-hugging highway, surfers hit the waves at San Juan (La Union), Pagudpud and Baler. The 16th-century west coast city of Vigan has the finest Spanish colonial architecture in Asia, while impenetrable east coast jungle shelters many of the country's endemic species.

Inland, the forest-clad Cordillera mountain range beckons with its Unesco-acclaimed tiered rice terraces, white-water rivers, hanging coffins and skull-filled caves. The highland villages of the country's richest cultural enclave, the Kalinga province, where headhunting has taken place within living memory, ring with myriad different languages and dialects. Further out to sea, the soporific, traditional life on the Batanes islands feels a world away from Manila's nightclubs.

GO IF YOU LIKE...

- 💜 *Sulawesi's hanging coffins, Indonesia*
- 💜 *Goroka, Papua New Guinea*
- 💜 *Yuanyang Rice Terraces, China*
- 💜 *remote islands*
- 💜 *Sa Pa, Vietnam*
- 💜 *unique indigenous culture*

Why go to North Luzon?

No less spectacular than Vietnam, Thailand, Indonesia or Malaysia when it comes to jungle treks, highland adventure and island-hopping, North Luzon has an edge over its neighbours: it's comparatively untrodden, and its rugged topography and little-visited islands still provide plenty of scope for authentic adventure – without a single banana pancake or full-moon party in sight.

Travelling in the Cordillera and the Batanes can be a challenge. Landslides close precipitous roads after heavy rains, self-driving in the mountains is not for the fainthearted, and a typhoon may strand you on a remote island sans wi-fi. But on the upside, you'll get to witness some of the most unique surviving indigenous cultures in Southeast Asia, while contributing directly to local communities and helping to ensure their survival for some time to come. With climate change posing an additional challenge to traditional livelihoods, the time to support them by visiting responsibly is right now.

GETTING THERE
Manila is connected to major towns in North Luzon, such as San Juan, Vigan, Pagudpud and Baler, by frequent, comfortable buses. More remote destinations in the Cordillera – Sagada, Baguio, Batad, Kabayan and various villages in the Kalinga province – can also be reached fairly easily by public transport. There are near-daily flights to the Batanes islands.

WHEN TO GO

Dec–May

The most pleasant time of year for hiking in the Cordillera. While the rice terraces are greenest and most picturesque between July and October, that's also typhoon season. Temperatures are higher April to July, but you'll encounter fewer crowds.

© JEREMY VILLASIS | GETTY IMAGES. © ART PHANEUF / ALAMY STOCK PHOTO. © DUY PHUONG NGUYEN / ALAMY STOCK PHOTO

FIRST-TIME TIPS

Arrange a <u>trekking guide in Bontoc</u> for hikes in the Kalinga province before you arrive, as the best guides get snapped up quickly.

The <u>best time to view</u> the five Unesco World Heritage rice terraces in Ifugao (the Cordillera) varies: they are greenest in Banaue, Bangaan, Nagacadan and Mayoyao from June to July and February to March, while in Batad it's April to May and October to November.

Visiting the Batanes islands without your rain gear? Follow the locals' lead and <u>don a kanayi</u> (vest made from voyavoy palm fibres) if you're a man, or a vakul (voyavoy-made, wig-like headpiece) if you're a woman.

AMAZING CROWD-FREE EXPERIENCES

 Experience Ivatan culture in the Batanes by taking a round-bottomed falowa boat from Batan to Sabtang, overnighting in a homestay. You'll find thatch-roofed *vahay* (traditional limestone houses) and a grassy pre-Hispanic *idjang* (fortress) near Savidug.

 Check out the centuries-old Echo Valley hanging coffins, a short trek from the mist-shrouded mountain village of Sagada.

 Hike to Batad to spy its spectacular rice terraces from a ridge that's reachable only on foot.

 Trek with a local Ibaloi guide to the Timbac Caves from Kabayan in the Cordillera. Here, mummified remains can be seen, entombed in the traditional foetal position.

 Get a traditional bamboo-needle tattoo from the grandnieces of Whang-Od, the Cordillera's most celebrated Kalinga *mambabatok* (tattoo artist) in Buscalan.

 Go jungle trekking in the wild frontier of Northern Sierra Madre Natural Park, accessed only by tiny plane and weather-dependent boat.

Clockwise from top left: The hanging coffins of Sagada; a mountain village in Banaue; Vigan is known for its Spanish colonial architecture

Incheon & the West Sea Islands

IN SEOUL'S SHADOW, AN HISTORIC PORT WITH ISLAND-HOPPING POTENTIAL

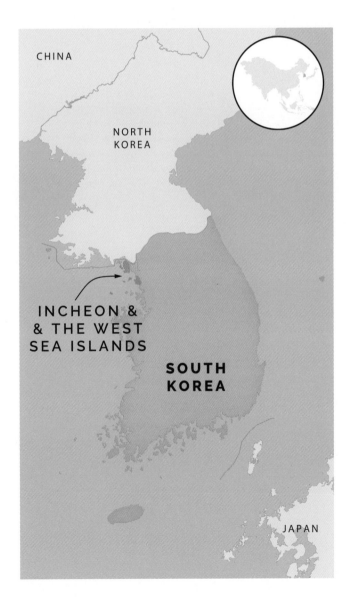

On the northwest coast of South Korea, just 27km (17 miles) from Seoul, is Incheon, the country's third largest city and home to its main international airport. Few visitors stick around to find out more about this historic port, home to 2.9 million people, preferring to head directly to the dynamic capital. Nevertheless, Incheon has plenty of fascinating attractions, including South Korea's only official Chinatown and a lively fresh fish market, alongside a similar contemporary urban vibe to Seoul, minus the tourist crowds.

Ferries from Incheon shuttle to the intriguing islands of the West Sea, all well off the international tourist trail. Options include Ganghwado, South Korea's fifth largest island, which was, for a brief period in the mid-13th century when the Mongols were rampaging through the mainland, home to Korea's capital. Or you can sail out to scenic and tranquil Deokjeokdo, 70km (43 miles) southwest of Incheon, to lounge on a blissful beach and hike up the island's main peak.

GO IF YOU LIKE...

- 🩶 *Yokohama, Japan*
- 🩶 *Busan, South Korea*
- 🩶 *heritage architecture*
- 🩶 *idyllic islands*
- 🩶 *freshly caught seafood*
- 🩶 *tranquil Buddhist temples*

Why go to Incheon & the islands?

In September 2020, Incheon became South Korea's first 'smart tourism' city, introducing AR (augmented reality) technology at attractions such as the Jajangmyeon Museum in its Chinatown. This atmospheric district, established in 1894 alongside the opening of the city's port of international trade, includes elaborately decorated *paifang* (gateway arches), murals, temples and delicious food. You might also recognise Incheon from scenes in Psy's *Gangnam Style* music video, which were shot around Songdo – Incheon's 'smart city'. Formed from reclaimed land along the waterfront, it's a district of buildings and infrastructure designed to be as sustainable as possible. Its Tri-bowl arts and culture complex is comprised of three giant bowl-shaped structures that appear to float on water.

In complete contrast is the beautiful hilltop temple of Jeondeung-sa on the island of Ganghwado. Enjoy a free vegetarian lunch here or spend the night as part of the national Templestay programme (eng.templestay.com).

GETTING THERE
Incheon International Airport is on the island of Yeongjongdo, an hour from Incheon city by bus. Alternatively, slow boats from China's port of Dalian arrive at Incheon's two International Ferry Terminals. To reach the West Sea Islands, ferries depart from the separate Coastal Ferry Terminal at Yeonan Pier.

WHEN TO GO

Jun & Sep

The best months for relaxing on the beaches of the West Sea Islands, with less chance of the heavy rains that can drench the region in July and August.

FIRST-TIME TIPS

Ganghwado's main town, Ganghwa-eup, is where all buses crossing the bridge from the mainland end up, and makes a logical base from which to embark on your tour of the island's attractions.

When travelling to the more remote West Sea Islands such as Deokjeokdo, be sure to take plenty of cash as you may struggle to find working ATMs.

Don't expect much in the way of fancy accommodation on the islands – this is your chance to connect with locals at simple pensions and minbak (private homes with rooms for rent).

AMAZING CROWD-FREE EXPERIENCES

 Stroll through Jayu, a picturesque hilltop park designed by a Russian civil engineer in 1888 that connects Incheon's historic Open Port and Chinatown areas.

 Chill out in Songdo's seaside Central Park and inspect the ambitious architecture of the Tri-bowl arts and culture hall.

 Climb a pine-covered hillside to the temple Bonmun-sa on the island of Seongmodo, accessed by ferry from Ganghwado, to view its grotto and 10m (33ft)-tall Buddha rock carving.

 Marvel at the Bugeun-ri Dolmen, a Bronze Age tomb made from a trio of giant stones on the island of Ganghwado.

 Explore the partially restored remains of the 13th-century Goryeogungji Palace in Ganghwa-eup, a relic of when Ganghwado was Korea's capital.

 Camp out on Seopori Beach, a spectacular 2km (1.2 mile) stretch of golden sand along Deokjeokdo's southern shore, backed by a thick grove of 200-year-old pine trees.

Above: Ganghwado island was briefly home to Korea's capital in the 13th century, when Mongols were sweeping through the country

Left: The shores of
Iskander Kul are
a popular place
for waterfront
cottage rentals

Fann Mountains

TALL PEAKS AND WARM WELCOMES IN ONE OF CENTRAL ASIA'S OLDEST REGIONS

Across the southern edge of the Syr-Darya watershed, on a route once trodden by Alexander the Great, Tajikistan's Fann Mountains offer the opportunity to explore imposing alpine landscapes and azure mountain lakes, cultural sites as old as civilisation itself, and community-based tourism initiatives connecting travellers directly with local families. Long on the radar of Soviet and CIS mountaineers, the region has widely escaped the notice of global tourism.

Though visitors more often climb east along the Pamir Highway, opting for this corner of northwestern Tajikistan reveals mountain ridges and cultural sites that match the history and grandeur of the more beaten path. The important Sogdian murals from Penjikent, linked to ancient Iran and now in St Petersburg's Hermitage Museum, speak of this area's diverse ethnic and religious heritage; while nearby Unesco-listed Sarazm grabs guidebook headlines — a wander through the ruins of either takes visitors back over four millennia to the first human settlements in Central Asia.

GO IF YOU LIKE...

💜 *Central Asian hospitality*
🤍 *Nepal teahouse treks*
🩶 *overland adventure*
💜 *remote alpine lakes*
💜 *overlooked Unesco sites*
💜 *Soviet-era relics*

Why go to the Fann Mountains?

Atop the Chukurak Pass (3180m/10,433ft), views fan out to every horizon – east to the sparkling Kulikalon Lakes and Alauddin Pass, west to Igrok Pass and Haft Kul's seven lakes, north and south to rugged peaks that attract alpinists from afar. Descending from the mountains in any direction, small village homestays welcome travellers for a night's rest and a hot meal – whether organised formally through the region's dual community-based tourism associations or resulting from the informal traditional welcome to passing guests. The combination of compelling landscapes and warm hospitality play out over and over across the Fann Mountains, forming a central element of the travel experience here. A surprisingly rich archaeological history shows life in the region has rolled this way for centuries – and with the 2018 reopening of the direct border crossing between modern Penjikent and Uzbekistan's Samarkand, travellers can once more travel overland along this strand of the ancient Silk Roads.

Right: Tajikistan's rugged peaks exert a magnetic pull on mountain lovers

Below: The spectacular rocky scree hike to Chimtarga Pass

FIRST-TIME TIPS

Tajikistan has announced <u>visa-free travel</u> for 52 countries from 2022 – if you're not on the list, leave a few weeks to process an e-visa (evisa.tj/index.evisa.html)

. . . .

<u>Dress modestly</u> – Tajikistan is still a conservative society.

. . . .

English-speaking <u>trekking guides are hard to find</u> – book early with one of Penjikent's community-based organisations: Zerafshan Tourism Board or Zerafshan Tourism Development Association.

. . . .

Travellers will benefit from a <u>basic vocabulary in Russian</u> (the lingua franca of Central Asia) or Tajik (a close relative of Farsi), particularly if utilising the region's homestay network to live with local families.

GETTING THERE

On a Tajikistan-only trip, fly into capital city Dushanbe and arrange a private or shared taxi for the five-hour drive to the Fann Mountains' city of Penjikent. On a longer Central Asia overland journey, cross between Penjikent and Uzbekistan's tourist hub of Samarkand in about 1.5 hours, allowing time for a brief stop for border formalities.

WHEN TO GO

Jun–Sep

In summer the snows have melted at lower elevations while the high passes are at least passable – in the middle altitude, lush green growth and colourful wildflowers linger into early summer. Expect heat on the plans near Penjikent.

AMAZING CROWD-FREE EXPERIENCES

 Dig into the history of the Sarazm Proto-Urban archaeological site, Unesco-listed ruins of one of the first human settlements in all of Central Asia.

 Climb the steep rocky scree hike to Chimtarga Pass below the stunning profile of Chimtarga Peak (5489m/18,008ft), which looms above.

 Bargain in the greatest Silk Roads tradition at modern Penjikent's busy bazaar for everything from foodstuffs to footwear, or wander in for endless people-watching.

 Splash out on a private cottage on the shores of Iskander Kul, a popular mountain lake where the Tajikistan president keeps a summer home.

 Stand awestruck at the ornate mausoleum of Rudaki, the literary giant of modern Persian, an unexpected sight in the tiny mountain village where he was born.

 Strap on sturdy hiking boots to explore the remote Yagnob Valley, home to the Yagnobi people and language, descended directly from ancient Sogdian.

Ko Tarutao Marine National Park

RESORT-FREE BEACHES IN A PROTECTED OUTPOST OF SOUTHERN THAILAND

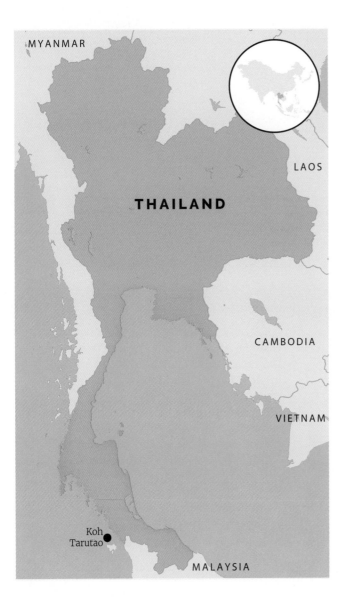

MYANMAR

LAOS

THAILAND

CAMBODIA

VIETNAM

Koh Tarutao

MALAYSIA

The Thai islands are Asia's favourite tropical escape, but peace and quiet on the beaches of Koh Samui, Koh Tao or Ko Pha-Ngan? Forget about it. Lucky, then, that there's one group of islands that have escaped the excesses of the developers – the Tarutao archipelago, so close to Malaysia you can almost see Langkawi Island.

How did this group of sand-circled islands escape the resort-builders? Thank the Thai officials who designated this former state prison a marine national park in 1974. Apart from Ko Lipe – a sea gypsy island with a buzzing backpacker scene – the 51 islands in the Tarutao group are preserved in time, with monkey-filled rainforest groves, resort-free beaches, fish-mobbed coral reefs, and precious few crowds. While camping on the national park beaches, spare a thought for the political prisoners who spent decades interred in front of views that people now regard as paradise. It's one of the last remaining snapshots of what all the islands of the Malay Peninsula looked like before mass tourism.

GO IF YOU LIKE...

💜 *Ko Phi Phi*
🤍 *Ko Chang*
🖤 *Koh Rong*
🤍 *coral atolls*
🤍 *beach camping*
💜 *peace & quiet*

Why go to Ko Tarutao?

You could always stay on Ko Lipe and day trip to the national park islands, but the best Tarutao experience is sleeping on the laid-back national park islands of Ko Tarutao and Ko Adang. The Department of National Parks maintains simple, inexpensive lodges, campgrounds and canteens on both islands, where you'll meet more Thai students than international backpackers. Staying at these agreeably institutional national park hubs, you can bask on beautiful beaches, hike through dense tropical forests teeming with wildlife, kayak the coastline and enjoy sunsets made even more special by the lack of tourists recovering from last night's full moon party. On Ko Adang, you can snorkel right off the beach.

The general lack of development and crowds means abundant nature. Reassuringly, the crocodiles and sharks that once discouraged prison escapes are absent today, but it's easy to spot mouse deer, crab-eating macaques, giant squirrels and boars, plus sea eagles and hornbills, all over the national park.

GETTING THERE

There's no airport in the archipelago so people arrive by boat from Pak Bara, close to Satun on the Thai mainland. You can reach Satun by bus from Bangkok, but it's more comfortable to cover the bulk of the distance by train (or air), travelling first to Hat Yai, on the international rail route between Bangkok and Padang Besar in Malaysia.

WHEN TO GO

Nov–May

The monsoon drenches the Ko Tarutao region from May to October, sometimes making sea crossings dangerous. Accordingly, the national park only opens during the dry season from November to mid-May.

FIRST-TIME TIPS

Check the political situation in the south – the islands are generally safe, but Hat Yai and other towns on the overland route towards Ko Tarutao have been targeted by Thai separatist rebels in the past.

....

Stock up on essentials before you go. If you're staying on Ko Lipe, you'll find the usual backpacker infrastructure (7-Elevens, beach bars and so on) but on the national park islands, resources are limited to simple park canteens and perhaps a basic shop.

....

Bring cash for meals, boat fares and paying the 200 Baht national park fee; the only ATMs are on Ko Lipe.

AMAZING CROWD-FREE EXPERIENCES

 Camp like Robinson Crusoe on the sands at one of the national park's campsites – There are three on Ko Tarutao, and one more on Ko Adang.

 Paddle the shoreline in a kayak, which can be hired from the park's headquarters at Ao Pante. Ko Tarutao's notorious saltwater crocodiles are extinct, so it's perfectly safe.

 Go birdwatching to spy hornbills, sunbirds, Brahminy kites and more – you don't need to be a committed spotter to be impressed.

 Hike the wilds from Talo Wao to Talo Udang along Ko Tarutao's 12km (7.5 mile) trail that follows the path once walked by political prisoners.

 Go diving and snorkelling around the marine park; operators on Ko Lipe can take you to sites resplendent with abundant marine life.

 Rent a longtail boat to reach empty beaches away from Ko Lipe, perfect for a quiet doze as you're unlikely to see another soul.

Above: Clear waters surround the Ko Tarutao Marine National Park, a haven for divers and snorkellers

Aral Sea

AN ECOLOGICAL DISASTER ZONE FINDING ITS WAY WITH COMMUNITY TOURISM

RUSSIA

KAZAKHSTAN

● Aral Sea

UZBEKISTAN

TURKMENISTAN

TAJIKISTAN

natural resources can have long-lasting repercussions.

In the 1960s, the Aral Sea – then the world's fourth-largest saltwater lake – supported a thriving fishing industry and supplied a quarter of the Soviet Union's fish. Then the ill-conceived Soviet monoculture farming schemes led to the diversion of the Amu-Darya and Syr-Darya rivers that fed the sea to water the production of cotton – a notoriously thirsty plant – in Uzbekistan and Turkmenistan. This set in motion irreversible ecological catastrophe on an epic scale. Today, tourism provides a trickle of income for communities whose historic livelihoods have been ruined.

I t's a scene of utter desolation: a handful of rusted boats – all that remains of the fishing fleet in Moynaq, Uzbekistan – reclining on a bed of scrubland-studded salt flats. Beyond lies a vast expanse of desert and what remains of the sea is now more than 200km (124 miles) away. Striking yet utterly tragic, a visit to the Aral Sea – either on the Uzbekistan side or from Kazakhstan – is an important lesson in how careless human misuse of

GO IF YOU LIKE...

💜 *Chernobyl, Ukraine*
💜 *Dead Sea, Israel*
💜 *Nevada National Security Site, USA*
💜 *Hiroshima Peace Memorial,*
💜 *Japan*

111

Why go to the Aral Sea?

Like a landscape out of a dystopian sci-fi movie, the ship graveyard in Moynaq and the metal hulks of fishing barges lying in the shallow water of the North Aral are a poignant and unforgettable sight. And this man-made disaster is now more topical than ever, as humanity struggles against climate change. The dilapidated Kazakhstan town of Aral, gateway to its namesake body of water, has seen the return of a modest fishing industry thanks to the construction of the Kok-Aral Dam in 2005, which has led to the slow rise of the water levels. It's now a base for NGO-led visits to the striking desert landscape surrounding North Aral.

On the Uzbekistan side, the South Aral gateway town of Nukus is well worth a stay for community-led camping, tomb explorations and outdoor adventure trips. It's also a surprising home for the Savitsky Museum, which holds the second most important collection of contemporary art in the former Soviet Union after the State Russian Museum in St Petersburg.

GETTING THERE

Once you've got your visa to Uzbekistan, getting to Nukus is straightforward. Most international visitors fly into Tashkent, the capital, and you can then combine visits to the Silk Road cities of Samarkand, Bukhara and Khiva with an extended train journey north to Nukus. On the Kazakh side, Aral is reachable via a 30-hour train ride from Almaty.

WHEN TO GO

Apr–Jun & Sep

The most pleasant times to visit, since you avoid the searing heat of summer. On the Kazakhstan side in particular, the desert near the sea is abloom with wildflowers in spring.

AMAZING CROWD-FREE EXPERIENCES

Clamber onto fishing vessel remnants in Moynaq, and gaze out over the desolation of the former seabed.

Seek out the *Aral Pieta* painting at the Savitsky Museum in Nukus, depicting the Aral Sea as an emaciated infant, cradled by a sorrowful mother.

Swim in the North Aral near the fishing village of Tastubek, and scramble up rock formations on a day excursion from Aral with Aral Tenizi NGO.

Take a two-day 4WD cross-country camping trip from Nukus with Ayim Tour or BesQala Tours. You'll get to watch the sun rise over what's left of the South Aral and float suspended in the super-saline water.

Marvel over the ancient tombs of Mizdakhan — a vital Silk Road city from the 4th century BC until the 14th century. It's a 40km (25 miles) roundtrip taxi journey from Nukus. Highlights include the 12th-century underground Mausoleum of Mazlum Khan Slu and the seven-domed Mausoleum of Shamun Nabi.

Clockwise from top left: Tastubek is one of the Aral Sea's few remaining fishing villages; the Silk Road tombs of Mizdakhan

Mountain-biking around Downieville
in California's Lost Sierra
© JOHN WATSON / WWW.THERADAVIST.COM

Americas

Waterton Lakes National Park

MOVE OVER BANFF AND GLACIER — THIS ROCKY MOUNTAINS BOLTHOLE HAS IT ALL

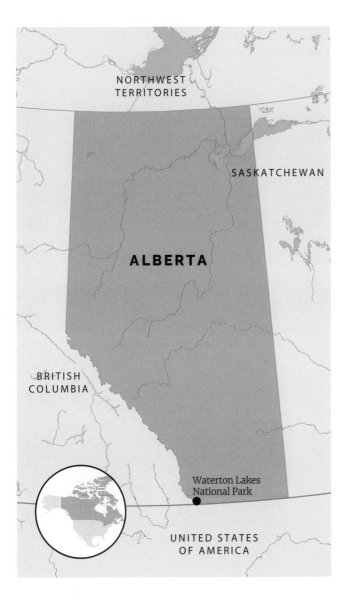

In the Rocky Mountains between the big-ticket national parks of Glacier in the US and Banff in Canada, Waterton Lakes enjoys less celebrity and less traffic than its esteemed neighbours. Yet this spectacular pocket of the Rockies has international pedigree. Inaugurated in 1895 as one of the world's first national parks, it has since been recognised by Unesco as a Biosphere Reserve and World Heritage Site. To add to its uniqueness, Waterton was conjoined with Glacier in 1932 to form America's first International Peace Park, as a symbol of the longstanding relationship between the two countries.

With its small town and handsome heritage hotel surrounded by chiselled mountains and a long navigable lake, Waterton is, in many ways, a microcosm of the larger Rocky Mountain parks to the north. But with all its sights stuffed into a compact 505 sq km (195 sq miles), its wilderness is refreshingly accessible. A rugged trail network emanates directly from Waterton's town and more than 800 wildflower species dot its brawny backcountry, along with bears, cougars and ungulates.

GO IF YOU LIKE…

- 💙 *Banff, Canada*
- 💙 *the Rockies*
- 💙 *Glacier National Park, USA*
- 💙 *lake cruises*
- 💙 *alpine hikes*
- 💙 *camping*

117

Why go to Waterton Lakes?

Waterton is famed for its high-altitude trails that deliver hikers almost instantaneously to lofty alpine terrain with expansive views over the Crown of the Continent, as the region is nicknamed. The best of them, the Carthew-Alderson Trail, is one of the finest above-the-treeline hikes in the Americas. A couple of smooth, serviceable roads, including the Akamina Parkway, provide good routes for cyclists and complement a compact network of single-track routes. Big fauna is abundant and easy to spot — sitting on the cusp of the mountains and prairies, Waterton is home to both grizzly bears and bison.

Thanks to its early development, the park supports a townsite (unusual in Canada) making it easy to organise activities and accommodation from a central base. Adventurous pursuits are juxtaposed with less hazardous hobbies — there's a vintage Swiss-meets-Scottish hotel, a lake cruise to the US border, and even a golf course.

GETTING THERE

Waterton lies in Alberta's southwestern corner, 270km (168 miles) south of Calgary. The one road entrance into the park is in its northeastern corner, along Hwy 5. Car rental is available at Calgary International Airport. Alternatively, buses from Calgary and Fort Macleod will get you as far as Pincher Creek from where you can get a taxi the final 56km (35 miles) to Waterton town.

WHEN TO GO

Jun–Sep

July and August offer the best weather and the most recreational opportunities, but also draw over half the annual visitors. Late spring is good for migratory birds and waterfalls. Early fall brings golden foliage, quiet trails and slightly cheaper accommodation.

AMAZING CROWD-FREE EXPERIENCES

 Negotiate the Crypt Lake Trail 'obstacle course', a hike involving a water taxi journey, ladder climbing, a crawl through a narrow tunnel and a scramble up a rockface.

 Visit placid Cameron Lake at the three-way meeting point of Montana, Alberta and British Columbia. It's an idyllic spot for picnics, hiking and boating.

 Follow the Carthew-Alderson Trail on the roof of the Rockies, a panoramic path through forests, meadows and rough scree from Cameron Lake back to Waterton.

 Circumnavigate Mount Crandell on the Crandell Lake cycle loop, a 16km (10 miles) trail mixing road-biking with single-track using Waterton's paths and parkways.

 Hike Upper Waterton Lake to North America's loneliest border post. It's 13km (8 miles) to the northern reaches of Glacier NP.

 Pitch a tent at Upper Twin Lakes camp ground on the 31km (19 mile)-long Tamarack Trail. Here you'll get to admire the night sky in the world's only trans-boundary International Dark Sky Park.

Above: Classic Rocky Mountain scenes await in Waterton Lakes, but fewer visitors than in Glacier National Park or Banff

Left: Far-reaching lake views surround the summit of Tin Hat Mountain

Sunshine Coast Trail

AN EPIC ADVENTURE TRAVELLING HUT-TO-HUT ACROSS BRITISH COLUMBIA

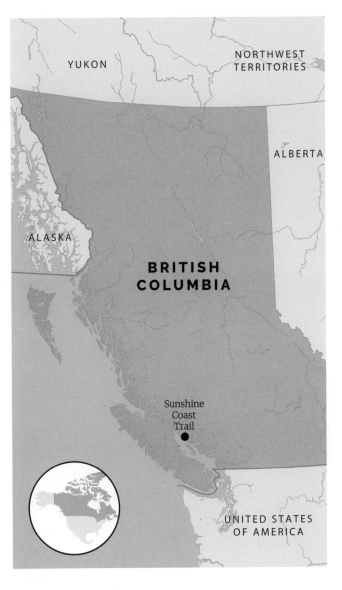

Canada's longest backcountry hut-to-hut hiking route travels through the forests and mountains of coastal British Columbia in the region known as the Sunshine Coast. Yes, it can be sunny as you traverse this 180km (112 mile) route above the Pacific Ocean, particularly during the summer months, but you're trekking in a temperate coastal rainforest, too. You'll cross mossy bridges, shade yourself among old-growth firs and cedars, and—if you're lucky—spot bald eagles soaring above the treetops as you hike.

There are 14 rustic huts in total – all free to use. Versatility is part of the beauty of this trail: those who don't want to tackle the entire route, which takes most experienced hikers 10 to 12 days, can day-hike sections, plan a shorter multiple-day backpacking trip, or organise an inn-to-inn adventure that combines hiking with craft beer tasting, canoeing and small-town exploring. Midway up the coast, the town of Powell River is a good base for tackling the trail in smaller segments.

GO IF YOU LIKE...

- ♥ *Tour du Mont Blanc, Switzerland*
- ♥ *Haute Route, Switzerland*
- ♥ *White Mountains, USA*
- ♥ *San Juan Huts, USA*
- ♥ *John Muir Trail, USA*
- ♥ *West Coast Trail, Canada*

Why go to the Sunshine Coast Trail?

Though its first section was completed back in 2000, the Sunshine Coast Trail is still relatively unknown among long-distance hikers, particularly outside the region. There are also fewer hikers here because it's harder to get to the trailhead – the Sunshine Coast itself, while technically part of British Columbia's mainland, is accessible only by ferry, making it feel more remote.

Although the Sunshine Coast Trail is rated moderate to difficult, there's something for everyone here. Some sections are family friendly, while others will challenge even the most hard-core hiker. Several segments have significant elevation gains, rewarding those who make the climbs with stellar views across the mountains and the sea. An added bonus to this long-distance adventure is that it lies close enough to Vancouver for you to be able to start or end your trip with an urban escape. Reward your exertions with visits to the city's museums, downtown parks and beaches, and casual farm-to-table restaurants. Just pack your urban blue jeans along with your hiking boots.

GETTING THERE

Vancouver is the international gateway. BC Ferries operate car ferry services from Horseshoe Bay, northwest of downtown Vancouver, to Langdale at the Sunshine Coast's southern end. From Langdale, it's a 80km (50 mile) drive north to Earls Cove, where you catch a second ferry to Saltery Bay, on the Upper Sunshine Coast, where the Sunshine Coast Trail begins.

WHEN TO GO

Jun–Sep

The driest months on the Sunshine Coast are during the summer and early fall; October to April are particularly rainy throughout coastal British Columbia. Snow can linger into May at higher elevations.

FIRST-TIME TIPS

The Sunshine Coast Trail Guidebook by RE (Eagle) Walz is the most detailed planning resource available. Order it via the Powell River Information Visitor Centre (tourism-powellriver.ca).

....

Check the trail's website (sunshinecoast-trail.com) or Facebook page (facebook.com/ SunshineCoastTrail) for updates on trail conditions.

....

Each hut sleeps eight to 12 people and beds are available on a first-come, first-served basis. It's wise to also pack a tent, in case a hut is full or you need to stop early.

....

Black bears live on the Sunshine Coast. Make noise as you hike to avoid surprising them and secure your food out of reach overnight.

AMAZING CROWD-FREE EXPERIENCES

 Take in the views of Desolation Sound from the water shuttle that runs from the town of Lund to Sarah Point, the northernmost entry to the Sunshine Coast Trail.

 Climb to a mountaintop lookout with a 360-degree vista when you overnight in the Tin Hat Hut at the trail's halfway point.

 Scan the trees and shoreline for wildlife as you hike. Great blue herons and eagles hide in the forests, and you can catch a glimpse of sea lions, seals and otters as the trail skirts the sea.

 Explore the old-growth forest surrounding the Troubridge Hut, a log cabin built of Douglas fir that sits below the summit of Mount Troubridge.

 Cool your tired feet in cool forest lakes. The huts at Inland, Confederation and Elk Lakes all have swimming beaches or secluded spots for a dunk.

 Sleep by the sea in the Fairview Hut at the trail's southern end, before catching the ferry back to civilisation.

Clockwise from top left: The overnight cabin at Tin Hat Mountain; the Sunshine Coast's Saltery Bay; paddling on Desolation Sound

Ontario's Black History Sites

THE UNDERGROUND RAILROAD LED MANY FORMERLY ENSLAVED PEOPLE TO CANADA

In the 1800s, the network of safe houses across the US known as the Underground Railroad sheltered formerly enslaved people escaping to freedom. At least 30,000 of the Black Americans who followed this route settled in Canada, the majority in southwestern Ontario. Several sites across this region, west of Toronto and east of Detroit, enable visitors to learn more about the lives that these new Canadians established and the experiences of their descendants. While many locations across the US educate visitors about slavery and the struggles for civil rights, fewer travellers are aware of the way history played out in Canada.

The Ontario communities with key Black settlements include Windsor, Sandwich, Amherstburg, Dresden, Buxton and Chatham. The latter became a hub of intellectual life for Black Canadians known as 'Black Mecca.' The region's attractions immerse visitors in railroad history, as you walk through 19th-century cabins and schoolrooms, examine shackles used on the enslaved, or listen to (virtual) dogs barking as if you, too, were fleeing to freedom.

GO IF YOU LIKE...

- ♥ *Black history*
- ♥ *Civil Rights narratives*
- ♥ *US Civil Rights Trail*
- ♥ *Ebenezer Baptist Church, USA*
- ♥ *Robben Island, South Africa*
- ♥ *Canadian Museum for Human Rights*

Why go to Ontario's Black History Sites?

As many North Americans reckon with ongoing racial injustices, and in light of the Black Lives Matter movement, learning about the history and narratives of both Black Americans and Black Canadians has become even more important. While Canada may have a reputation as an open, just society, the nation's history does not fully support that image. Slavery was legal in the country throughout the 1600s and 1700s.

In 1793, the legislature of Upper Canada (encompassing present-day Ontario) passed an act decreeing that no new slaves could be brought into the territory. However, it wasn't until 1833 that the British Slavery Abolition Act freed enslaved people in Canada and elsewhere across the British Empire. This 19th-century law helped pave the way for formerly enslaved Americans to travel north to freedom, leading to the establishment of significant Black settlements in Southwestern Ontario.

GETTING THERE

Toronto Pearson International Airport is the main Canadian air gateway to Southwestern Ontario, but Detroit Metro Airport, across the border in the US, is also convenient. Via Rail trains travel between Toronto and Windsor, which makes a good starting point for explorations. Once you reach the region, public transit between communities is limited, so it's easiest to explore by car.

WHEN TO GO

May–early Oct

Summer has the warmest temperatures and everything is open; September and October are good months to visit if you want to combine your trip with autumn leaf-peeping and crisp days.

FIRST-TIME TIPS

Check opening hours for each site before visiting as they can change seasonally and not all are open year-round. Some require advance reservations.

....

If you're unfamiliar with this history, don't hesitate to ask questions as you're visiting these sites, but always be respectful.

....

The Slavery to Freedom site (heritagetrust.on.ca/en/pages/our-stories/slavery-to-freedom), created by the Ontario Heritage Trust, provides excellent background information about Black history in the province.

....

The Southwest Ontario Tourism Corporation's website (ontariossouthwest.com) is a helpful resource for planning travel to the region.

AMAZING CROWD-FREE EXPERIENCES

 Sit at a desk in one of North America's first integrated schools at the Buxton National Historic Site and Museum; Buxton was once Canada's largest Black settlement.

 Learn about Ontario's prominent Black citizens at Chatham's Black Mecca Museum and take a walking tour through the neighbourhood's heritage.

 Hear stories that inspired Harriet Beecher Stowe's famous abolitionist novel at the Uncle Tom's Cabin Historic Site, near Reverend Josiah Henson's Dawn Settlement.

 Walk through a formerly enslaved family's cabin at Amherstburg Freedom Museum, where you can also visit one of Canada's earliest Black churches.

 Imagine your own route on the Underground Railroad at the immersive John Freeman Walls Historic Site and Underground Railroad Museum.

 Tour one of Canada's oldest still-active Black worship sites, the Sandwich First Baptist Church National Historic Site, and learn about its Underground Railroad links.

Clockwise from top left: Windsor's Tower of Freedom Underground Railroad Monument; the Harriet Tubman statue at St Catharines; Henson House at Uncle Tom's site

Shannon Prince
curator, Buxton National Historic Site & Museum

WHY I LOVE BUXTON

Buxton was an integrated school from its founding in 1849, when all the other schools around were segregated. My husband and I, our parents, our grandparents — we all went to this school. It was an honour and privilege.

Must-have local experience?
In Chatham, they have a cool walking tour of different Black businesses and Freedom Park, where there's a bust of Mary Ann Shadd, who founded The Provincial Freeman [making her the first Black newspaper publisher in Canada].

Favourite season?
Summer is the winner to do things outside, but it's nice in fall, too.

Left: Where the Río Magdalena meets the sleepy town of Mompós

Bolívar

DELVE BEYOND BUSY CARTAGENA INTO REVOLUTIONARY RURAL COLOMBIA

Named after Simón Bolívar, who led Colombia to independence from the Spanish empire in 1819, this region of Colombia is profoundly unique – both culturally and topographically. Feeding off the glorious and mighty Río Magdalena, it begins at the northern coast and extends south into the nation's heartland. Gateway to the region is the popular Caribbean port city of Cartagena – a favourite dock for passing cruise ships

— but the rest of Bolívar receives far fewer tourists and is arguably more remarkable, giving visitors an insight into Colombia's sleepy and charming rural culture.

Driving south, the pace goes quickly from the loud and vibrant streets of Cartagena to the laconic vibration of small-town life. Seeing the same grand Spanish architecture you would expect in larger Colombian cities decorating the region's tiny historic towns – some with revolutionary ties – makes Bolívar feel quite unlike any other place in the world. Its magic was not lost on Nobel Prize winner Gabriel García Márquez, who found inspiration for his magic-realist novel *One Hundred Years of Solitude* in this isolated, enchanted locale.

GO IF YOU LIKE...

- ♥ *friendly locals*
- ♥ *charming small towns*
- ♥ *literary history*
- ♥ *Spanish architecture*
- ♥ *road trips*

Why go to Bolívar?

As the second-most biodiverse country on the planet and one of the 20 founding members of the important Future of Tourism Coalition, Colombia is one of the few nations in the world to have put legislation behind their sustainability pledge. In Bolívar specifically, the Magdalena River is a goldmine for sustainable tourism and ecotourism. Community-based initiatives in Afro-Latino communities give directly back to the area. Visitors can go on locally run fishing trips, take dance lessons, join boat trips on wooden canoes helmed by local captains and stalk through the jungle on exotic birdwatching tours.

For wildlife junkies, the misty riverbanks of the Magdalena are a delight, home to the spectacled caiman, the American crocodile, the brown pelican and the West Indian manatee. And this region has even more: offshore from Cartagena lie Caribbean islands including Isla Barú and Islas del Rosario — a marine paradise and a little-known pearl-harvesting region, home to some of the most lustrous gems in the world.

GETTING THERE

Cartagena's Rafael Núñez International Airport is the main gateway to the region. From Cartagena, it's about 5hr 30min by car to Magangué, the main city of Bolívar's interior region. Ferries and water taxis run from Magangué across the Magdalena River to Mompós. To get to offshore islands such as Barú and the Rosarios, take a speedboat or locally operated ferry from Cartagena.

WHEN TO GO

Dec–Feb

The best time to visit Bolívar is early December to mid-February. The peak window is small and prices will be higher, but the weather is truly gorgeous and well worth it. At other times of year, the heat is oppressive and the skies can be overcast.

FIRST-TIME TIPS

Wear loose, breathable clothing if possible. Temperatures in Colombia's interior increase swiftly around midday.

....

Grocery-shop locally. Rather than dining out, buy exotic fruits from a market or low-priced vegetables from vendors.

....

Buy a copy of Gabriel García Marquez' One Hundred Years of Solitude or Love in the Time of Cholera, both set in Bolívar, and follow in the footsteps of the author's famous characters.

....

Bring a swimsuit. The interior may not have the beaches of the Caribbean, but there will be many opportunities to jump in the Magdalena River.

AMAZING CROWD-FREE EXPERIENCES

 Attend a local church service in Mompós at 17th-century Iglesia de Santa Barbara. It's one of the most beautiful churches in the country and, arguably, the world.

 Take a boat ride down the mighty Río Magdalena. This river is the irrigation source for the entire region and an emblem of national pride.

 Buy locally made silver souvenirs in Mompós. The town is known for its skilled silversmiths and their wares, made with some of the world's finest silver.

 Watch the full moon rise over a river town. In charming towns like San Agustín and Mompós, it's a prime local activity to stroll along the river after dusk.

 Attend a *novena* celebration for the nine days of Christmas. Rural Bolívar goes all out with fireworks, hours-long dinners, and the singing of *villancicos* (religious folk songs).

 Stay at Isla Baru's sustainable Las Islas Hotel, which supports community initiatives and helps fund marine habitat conservation on this pearling island.

Above: Mompós, officially called Santa Cruz de Mompox, has Spanish colonial architecture and a revolutionary past

Camagüey

THIS ELEGANT FILM-SET CITY IS AS COOL AS THE CUBAN CAPITAL

You are walking the labyrinthine streets of a debonair Cuban city. Baroque cupolas soar above cobbled thoroughfares. An alleyway opens into a bright plaza where musicians perform and smartly dressed old men play chequers. Suave cafes and restaurants tastefully decorated in memorabilia illuminating the city's glamorous past serve excellent coffee, rum and seafood. A refurbished museum or three reveal all about the internationally renowned local personalities (a game-changing revolutionary, a seminal poet, a ground-breaking doctor). Dignified old movie theatres point to a strong cinema-going tradition here. A festival is often on, for this is a culturally proud place and the city tempo is *allegro* with a huge 'A'.

As the day draws on, you return to your *casa particular* (homestay) – a palatial historic building that would be remarkable were it not for the fact that so much of this cityscape is palatial and historic. It might sound like Havana, but this is Camagüey: less-crowded and more mellow, but with all the sophistication of the capital.

GO IF YOU LIKE...

- 💚 *Havana*
- 💚 *old-fashioned elegance*
- 💚 *Baroque architecture*
- 💚 *centuries-old streets*
- 💚 *cinema*
- 💚 *revolutionary heroes*

Why go to Camagüey?

A good-looking, culturally buoyant city might not be such a talking point in many corners of the world, but in Cuba, where most settlements are crying out for TLC, well-kept Camagüey stands out. Recipient of a dazzling makeover for its 2014 quincentenary, its buildings, streets and public spaces now sparkle with vitality. This is somewhere to come to see Cuban culture making bold, bright new moves.

Camagüey is a city showcasing its pedigree with grace. Take a spruced-up street like Calle Cinema, its businesses full of fresh paint and insights into the city's cinematographic legacy. Take magical places to stay like Los Vitrales, a former convent converted into superlative accommodation. Or take a rejuvenated plaza like San Juan de Dios, where one of Cuba's grandest restaurants awaits. Along with urban sophistication, Camagüey has a central location that makes it one of the best bases for exploring — you could be cooling off in a resort backing onto one of Cuba's longest, loveliest beaches in less time than it takes to reach Varadero from Havana.

Right: The streets of Camagüey are a riot of colourful buildings dating back 500 years

Below: Camagüey has many of the same attributes as Havana — 1950s cars and interesting history

FIRST-TIME TIPS

Although not as bad as in Havana, Camagüey is not without its jiniteros (street touts), who can pester you for all manner of services. The best way to deal with them is to politely but firmly decline and continue walking.

The city has several fantastic accommodation options and lots of average ones; to score the best rooms, book a week or two in advance.

Consider embellishing a city visit with a trip to Camagüey Province's north coast, under two hours away, where a 20km (12 mile) stretch of sandy beach beckons at the Playa Santa Lucía resort complex.

GETTING THERE

Bus is the most convenient and practical way to reach Camagüey; national operator Viazul runs from Havana (8–9hr) in the west and Santiago de Cuba (6hr) in the east. Camagüey is also on the long-distance train line between Havana and Santiago de Cuba and, pre-covid, efforts had been made to improve the service; journey time from Havana is around 10 hours.

WHEN TO GO

Nov–Apr

These dry-season months are best for visiting Cuba, especially as they dodge hurricane season. Weather aside, good months for festivities are February, June and September.

AMAZING CROWD-FREE EXPERIENCES

 Stroll the maze of characterful cobbled streets, supposedly built so higgledy-piggledy to confuse invading pirates, gazing at the graceful colonial buildings.

 Book a table at classy Restaurante 1800, a stunning example of the huge stride forward Cuba's independent restaurant scene has taken in recent years.

 Visit the city's ecclesiastical jewel, the 1748 cream-and-terracotta Iglesia de Nuestra Señora de la Merced, steeped in legend and with a solid silver coffin inside.

 Get to grips with Camagüey's famous revolutionary son at the house where he was born — now the Museo Casa Natal de Ignacio Agramonte. Agramonte led the fight for Cuban independence from Spain.

 Take a turn in Casino Campestre, Cuba's largest urban park. This leafy spot is peppered with monuments.

 Pay homage at the vast Necropolis de Camagüey, the final resting place of famous figures from Camagüey's past, including Agramonte.

Tubagua

THATCHED JUNGLE CABINS AND COMMUNITY TOURISM BEYOND THE BEACHES

In a country where few tourists make it beyond the swim-up bar of their all-inclusive resort, Tubagua is a refreshing alternative. Perched on the cusp of the Cordillera Septentrional and bisected by the Ruta Panorámica, a serpentine road linking the Dominican cities of Puerto Plata and Santiago de los Caballeros, it's home to one of the Caribbean's best ecolodges. Within the small strung-out village of Tubagua, where simple one-storey houses are interspersed with grassy cow pastures, the lodge sits in a spectacular lofty position, built in the style of a traditional indigenous village. Here, amid lush foliage and rolling hills, pop-up roadside stalls ply an A to Z of tropical fruit, and villagers on motor-scooters fill up on gas sold in recycled rum bottles.

Radically different to the coast in tempo and culture, Tubagua is a perfect place to absorb the nuances of authentic Dominican life through community tourism projects. If you're willing to forsake air-con for gentle mountain breezes and poolside merengue for a shrill chorus of cicadas, this could be your nirvana.

GO IF YOU LIKE...

💜 *Cuba*
🤍 *Jamaica's Blue Mountains*
💜 *Dominican village life*
🤍 *coffee*
💜 *rice & beans*
💜 *tropical fruit*

137

Why go to Tubagua?

As well as providing a rustic escape from the commercial trappings of the Dominican Republic's big resort strips, Tubagua acts as a hub for community tourism along the northern coast. Surrounded by tropical vegetation and built with palm thatch and wood, the tranquil Tubagua Ecolodge is the best base for exploration. From here, it's possible to organise a handful of excursions into the immediate countryside using local guides.

The Doña Julia coffee plantation in the nearby village of Pedro García is one of over 50 local farms reestablished in the last decade after the regional water table was damaged by deforestation and cattle-grazing. Further south, the El Cumbre amber mines take you underground to where locals excavate the vivid gems by hand. A hiking circuit through pastoral countryside leads out directly from the ecolodge to a luminous blue swimming hole, meandering past isolated homesteads en route including the birthplace of Dominican painter Jaime Colson.

Right: Tubagua sits in a spectacular hilltop position, with views over the jungle canopy

Below: Thatched rural huts in DR's interior are a world away from the popular beach resorts of the coastal areas

© HUDSON FLEECE / ALAMY STOCK PHOTO

FIRST-TIME TIPS

For more flexibility, <u>rent a car</u>. With four wheels, it's easier to get out and explore the villages that dot the recently upgraded Ruta Panorámica (Ruta 25).

....

Eat at the Tubagua Ecolodge (https://tubagua.com). The <u>homespun food</u> made from local ingredients and served in huge portions is as spectacular as the view.

....

<u>Save time for a beach day</u> in Cabarete, Dominican Republic's laidback kite-surfing mecca. Hotel-backed Kite Beach is a 30-minute drive from Tubagua and sees upwards of 40 kite-surfers braving the waves at any one time. For more tranquility try Playa Encuentro, 4km (2.5 miles) to the west.

GETTING THERE

Tubagua is 18km (11 miles) southeast of Puerto Plata on the DR's north coast. Due to a lack of reliable public transport, it's best to rent a car or get a taxi to pick you up from Gregorio Luperón International Airport. Taxis can be pre-booked through the ecolodge and car rental is available at the airport.

WHEN TO GO

Nov–Mar

As with most Caribbean destinations, peak season is from November to March when the weather is calmer and drier, and the temperatures are a little more bearable.

AMAZING CROWD-FREE EXPERIENCES

 Hike between a series of swimming pools and waterfalls that feed into a tree-shaded mountain river; the circuitous 11km (7 mile) trail is best tackled with a local guide.

 Visit a local coffee plantation and farm and watch as your beans are roasted, ground with a wooden *pilón*, and filtered into cups for drinking.

 See how amber is excavated in El Cumbre, where mines dug with small shovels and pick-axes bring to light gold-tinted gemstones filled with ancient fossils.

 Stroll around Taíno Valley Tropical Park on the south side of Tubagua with its petting zoo, abundant foliage and several kilometres of trails.

 Chill out in the oasis environment of Tubagua Ecolodge, spending a day or two admiring the view, sipping beer from the honesty bar and soaking in the small pool.

 Take a car or moto-ride along the Ruta Panorámica, stopping at road-side stalls in the villages of Tubagua and Yásica to sample local cheese, honey and fruit.

Left: Pastel-hued favela on the Cerro del Carmen, one of several hillside city neighbourhoods

Guayaquil

THE YING TO ECUADOR'S HIGHLAND YANG, THIS LIVELY PORT CITY HAS SWAGGER

Steamy tropical air, an enchanting riverfront and fresh-off-the-boat seafood: Guayaquil feels a world removed from Ecuador's foggy highland cities like Quito. Many visitors only pass through en route to the Galápagos, but Ecuador's largest and most underrated city has an impressive array of attractions. The Museum of Anthropology and Contemporary Art houses one of the finest pre-Columbian collections in the country, while the city hosts an outstanding dining and drinking scene — which, unlike in Quito, is an entirely local affair.

The wide, fast-flowing Río Guayas has shaped Guayaquil's development, from its early days as a major port and shipbuilding centre to its 21st-century revitalisation. Today, its grand waterfront promenade is dotted with parks and monuments. Though the city was partially razed by fire in 1896, the hilltop district of Santa Ana, settled in the 1500s, retains its cobblestone streets and colourful buildings. The climb to it up more than 400 steps winds past galleries and family-run restaurants, to a hilltop fort with breezy views over the metropolis.

GO IF YOU LIKE...

- 💚 *historical sites*
- 💚 *art galleries*
- 💚 *waterfront walks*
- 💚 *seafood*
- 💚 *nightlife*
- 💚 *tropical scenery*

Why go to Guayaquil?

In 2021, Ecuador elected a new president, the Guayaquil-born businessman Guillermo Lasso, who aims to revitalise the nation's tourism industry. Nomad visas, for remote-working digital nomads, are launching in 2022. On a local level, Guayaquil continues to invest in infrastructure and green spaces. In 2020, Ecuador's first urban gondola lift opened, linking Guayaquil with Durán across the river. The sustainable 4km (2.5 miles) route soaks up sweeping views over the Río Guayas, while also providing a key transport link for commuters.

Despite the burgeoning size of the metropolis, nature lurks in surprising places even in the centre of town. New pedestrian bridges cross the river to the wildlife-filled mangroves of Isla Santay, while the Parque Bolívar is home to free-roaming land iguanas, some over a metre in length. Just 15km (9 miles) west of Guayaquil, jaguars, macaws and howler monkeys inhabit the protected reserve of Cerro Blanco.

GETTING THERE

Guayaquil's modern Aeropuerto José Joaquín de Olmedo has direct flights to Miami and New York, as well as Madrid and Amsterdam. Although there are frequent flights from Quito, it's well worth taking the eight-hour bus, which offers some mesmerising views of the Andes along the way.

WHEN TO GO

Jun–Nov

The dry season brings cooler temperatures and fewer showers, good for strolls and fine beach escapes. Some of the city's best festivals happen during this period, like the music-filled nights surrounding 25 July, Guayaquil's foundation day.

AMAZING CROWD-FREE EXPERIENCES

 See finely crafted works created by early peoples at the MAAC (Museo Antropológico y de Arte Contemporáneo), then catch an independent film at the museum's cinema.

 Take a whimsical journey through Guayaquil's history at the Museo en Miniatura, a museum made up of elaborate miniature sets.

 Bike to Isla Santay across the vehicle-free bridge. This mangrove-covered island hosts over 120 bird species and toothy caimans.

 Climb the 444 steps to the top of Cerro Santa Ana to watch the sunset over Guayaquil. Afterwards, have drinks at the festive La Taberna.

 Take a stroll along the Malecón 2000, Guayaquil's 2.5km (1.5 mile) riverfront promenade. Stop by outdoor monuments, recharge at an outdoor cafe and take a ride on the lofty Ferris wheel La Perla.

 Dine on *arroz con mariscos* (seafood rice) and other local specialities at Lo Nuestro, one of Guayaquil's best restaurants.

Hermel Quezada
Ecuadorian artist

WHY I LOVE GUAYAQUIL

Guayaquil welcomed me 54 years ago and allowed me to grow and flourish as an artist. I love the spontaneity of the people — always full of joy — and I love the food.

Must-have local experience?
Take an afternoon stroll along the Malecón and then walk up to the neighbourhood of Las Peñas. Aside from the great view, this is an ideal place to try Guayaquileño dishes such as encebollado *(seafood soup).*

Favourite season?
I prefer the cool days without rain during the summer (also known as our dry season), which runs from June to November.

Top: Parque Bolívar is a pocket of nature for city residents
Bottom: huge land iguanas are easily spotted in Guayaquil

Rupununi

ECO ADVENTURES IN ONE OF SOUTH AMERICA'S FINAL FRONTIERS

South America's only English-speaking country, Guyana grooves to a very different rhythm to its neighbours. And this is partly what makes it so fascinating. Yet while visitor numbers have been increasing since 2015, only around 315,000 tourists a year make the effort to visit. Fewer still venture to Guyana's jungle interior (beyond the famed Kaieteur Falls) where some of the world's best wildlife-spotting comes together with opportunities to connect with indigenous Amerindian culture in the Rupununi region, named for its mighty river.

Most easily arranged via a local operator such as Wilderness Explorers (wilderness-explorers.com) due to poor transport connections, an adventure to the North Rupununi region will see you boat down rainforest-fringed waterways in search of macaws, monkeys and more, staying in rustic ecolodges that create sustainable livelihoods for Amerindian communities and serve delicious Guyanese food. The jungle gives way to wild savannah in the South Rupununi, where ranch stays support wildlife conservation.

GO IF YOU LIKE...

- 💚 *the Amazon*
- 💚 *exotic wildlife*
- 💚 *community tourism*
- 💚 *off-grid adventure*
- 💚 *hot (pepper) sauce*
- 💚 *rum*

145

Why go to Rupununi?

If you've always wondered what it might have been like for early Western explorers to visit the Amazon Rainforest, the North Rupununi region offers a taste. Here a clutch of remote ecolodges (some only accessible by boat) dot jungles bursting with rare wildlife more easily spotted here than in South America's busier Amazon tourism hubs – especially with the help of Amerindian guides. Further south, staying on a ranch in the Rupununi savannah offers a fascinating window into *vaquero* (Guyanese cowboy) life on the fringe of the forest, where giant anteaters graze alongside cows.

With only one dodgy (dirt) road connecting the region to the capital Georgetown to the north, and Brazil to the southwest, the Rupununi's relative inaccessibility has helped to protect it. As plans to pave the road gather steam, there's no better time to explore this magnificent slice of nature and culture before it potentially changes forever.

GETTING THERE
The capital Georgetown has two international airports. Shuttles run nightly from the city to the Brazilian border town of Lethem in the South Rupununi. Alternatively, small planes typically fly to the Rupununi from Georgetown's Eugene F Correia International Airport.

WHEN TO GO

Sep–Apr

Access to the interior can be difficult or impossible during the wetter months from May to early August, when roads can flood.

AMAZING CROWD-FREE EXPERIENCES

Learn about Amerindian culture at community-owned lodges Rewa Eco-Lodge (rewaecolodge.com) and Surama Eco-Lodge (suramaecolodge.com).

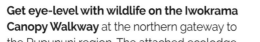
Get eye-level with wildlife on the Iwokrama Canopy Walkway at the northern gateway to the Rupununi region. The attached ecolodge is frequented by hummingbirds.

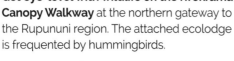
Learn about pioneering wildlife conservation work at Karanambu Lodge (facebook.com/karanambu), which rehabilitates giant otters.

Join local researchers on nightly caiman tagging patrols as a guest of Caiman House (caimanhouse.com) located in the Amerindian village of Yupukari.

Get seriously off-grid at Mapari Wilderness Camp (mapariwilderness camp.com), only accessible by boat, and hope to spot jaguar and giant armadillo.

Explore the South Rupununi savannah on a ranch stay such as Waikin Ranch (waikinranch.com) or conservation-driven Wichabai Ranch (wichabai.com).

Above: Squirrel monkeys are just one of the many jungle species that can be spotted in Guyana'a unspoilt Rupununi region

Leroy Ignacio
*president,
South Rupununi
Conservation
Society (SRCS)*

WHY I LOVE THE RUPUNUNI REGION

Part of the Guiana Shield, the Rupununi is a very unique environment that allows a rich biodiversity to thrive. Ancient culture and language is also present here, with petroglyphs and signs of past cultures all over.

Must-have local experience?
Heading out with SRCS guides to spot the red siskin, a bright little endangered bird species that inspired the formation of the SRCS and important conservation work.

Favourite season?
The dry season for fewer insects and less rainfall —ideal for camping. It's also better for seeing the Rupununi's amazing wildlife.

Monte Albán

IN THE OAXACA CLOUDS LIES A PRE-COLUMBIAN CITY TO RIVAL CHICHÉN ITZÁ

Though it bears a strong resemblance to Chichén Itzá, Mexico's hilltop complex of Monte Albán pre-dates its Yucatán cousin by 750 years and receives just a fifth of the visitors. Set high above Oaxaca City, it was built by the Zapotecs around 500 BCE but eventually faded into slow obscurity until Leopoldo Batres began excavations in 1902, discovering a trove of important gold and striking pyramids. Alongside Chichén Itzá and the pre-Aztec Teotihuacan ruins outside Mexico City, Monte Albán is one of the most important pre-Columbian archaeological treasures of Mesoamerica.

The site's strategic hilltop location puts it level with the clouds above Oaxaca's Central Valleys, and as visitors stroll the grounds they can ponder the astronomical observations made from the site centuries ago. The Zapotec god of rain, Cocijo, was the main deity worshipped here, perhaps because the 400m (1312ft) elevation gives the perfect vantage on any storm clouds moving in. Come on a weekday and it can feel like a place where time has collapsed, far from the busy city below.

GO IF YOU LIKE…

- 💚 *Chichén Itzá, Mexico*
- 🤍 *Teotihuacan, Mexico*
- 💚 *Tikal, Guatemala*
- 🤍 *pyramids of Giza, Egypt*
- 💚 *Sukuh Temple, Indonesia*
- 🤍 *Machu Picchu, Peru*

Why go to Monte Albán?

For years, Oaxaca has deservedly been touted as the go-to destination for Mexico's best cuisine. More recently the area has also made its name as the home of mezcal. But the ruins perched 10km (6 miles) outside the city centre still feel like a secret, a portal back to pre-Columbian Mexico and even to a time before the Aztecs. Built in the Pre-Classic period and likely housing as many as 35,000 people in its heyday, Monte Albán's many pyramids were sites of religious ritual and locuses of state power; hieroglyphics on stelae here still tell of peaceful transfers of power between rulers.

A visit is a vital experience for anyone wishing to understand Mexico's rich history before the Spanish conquest. Unlike at Chichén Itzá, it's still possible to climb up the major pyramids here. And though much of the site's gold is now in Mexico City's National Museum of Anthropology, Monte Albán is still revealing its secrets: in 2020, radar imaging discovered the existence of a buried pyramid underneath the site's main plaza.

Right: Hieroglyphics and engravings on stelae tell tales of ancient rulers

Below: From Monte Albán's spectacular hilltop position, the Zapotecs used to practise astronomy

© MARK READ | LONELY PLANET

GETTING THERE

Monte Albán is only 10km (6 miles) from Oaxaca International Airport, with direct flights from airports including Mexico City and Houston's IAH. If you're not pressed for time, it's also easy to visit Oaxaca travelling by road from Mexico City.

WHEN TO GO

Oct–Nov

October marks the start of the dry season, with ideal temperatures and clear skies. Time your trip right (in the lead up to 1-2 November), and you can view the local Day of the Dead altars in Oaxaca City during your stay.

FIRST-TIME TIPS

Bring your own water – vendors may not be on hand and Monte Albán can be exposed to the sun (hats and sunscreen are a good idea as well).

....

Taxi drivers can take you to the entry and local buses also depart from the parking lot here.

....

Though Monte Albán is technically open until 5pm each day, it's better to arrive early afternoon, before 2pm if possible, just in case it closes early.

....

If flying in or out of Oaxaca City, look for the ruins — you may be able to get a first or final glimpse of Monte Albán from your plane while ascending or descending over the city.

AMAZING CROWD-FREE EXPERIENCES

 Climb the North Platform. Dominating one end of the Gran Plaza, the top of this platform boasts its own ceremonial complex from 500-800 CE.

 Visit the Juego de Pelota. This well-preserved ball court is believed to have been used mainly to arbitrate disputes, similar to a court of law today.

 Take in the Edificio de los Danzantes. Original carvings of men thought to be sacrificial victims can be seen inside this structure, which dates to 500-100 BCE.

 Explore the nearby tombs. Above the parking lot and outside the official bounds of the site, additional excavation sites mark ceremonial tombs.

 Scope out the Stelae. The on-site museum holds more of the excavated finds, while there are other pieces nearby in the Museo de las Culturas de Oaxaca.

 Dive into the Oaxacan food scene. The bus back to town drops off near the Mercado 20 de Noviembre, still mainly a locals-only haunt crammed with food stalls.

Left: Surfer favourite
Santa Catalina gets
compared to Costa
Rica 20 years ago

Santa Catalina

THE ONLY PARTY IN THIS BAREFOOT SURFER DEN IS OUT ON THE EPIC BREAKS

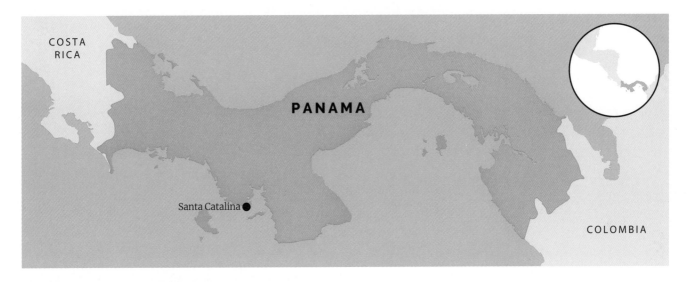

You've never heard of Santa Catalina, Panama? The folk who come to this laid-back, old-school surf hub will be glad to hear it. While the Pacific shoreline of nearby Costa Rica rings with the sound of strummed guitars, clinking beer glasses, unzipping wetsuits and late-night techno, Santa Catalina sits quietly off the mainstream radar. There's a surf scene here – of course there is – but it's low key and barefoot, and while powerful breaks roll left and right, the waves are rarely mobbed.

Devotees of Central America's Pacific swells compare Santa Catalina to Costa Rica 20 years ago. You'll find board rentals, surfing lessons. beach cafes, pizzerias and bakeries, plus fan-cooled beach cabanas for cheap overnight stops, but the nights are reserved for the hum of the tropics rather than the hum of tourist bars. This is a place to surf your heart out by day, then pour your heart out to your best bud by night over a take-out beer on the beach beneath a canopy of stars.

GO IF YOU LIKE...

- 💚 *Costa Rica*
- 💚 *Bali, Indonesia*
- 💚 *Byron Bay, Australia*
- 💚 *beach hut living*
- 💚 *uncrowded surf breaks*
- 💚 *early nights*

Why go to Santa Catalina?

When the surf's up in Central America, Costa Rica is the pulsing heart of the action, but the wait for a wave at prime surf beaches such as Playa Tamarindo can rival the queues for the loos during Spring Break. At Santa Catalina, there's enough of a buzz to feel part of a scene, but thanks to the the chilled-out mood you won't feel like just another punter on the conveyor belt of tourism. Surfing isn't the only trick Santa Catalina has up its sleeve, either. Just 46km (29 miles) offshore, the marine national park at Isla de Coiba is an underwater playground for divers, snorkellers and visiting megafauna.

The trade-off for this right-place-at-the-right-time vibe is the hassle of getting here. It takes three buses to reach Santa Catalina from Panama City. On arrival, you'll be getting around by foot power, which is just how aficionados like it.

Right: Surfer walking out to the point, which breaks left and right

Below: Santa Catalina's quiet streets have quite the opposite vibe to some other Central American surf towns

FIRST-TIME TIPS

If entering Panama overland – for example, via the crossing from Costa Rica at Paso Canoas – you may need to show proof that you have onward transport booked for travel out of Panama.

....

Beachwear is fine on the sands, but wandering around local fishing villages in skimpy outfits may raise eyebrows.

....

Check the tide times – waves that even beginners can tackle at high tide are only suitable for pros at low tide, when the risk of wiping out on razor-sharp lava rocks is ever-present.

....

Santa Catalina has a respectful surf scene; never 'drop in' if you see another surfer is already riding a wave.

GETTING THERE

From Panama City, take a bus to Santiago, then another bus to Soná, which is directly connected to Santa Catalina by another bus. The entire journey can be done in a day, but it can take two days if the connections don't match up.

WHEN TO GO

Apr–Sep

There's surf in Santa Catalina year-round, but the swells from April to October produce particularly impressive rides.

AMAZING CROWD-FREE EXPERIENCES

 Experience Santa Catalina's varied breaks. The point at Santa Catalina breaks left and right, and there are sections for riders of all abilities, both here and at nearby Punta Brava and Punta Roca.

 Hone your technique at a local surf school or camp. The waves here can be challenging, but instructors can help novices up their game.

 Find peace swinging in a hammock — surfing wasn't the only reason you took three buses to get away from the crowds.

 Take an overnight boat trip to dive or snorkel at Isla de Coiba. The reefs here draw megafauna such as manta rays, whale sharks, hammerheads, dolphins and even humpback whales.

 Mount up for a horseback trip along the beach and into the jungle. Guesthouses, hotels and cabanas can fix you up with a horse and guide.

 Tantalise your palate feasting on fresh seafood, with everything from coconut curry to local lobster and squid ceviche.

Left: Like Machu Picchu, Choquequirao occupies a remote mountaintop

Choquequirao

ALL OF MACHU PICCHU'S ALLURE BUT JUST A TINY FRACTION OF THE VISITORS

It is tough talking about remote Inca citadel Choquequirao without framing its appeal in the context of Machu Picchu, one of South America's most-visited tourist attractions, which sits 40km (25 miles) away across the Peruvian Andes. Choquequirao often gets called Machu Picchu's 'sacred sister', due to similarities in their stunning locations and architecture. Like Machu Picchu, it ranks among Peru's vastest Inca ruins, spread over more than 1800ha between broccoli-green mountain slopes. It too can be accessed via tantalising multiday treks: two days' hike from the nearest civilisation, or five days from Machu Picchu.

Choquequirao, however, receives little more than 20 visitors a day, while Machu Picchu has well above 2000. If they're siblings, Choquequirao is the infinitely more mysterious one without her picture plastered everywhere. Its five-centuries-old building techniques still bedazzle. Among the labours that would wow Hercules are a ceremonial plaza created by truncating a hilltop and decorated stone farming terraces on precipitous mountainsides.

GO IF YOU LIKE…

- ♥ *Machu Picchu*
- ♥ *the Andes*
- ♥ *ancient civilisations*
- ♥ *Indiana Jones archaeology*
- ♥ *multiday hikes*
- ♥ *camping*

Why go to Choquequirao?

You are on a mountain track in morning mist. Cloud dissipates on your 1500m (4921ft) descent down a river's rocky valleyside. The terrain's stark scale becomes apparent: high enough to have *nevados* (snow-capped peaks), yet dropping low enough to become almost tropical by the glass-blue Apurímac River on the valley bottom. Droves of donkeys and their herders – and occasional out-of-breath backpackers – pass by, emphasising the scene's immensity.

The steeply graded climb up the far valleyside punishes even seasoned trekkers, but the reward is huge. The 16th-century city of Choquequirao, one of the last Inca strongholds, has an astounding 12 sectors clinging to vertical mountainside. And an estimated 60% of the city still awaits excavation. Cascades of agricultural terraces depict stone likenesses of llamas, and the city's architects hacked the top off a peak to create a flat plain for Choquequirao's celebrated ceremonial space. Hardly anyone is here, though plans are afoot to install a cable car in an effort to ratchet up tourism.

GETTING THERE
From Lima airport, first travel to Abancay (58km/36 miles southwest of Choquequirao) or Cuzco (166km/103 miles east). Flying Lima to Cuzco saves a day's journey by road. Both cities have agencies offering Choquequirao tours. It's also possible to travel to the site independently, combining bus travel, walking and by hitching lifts with trucks or shared taxis.

WHEN TO GO

Apr–Oct

You can hike to Choquequirao year-round, but the dry season months between April and October make the challenge easier as the steep trail has significantly less slippery mud at this time of year.

FIRST-TIME TIPS

You need good levels of long-distance <u>hiking fitness</u> to tackle the trail to Choquequirao.

Choquequirao can be hiked independently without pre-booking. <u>Guided tours</u> need to be arranged with an agency at least several weeks beforehand.

A few local family homes along the trail offer basic meals but, if going independently, <u>bring back-up supplies</u> for two to four days' walking. Also bring kit to purify drinking water, which is not always available en route.

Bring your own tent as <u>you'll need to camp</u> each night at one of the designated campgrounds. Expect basic facilities, with little beyond a toilet.

AMAZING CROWD-FREE EXPERIENCES

 Hone your Andes adventuring skills, travelling by spluttering local bus and *colectivo* (shared taxi), meandering through the mountains to the starting point of the hike.

 Experience a real, no-frills Andean settlement in Cachora, mingling with the villagers over a traditional restaurant supper and drinking in the winsome views.

 Gasp at the majestic Apurímac Valley from above, at Mirador de Capuliyoc.

 Collapse for a breather at pretty Playa Rosalina, taking a refreshment by the aquamarine Apurímac River.

 Marvel at the first sight of Choquequirao, which becomes visible from the hilltop the citadel's builders truncated themselves.

 Discover the llama sector's unique stone depictions, clambering over terraces for an eyeful of these animals cascading down the mountainside.

Clockwise from top left: Thatched huts overlooking Apurímac Valley; Choquequirao's stone llamas; pack mule on a high trekking pass

Left: Pigeon Point Beach is the stuff of Caribbean dreams

Tobago

WHERE BIRDS SOAR AND LOCALS DICTATE THE RHYTHMS OF ISLAND LIFE

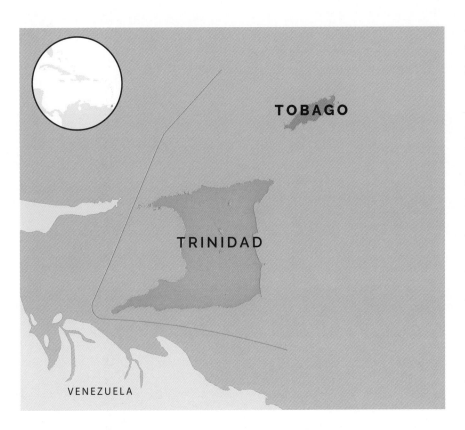

White-sand beaches, slowly lapping turquoise waves in quiet coves and crystal-clear warm waters: Tobago has all the makings of an unforgettable dreamscape. Yet, somehow, this unassuming Caribbean island off the northern coast of South America often gets overlooked. Casually bundled into the catch-all national moniker Trinidad and Tobago, most visitors to the area head directly to Tobago's larger sister island Trinidad for Carnival, or to the nearby resorts of Barbados or St Lucia.

Hiding in the shadow of its sibling has allowed sleepy Tobago to remain a little slice of heaven for decades, while local dependence on agriculture keeps the island sustainable by default. Fruit, vegetables and meats are often grown or farmed on the island, with many locals selling life-boosting juices from their own groves alongside fish caught just that very morning. The island's bays are also a haven for Tobagonian-owned sleeping options set against perfect beach backdrops. This island's quaint, quiet and humble magic is a glory not to be missed.

GO IF YOU LIKE...

- 💚 *white-sand beaches*
- 💚 *friendly locals*
- 💚 *snorkelling*
- 💚 *birdwatching*
- 💚 *Caribbean music*

Why go to Tobago?

Only a twin-island republic as fun and joyous as Trinidad and Tobago could have brought the world cultural phenomena such as steel pan music and the limbo dance. In the past two years, Tobago has promoted Tobagonian experiences and culture to visitors. Tourists can now take a beachfront workout class led by a local fitness guru, hitch a ride with fishers to harder-to-reach beaches, or join a mural painting class. Local artwork is promoted at many establishments across the island, in support of the flourishing Tobagonian art scene. And small independent holiday accommodations are championing local food producers on their menus.

Tobago is also an island of extraordinary biodiversity. Fun fact: the island's Main Ridge Forest Reserve – almost 4000ha of tropical rainforest – is said to be the oldest protected land reserve in the Western Hemisphere, declared in 1776 by the British crown. The island is particularly well known as a birdwatching destination, with more than 200 species including parrots and the ruby-topaz hummingbird.

GETTING THERE

Tobago's airport is ANR Robinson International Airport, but the only direct flights here run from the US and the UK. If landing in Trinidad at Piarco International Airport, it's a short cab ride to the Inter-island Ferry Service, which makes the 32km (20 mile) trip between Port of Spain, Trinidad, and Scarborough, Tobago in 3hr 30min.

WHEN TO GO

Jan-May

During the island's idyllic dry season, rainfall is minimal and temperatures hover around 26°C (80°F). Afternoon rainclouds roll through the skies daily during the other six months of the year.

FIRST-TIME TIPS

If you can, stay at a small <u>locally owned beachfront property</u>. It is a great way to experience the local community and fall asleep to ocean sounds.

This is the tropics: bring a strong <u>insect repellent</u>. While hiking, wear long loose trousers to avoid any pesky bites.

A <u>wide-brimmed hat</u> is useful, as the sun here is powerful and unforgiving.

<u>Bring closed-toe shoes</u> – running shoes or hiking boots – for the backroads and hiking trails.

AMAZING CROWD-FREE EXPERIENCES

 Stay in the tiny, unspoilt fishing village of Castara Bay, with its under-the-radar beach, perfect oceanside guesthouses and stunning views.

 Voyage to No Man's Land, a secluded beach accessible only by boat that's perfect for sunbathing or a beach picnic.

 Hike or boat with a local fisherman to Pirate's Bay. This beautiful, forest-backed curve of sand has such strong Robinson Crusoe vibes that it featured on screen in the original 1952 *Robinson Crusoe* movie.

 Explore island history at Tobago Museum. This charming collection within Fort King George displays Amerindian artefacts, colonial relics and maps from the 1600s.

 Get your wildlife fix on Turtle Beach — the nesting grounds for leatherback, hawksbill, green, loggerhead and olive ridley turtles.

 Trek through the forests of Petit Trou Lagoon, with its bramble of sky-high tree roots and mysterious paths. Its Mangrove Boardwalk is a good place to spot marine life, including crabs, and birds galore.

Clockwise from top left: A copper-rumped hummingbird; the white-sand crescent of Parlatuvier Bay; green turtles nest at Turtle Beach

Suriname

MAROONS AND AMERINDIANS RULE THIS WILD POCKET OF SOUTH AMERICA

GUYANA

SURINAME

FRENCH GUIANA

BRAZIL

capital Paramaribo is packed with Unesco-listed architecture, buzzy nightspots and some excellent restaurants featuring the spicy fusion cuisine of its ethnically diverse population, largely descended from escaped enslaved Africans (known as Maroons), Indian, Indonesian and Chinese indentured laborers, English and Dutch colonists and indigenous Amerindians.

Old plantation houses symbolise a dark chapter of Suriname's history, when it was one of the world's most brutal slave colonies. Just a few hours away by road or boat, the nation's untamed jungles cover more than 90% of its territory, with wildlife-spotting opportunities and a window into Maroon culture.

Suriname isn't just South America's smallest country, but also its least visited. It's any wonder why, for this little-known corner of the continent, well off the Gringo Trail, offers a refreshingly different South American experience. Following coups and a civil war in the 1980s, today's Suriname is also statistically one of South America's safer countries to visit. Tucked inside the mouth of the Suriname River, the sultry Dutch-colonial

GO IF YOU LIKE...

- 💜 *the Amazon*
- 💜 *community-based tourism*
- 💜 *off-grid adventure*
- 💜 *Dutch-colonial architecture*
- 💜 *Maroon culture*
- 💜 *wildlife*

Why go to Suriname?

For many visitors to Suriname, experiencing the Maroon way of life is a travel highlight. While many Maroon people now live in the capital, Suriname's jungle interior remains the heartland of their culture, where six politically distinct groups continue to occupy traditional territories hugging the nation's mighty rivers.

The classic travel experience includes a longtail boat trip to the Upper Suriname River to stay at a rustic Saramaka community-run ecolodge such as Danpaati River Lodge (facebook.com/FB.Danpaati), which supports a clutch of local villages. The scenic journey only takes a few hours, but you'll feel like you've stepped back into bygone era, where cultural traditions run deep. Off-grid wildlife experiences beckon at the nation's remote and untamed national parks and lodges, while Paramaribo offers a more accessible cultural adventure, including a museum dedicated to another byproduct of Suriname's once-booming sugar industry: rum. The Surinaamsch Rumhuis (Surinamese Rum House) also offers tastings.

GETTING THERE

A coastal road connects Paramaribo to Georgetown, Guyana, to the west (450km/ 280 miles), and Cayenne, French Guiana to the east (400km/248 miles). Both journeys require a ferry crossing, and take the better part of a day to complete the bus-ferry-bus shuffle. There are direct flights to Paramaribo from Amsterdam with KLM.

WHEN TO GO

Feb–late Apr & Aug–early Dec

Suriname's dry seasons are the best times for a visit. Boat travel can be dicey in the wet season.

FIRST-TIME TIPS

Dutch may be Suriname's official language, but an exceptional array of <u>languages and dialects</u> are spoken across the country (including eight recognised indigenous languages). Sranan Tongo, a Creole language, is commonly spoken on the streets of Paramaribo. Some English is spoken in hotels and in Suriname's tourist areas.

<u>Photography is not allowed</u> in Maroon communities (or Paramaribo's Witches Market) without permission. This includes on boat trips on the Upper Suriname River.

Suriname is essentially <u>a cash economy</u>, so stock up before heading into the jungle. The official currency is the Surinamese dollar (SR$), but some businesses take euros and US dollars.

AMAZING CROWD-FREE EXPERIENCES

 Take a longtail boat trip up the Suriname River from Atjoni to immerse yourself in the jungle and Maroon culture while staying at a community-run ecolodge.

 Book a multiday tour to Central Suriname Nature Reserve – 1.6 million hectares of primary tropical forest with the nation's best wildlife-watching.

 Explore the Unesco-listed centre of Paramaribo. Don't miss Fort Zeelandia, a star-shaped, 18th-century fort built on the site where Suriname's first colonists alighted.

 Fly over the jungle in a small plane to Kabalebo Nature Resort (kabalebo.com), a wildlife-spotting haven run by descendants of Maroons and Amerindians.

 Discover historic riverside plantations along the Commewijne River, near Paramaribo, by bicycle or on a boat tour, possibly spotting pink estuarine dolphins.

 Spot tropical birds, monkeys and more at Brownsberg Nature Park, about 100km (62 miles) from Paramaribo. It's the best place to see wildlife on a day trip from the capital.

Above: A longtail boat glides down Suriname River around Brokopondo

The Lost Sierra

WHERE OLD GOLD-MINING COMMUNITIES ARE REVIVING TRAILS FOR ADVENTURERS

Speeding downhill, your shoulders skimming the trunks of giant trees and the wheels of your bike bouncing over rocks and roots, it's impossible to take your eyes off the trail ahead. But pull over occasionally to appreciate your surroundings among ponderosa pines or red fir trees, blue jays hopping from branch to branch, the only sound a river churning with snowmelt below. And there won't be another soul in sight.

This is because you're in the Lost Sierra, a triangle of 2591m (8500ft) peaks and glacial lakes roughly between the towns of Quincy, Graeagle and Downieville, a four-hour drive northeast from San Francisco. The closest comparison in California's northern Sierra Nevada is Lake Tahoe nearby, but the Lost Sierra has none of that region's visitor traffic. You don't need to ride a bike to discover the Lost Sierra, either. The region is threaded with trails pioneered by gold miners 170 years ago but newly restored for hikers, horse riders and off-road motorcyclists by local groups determined to put the Lost Sierra back on the map.

GO IF YOU LIKE...

- 💙 *world-class activities*
- 💙 *fresh mountain air*
- 💙 *navigating wildernesses*
- 💙 *big trees — and perhaps big cats*
- 💙 *authentic Americana*
- 💙 *dips in icy water*

Why go to the Lost Sierra?

The flowering of the Lost Sierra as an outdoor adventure destination has largely occurred thanks to grassroots efforts, in particular by the Sierra Buttes Trail Stewardship (SBTS), co-founded by Greg Williams, a descendant of the local Miwok people. The SBTS' latest project is called Connected Communities and is based around the development of 965km (600 miles) of multi-use trails to link 15 former gold-mining towns in the Lost Sierra. Sections of trail will be completed from 2023 to 2030 and are expected to encourage new businesses to open, supporting the trails' hikers, horse riders and bikers.

Towns such as Sierra City and Downieville have fewer than 300 permanent residents but retain Gold Rush-era architecture that is now home to restaurants, guesthouses and other amenities. Parts of the Lost Sierra have been affected by fires in recent years and visitors will aid the economic recovery: the Quintopia brewery, Quincy's first brewery in a century, has already risen from the ashes.

GETTING THERE

The closest airports are Reno-Tahoe, Sacramento, Oakland and San Francisco (the latter two most used by international visitors). From the west, Hwy 49 is the main (and twisty) route. From the north and east, you'll likely use Hwy 89 or 70. There's no practical way to explore the Lost Sierra without a vehicle of your own.

WHEN TO GO

May–Oct

Higher trails may still be snow-bound in early June, although lower elevations are open all year. Ever-shorter winters bring snows, perfect for snow mobiles and snow shoeing. Fishing season is April to November. Fire season gets longer each year.

FIRST-TIME TIPS

If you're visiting to ride, you can rent a demo mountain bike for the day (including electric bikes for $200/day) from Yuba Expeditions in Downieville and Quincy (yubaexpeditions.com) instead of transporting your own.

....

There are no reasonable public transport options — you'll need to have your own wheels or rent a vehicle. There are few gas stations here and even fewer electric vehicle charging points, so top up when you can.

....

If you have special dietary needs or require flexibility with food, bring your own supplies. Smaller towns, such as Downieville, have at least a general store and a couple of eating options, but they may have limited choice and opening hours.

AMAZING CROWD-FREE EXPERIENCES

 Cast a line into lakes and rivers to fish for native trout. Salmon and Sardine lakes are favourites, or the North Yuba and Middle Feather rivers.

 Mountain bike Downieville's renowned trails, Mills Peak and Mt Hough; shuttles to the trailheads from local bike shops allow you to skip the climbs.

 Explore the Gold Rush history of Lost Sierra towns, for example at the Kentucky Mine Museum in Sierra City, near where one of California's largest nuggets was found.

 Hike or bike a portion of the new 965km (600 mile) Lost Sierra Trail network, connecting 15 mountain communities in the region, starting with Quincy and Taylorsville.

 Camp under star-filled skies at one of the Lost Sierra's many campgrounds in the affordable Forest Service-managed recreation areas of Lakes Basin, Mt Hough and beyond.

 Canoe, kayak or SUP the chilly waters of the Lakes Basin Recreation Area; Lower Sardine Lake is one of the more accessible.

Above: A forest trail in the Lost Sierra; wooden storefronts on Downieville's Main Street; hikers cool off in a Lost Sierra river

Trinity Stirling
Project coordinator,
Connected Communities,
Sierra Buttes Trail
Stewardship

WHY I LOVE THE LOST SIERRA

Born and raised in the region, I appreciate that we have 66% public land as opposed to the national average of 28%. It's this public land access and strong sense of community that I love the most.

Must-have local experience?
Hiking, biking, horseback riding or motorcycling around Downieville, Graeagle or Quincy, followed by good food

and drinks at a local brewery. Our vision is to bring this style of adventure to the entire region.

Favourite season?
Summer is best. The lakes and rivers are warm and it's the time of year when the region comes out of hibernation with seasonal businesses open and community events.

Buffalo

NEW YORK CITY'S LITTLE BROTHER IS A MODEL OF REVIVAL AND RESILIENCE

Thanks to its location on Lake Erie, Buffalo boomed in the early 1900s. Industries like steel manufacturing and car production thrived, and it was a major hub for transporting agricultural products from the Midwest. With power on tap from nearby Niagara Falls, it was the first American city to have electric streetlights. Talented architects were commissioned to design buildings and landscape the city's parks, including Louis Sullivan,

HH Richardson and Frederick Law Olmsted. Industrial collapse across the rust belt in the late 20th century left Buffalo a shadow of its former self, but in the last decade revival has been in the air.

New York State's second-largest city has been restoring its architectural gems, turning them into classy hotels and restaurants and incorporating them into public spaces. View impressive early career works by Frank Lloyd Wright, sip your way through a burgeoning craft beer scene and check out the redeveloped waterfront districts. This is a city that can hold its own against New York and Chicago, but which receives a fraction of their visitor numbers.

GO IF YOU LIKE…

- 💜 *New York*
- 💜 *Chicago*
- 💜 *architecture*
- 💜 *Frank Lloyd Wright*
- 💜 *museums*
- 💜 *parks*

Why go to Buffalo?

Frank Lloyd Wright fans can tour several of the celebrated architect's projects: the Martin House Complex and the Lake Erie summer house Graycliff, two meticulously restored properties Wright created for his friend and patron Darwin D Martin; the Filling Station, designed in 1927 but only built in 2013 inside the Pierce Arrow Museum; and the Blue Sky Mausoleum, constructed in 2014 from Wright's 1920s plans. Buffalo also celebrated Frederick Law Olmsted's 200th birthday in 2022, with a number of events in the three city parks he designed here.

Inspired reuse of ageing buildings is something of a Buffalo speciality. The 1874 Delaware Avenue Methodist Church has morphed into Babeville, a multi-use arts centre. In 2019, microbrewery Resurgence Brewing moved its popular taproom to the E&B Holmes Machinery Company Pattern Building, a 1910 factory that once made wooden barrels. And the city's monumental, defunct grain silos are being transformed into the various facilities of Silo City, a living laboratory of ecological regeneration.

GETTING THERE

Amtrak trains run to Buffalo's downtown Exchange Street Station from New York City (8hr 30min), Niagara Falls (1r), Albany (5hr) and Toronto (4hr 30min). All services also stop at Buffalo-Depew Station, 13km (8 miles) east of the city centre, which links in with trains from Chicago (10hr 30min). Alternatively, fly to Buffalo Niagara International Airport.

WHEN TO GO

May–Aug

Summertime is the city's high season, but the weather can't be beat: average highs are in the mid to upper 20s°C (upper 70s°F to low 80s°F).

© PIERRE WILLIOT | SHUTTERSTOCK. © DEMERZEL21 | GETTY IMAGES. © LAWRENCE WORCESTER | LONELY PLANET

FIRST-TIME TIPS

Take a guided tour. Explore Buffalo (explorebuffalo.org) offers an amazing range of architectural, history and other themed tours around the city on foot or by bus, bicycle or even kayak.

....

In downtown Buffalo, Metro Rail trains are free to ride for the stops between the Theater District and Harborcenter along Main St.

....

Find your bar scene. Chippewa St (aka the Chip Strip) caters primarily to a mainstream college crowd, while nearby Allentown has a more eclectic scene.

....

For events listings detailing Buffalo's thriving live performance and music scene, check out Artvoice (artvoice.com) and The Public (dailypublic.com).

AMAZING CROWD-FREE EXPERIENCES

 Wander through the Frederick Law Olmsted–designed Delaware Park, which includes meadows, forests, lakes, rose and Japanese-style gardens, and the grounds of Buffalo Zoo.

 Be amazed by the art collection of the Albright-Knox Art Gallery, which includes paintings by Degas, Picasso, Rauschenberg and other abstract expressionists.

 Take a tour of City Hall, an art deco masterpiece and one of the largest public buildings in the US.

 Admire the splendidly restored Guaranty Building, clad in ornamental terracotta tiles – the beautiful beaux arts design is by celebrated architect Louis Sullivan.

 Explore 264 acres of restored habitat at the Tifft Nature Preserve, with 8km (5 miles) of trails and boardwalks at the edge of Buffalo's Outer Harbor.

 Satisfy your sweet tooth at Parkside Candy, a historic candy shop with original retro decor as delicious as the confections it sells inside.

Clockwise from top: Buffalo's Guaranty Building; Frank Lloyd Wright's Darwin D Martin House; a northern cardinal in Tifft Nature Preserve

Left: Big Bend's lush river corridor has helped make the national park a bird paradise

Big Bend National Park

BLISSFUL ISOLATION KEEPS THIS TEXAN PARK FROM BEING OVERRUN

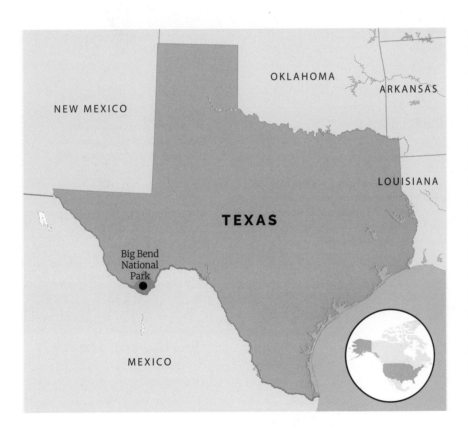

of stargazing in one of the world's largest Dark Sky Parks. Big Bend is also an avian paradise, with over 450 bird species — the most of any national park in the US.

Make no mistake: Big Bend is remote. It's more than three hours from the nearest airport, and by road it's a long way from anywhere (it's at least an eight hour drive from Dallas and Houston). Its isolation, however, has saved it from overdevelopment. The national park receives less than 10% of the visitors the Grand Canyon receives, and multiday excursions — like rafting on the Rio Grande — don't require booking many months in advance.

The mountains meet the desert in Big Bend, a vast national park tucked into a remote corner of west Texas. Set with steep-walled canyons, craggy peaks and a verdant river corridor carving through the scrubland, this expansive wilderness offers a wide range of adventures. You can spend your days hiking rugged trails, paddling along smooth rivers and soaking in natural hot springs, followed by an evening

GO IF YOU LIKE...

- 💚 *mountain hikes*
- 💚 *river rafting*
- 💚 *desert landscapes*
- 💚 *stargazing*
- 💚 *birdwatching*
- 💚 *scenic drives*

177

Why go to Big Bend National Park?

You'll find eons of history in Big Bend National Park, but you won't be stumbling over crowds to experience them. The Fossil Discovery Exhibit, an open-air prehistory museum of sorts, takes you 130 million years back in time. One of its most important displays is the skull of Bravoceratops, a new species of horned dinosaur discovered in Big Bend in 2013. Geology surrounds you in Big Bend too. You can even see rock strata known as the Javelina Formation, which records the mass extinction event that ended the era of the dinosaurs.

Big Bend has plenty of surprises, which makes it well worth your time to stick around a while rather than trying to cram everything into a fleeting visit. You can even drop by a hidden enclave of Mexico: the border crossing over the Rio Grande finally reopened in late 2021 after being closed for nearly two years.

GETTING THERE

A car is essential to reach Big Bend. The nearest airports are in Midland, three hours north, and El Paso, five hours west. Rental cars are available at either airport. Main park roads are accessible to normal vehicles, but if you want to go deeper (and pitch a tent at remote backcountry road sites), you'll need a 4WD.

WHEN TO GO

Oct–Apr

Outside of the blazing summer months, you'll find cooler temperatures as well as wildflowers in the spring (March through April). Winter is mild, though light snow is a possibility, and park trails are empty.

FIRST-TIME TIPS

The Chisos Basin is a key gateway, with a visitor centre, campground and trailheads (including access to Emory Peak). The Chisos Mountains Lodge, the park's only non-camping accommodation, is also here.

....

Temperatures can soar even outside summer, so avoid hiking in the middle of the day, and bring lots of water as well as ample sun protection (long sleeves, hat, etc).

....

If you're not staying in the park, bed down in Terlingua. It's a 45-minute drive west of the Chisos Basin visitor centre and your best bet for lodging/dining.

....

Don't forget to carry your passport if planning to make the river crossing into Mexico.

AMAZING CROWD-FREE EXPERIENCES

Climb to the top of Emory Peak, the highest point in the national park. From the summit, you'll have sweeping views over the Chisos Mountains.

Go rafting through the Santa Elena Canyon, one of Big Bend's most dramatic formations. You'll pass beside sheer, limestone walls and camp along the way.

Soak in the Langford Hot Springs after a day of walking the trails. The setting along the Rio Grande is magical.

Hike the Chihuahuan Desert Nature Trail, where you can see desert habitats as well as an oasis filled with cottonwood trees.

Visit Mexico at Boquillas Crossing. After getting your passport stamped, you can take a rowboat across the Rio Grande, then continue by mule or vehicle into the tiny village of Boquillas.

Have a drink in the ghost town of Terlingua. An abandoned cinema reborn as the Starlight Theater serves up the best food and drink for miles around.

Clockwise from top left: The open road framed by tall grasses in Big Bend; rock formations dot the park; the Starlight Theatre in Terlingua

Charlie Angell
founder & guide, Angell Expeditions

WHY I LOVE BIG BEND

It's so diverse! You can mountain bike a dirt road, hike up to towering peaks, or go paddling through one of the river canyons past 1500ft cliffs.

Must-have local experience?
Go at sunset to Terlingua, the ghost town just outside the park. You can check out the historic cemetery and see the Chisos Mountains light up with fiery colours.

Favourite season?
In the fall [October and November], the weather is cooler and it's the end of the rainy season, so the river is usually at its highest and you can have some great rafting trips.

Waterpocket Fold, Capitol Reef

UTAH'S GRAND CANYON HAS BAGS OF DRAMA BUT NONE OF THE TOURISTS

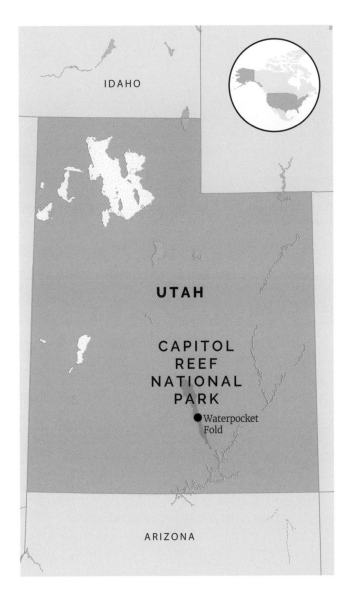

If you're fantasising about the kind of big deserts, red-rock mesas, searing blue skies and blazing-fire sunsets that only America's wild, wild west can deliver, you've probably got the Grand Canyon in mind. It's astonishing, no question, but it has also succumbed to the Unesco touch – popular trails, viewpoints and campgrounds get swamped in peak summer. Whereas a giant 563km (350 mile) leap north brings you to the delightfully under-the-radar Capitol Reef National Park, which receives just a trickle of the visitors, yet has an equally staggering geological marvel up its sleeve.

Out on its lonesome in Utah's red rock country, Capitol Reef is remote enough to remain peaceful even during peak season. The park is a geologist's dream, centring on the Waterpocket Fold, a near-160km (100 mile) wrinkle on the earth formed by the same forces that lifted the Colorado Plateau 65 million years ago. As the land buckled, it gave rise to a rocky spine of canyons, bridges, white-tipped domes, rust-red cliffs, fossils and skinny slot canyons, whittled into form over many millennia.

GO IF YOU LIKE...

- 💜 *the Grand Canyon*
- 💜 *desert drama*
- 💜 *the Wild West*
- 💜 *Mormon heritage*
- 💜 *quiet hiking trails*
- 💜 *stargazing*

Why go to the Waterpocket Fold?

Go to contemplate the foundations of the earth and the unstoppable force of nature as you gaze in quiet wonder at this tidal wave of rock, a monocline that is 2134m (7000ft) higher in the west than in the east. Laid bare to time and the elements, it forms the backbone of Capitol Reef's extraordinary rockscapes, painted with ever-changing tones of pink, ochre, red, taupe and grey. This stark, grippingly beautiful landscape is as ancient as it feels, with 250-million-year-old rocks around since early dinosaurs walked the earth.

The Waterpocket Fold can be admired from many angles: Strike Valley Overlook, reached on foot or by 4WD, and Sunset Point on the park's 13km (8 mile) Scenic Drive among them. As day melts into fiery twilight and the ringtails and racoons come out to play, peer up to the glitter of meteors, planets and the Milky Way in this International Dark Sky Park, which offers some of the clearest night skies in the west.

GETTING THERE

You're going to need your own wheels – and make it a 4WD if you plan on exploring the park's remotest reaches. The closest international airport is Salt Lake City, 370km (230 miles) north. Alternatively, fly to Las Vegas, 547km (340 miles) southwest.

WHEN TO GO

Mar–early Oct

Spring brings mild days perfect for hiking and orchards in full bloom; fall is just as glorious (bring layers for chilly nights in both seasons). Days are hot and arid in summer.

AMAZING CROWD-FREE EXPERIENCES

 Catch a fiercely blushing sunset at Goosenecks Overlook, which thrusts up above the marvellous deep-cut canyon of Sulphur Creek.

 Drive south from Torrey to Bryce Canyon along Scenic Byway 12, which is way up there with America's most beautiful drives.

 Experience the silence and the seclusion of a slot canyon. Burro Wash, Cottonwood Wash and Sheets Gulch burrow deep into the Waterpocket Fold. Trails are largely unmarked, so take a topographic map.

 Dive into the wilds backcountry camping. There are two free, very basic but staggeringly scenic campgrounds, in Cathedral Valley and at Cedar Mesa.

 Hike the Grand Wash in the morning cool. A steep, sudden detour rises to the Cassidy Arch, named after legendary outlaw Butch Cassidy, who hid out here in Utah's maze of canyons.

 Go off piste in rugged Cathedral Valley. Thrillingly remote, its red sandstone monoliths look shaped by a Godly hand.

Above: Capitol Reef's Waterpocket Fold, with its deep canyons and rust-red cliffs, offers awesome roadtripping potential

Milwaukee

THE BLUE-COLLAR BREWSKI CITY WITH ENOUGH GUTS TO RIVAL NEARBY CHICAGO

MINNESOTA

WISCONSIN

MICHIGAN

IOWA

Milwaukee ●

ILLINOIS

Milwaukee gets overlooked, standing as it does in Chicago's shadow, and that's a shame. Because like its big-city sibling, Milwaukee also flaunts a top-tier art museum, buzzing beer scene and beaches aplenty set against a Lake Michigan backdrop, but with only half the number of visitors partaking in the bounty. Those who make the trip 145km (90 miles) north are rewarded with a city that's more relaxed, compact and

inexpensive. Plus Milwaukee has several peculiar attractions you won't find anywhere else, like the Bobblehead Museum, where more than 6500 dolls' noggins bounce, and the American Geographical Society Library, filled with old maps, globes and Captain Cook's hand-drawn charts.

Milwaukee developed its singular personality early on. Germans settled the city in the 1840s and many started breweries. By the 1880s Pabst, Schlitz, Blatz, Miller and 80 other breweries made suds here, and Milwaukee became known as the 'nation's watering hole.' These days, Miller and a slew of microbreweries carry on the legacy.

GO IF YOU LIKE...

- 💜 *Chicago*
- 💜 *beer*
- 💜 *art*
- 💜 *festivals*
- 💜 *motorcycle culture*
- 💜 *lakefront beaches*

185

Why go to Milwaukee?

Part of its appeal is that Milwaukee doesn't shy away from its reputation as a blue-collar town of brewskis, bowling alleys and polka halls. Now it just melds its renown with eye-popping modern marvels such as the Santiago Calatrava-designed art museum, with its kinetic 'wing' that soars open and shut, and the glass-and-steel Harley-Davidson Museum that pays homage to the motorcycles invented here.

The city's ever-growing bike share scheme makes it easy to take advantage of the lakefront, where cycling trails and beaches await and celebrations let loose most weekends at Henry Maier Festival Park. The RiverWalk cuts through downtown and beckons with waterside bars and cafes. And for the chowhounds in the crowd? Cool-cat eateries powered by area farms, orchards and creameries continue to pop up in neighbourhoods such as Bay View, the East Side and Third Ward.

GETTING THERE

Getting to Milwaukee is a cinch, thanks to frequent train and bus services from Chicago right into downtown's core. Milwaukee's mid-sized airport has direct flights to 40 US cities. International flights typically go through Chicago.

WHEN TO GO

Apr–May & Sep–Nov

Summer (June through August) is warm and festival laden, though it's also the busiest time to visit. Spring and fall have fair weather and plenty of outdoor action, but with fewer crowds.

FIRST-TIME TIPS

Stay over on a Friday evening so you can experience the traditional fish fry, a communal meal of beer-battered cod and coleslaw, when locals gather and mark the workweek's end.

....

Pack a warm coat. Milwaukee's location by Lake Michigan makes for chilly, changeable weather. Even in summer the temperature can drop fast, so bring a sweater when you head out for the day.

....

Get tickets online in advance for the Milwaukee Art Museum and Lakefront Brewery tour.

....

Book accommodation in advance and expect higher prices from late June through early September, when the city's calendar of festivals draws crowds.

AMAZING CROWD-FREE EXPERIENCES

 Visit the Milwaukee Art Museum to gape at world-class folk art, Georgia O'Keeffe paintings and the building's wild moving architecture that flaps like a bird's wing.

 Sit in the saddle of a classic motorcycle at the Harley-Davidson Museum and admire badass bikes through the ages, including those of Elvis and Evel Knievel.

 Tour eco-friendly Lakefront Brewery to sip abundant ales, sing the *Laverne & Shirley* sitcom theme song and munch on cheese curds in the beer hall.

 Stroll Walker's Point, a neighborhood packed with LGBTQ+ bars, Latin cafes and one-of-a-kind sights like the Bobblehead Museum and Cheesehead Factory.

 Rent a bike to cycle Lake Park. Lounge on the beach and climb the lighthouse for views before pedalling along the Oak Leaf Trail.

 Pop into a cheese shop or creamery, such as Clock Shadow Creamery or the Wisconsin Cheese Mart, to sample Wisconsin's signature product and stuff your face with gruyere, buttermilk blue and beer cheddar.

Phil Sklar
co-founder & CEO, National Bobblehead Hall of Fame & Museum

WHY I LOVE MILWAUKEE

It's a really vibrant city with a great art scene and museums. And it has several unique attractions that make it fun, everything from the Bobblehead Museum and Cheesehead Factory to the breweries.

Must-have local experience?
Tour the Cheesehead Factory, which is where they make the foam blocks of cheese that Green Bay Packers fans wear on their heads during football games. Wisconsin has become synonymous with the cheesehead.

Favourite season?
Spring. Once winter ends, everyone heads outside to take long walks by the lake and eat on patios.

Clockwise from top left: Cheese shops are a Milwaukee trademark; the summer Wisconsin State Fair; a slice of Milwaukee on water

Utuado

TAÍNO CULTURE AND RIVER ADVENTURES IN THE MOUNTAINS OF PUERTO RICO

Utuado
•
PUERTO RICO

U.S. VIRGIN
ISLANDS

Tourists flock to Puerto Rico's beaches but the island's cultural heartbeat lies folded into the mountains of Utuado. Once home to the Taíno, the indigenous people who inhabited much of the Caribbean before European contact, this lush area is a place for nature adventures and unique rentals. While only 1.5 hours from San Juan, tourists who base themselves here will find an emphasis on wellness and scenic tropical views reminiscent of Bali's Ubud.

Utuado is one of the least populated areas of Puerto Rico. Peace and quiet reign – instead of the sounds of pumping nightlife, guests are serenaded by the dusk-induced song of coquís, small native tree frogs. Utuado feels secluded and mystical, providing a portal back

in time through impeccably preserved petroglyphs at Caguana Indigenous Ceremonial Park, one of the most important archaeological sites in the Caribbean. To get there requires navigating winding, narrow roads but those who make the effort are rewarded with a connection to Puerto Rico's ancestral pulse.

GO IF YOU LIKE…

💜 *Ubud, Bali*
💜 *Costa Rica*
💜 *Colombia*
💜 *mountains*
💜 *lake houses & glamping*
💜 *indigenous culture*

Why go to Utuado?

Experience a detox from overstimulation and a return to basics. Spotty phone service should be interpreted as a sign to slow down and disconnect. This is Puerto Rico in its purest form, with trails through lush greenery and natural freshwater swimming pools, all undisturbed and open to the public.

Attractions include lakes and manmade structures that belong to a green energy initiative the island is seeking to reinvigorate. Wellness retreats, such as Casa Grande, facilitate spiritual growth and healing, drawing on their surroundings which include an abundance of flora native to the area that has historically been used for medicinal purposes. Camping is popular, providing an opportunity for travellers on a tight budget to immerse themselves in the area's mountain panoramas. And new short-term rental options, ranging from bubble domes to contemporary lakefront suites, have made the region increasingly appealing for visitors.

Right: A stone circle at Caguana Indigenous Ceremonial Park near Utuado

Below: Limestone arch at Tanama River, home to one of the longest underground caves in the world

Melina Aguilar Colón
independent tour guide

WHY I LOVE UTUADO

Utuado is the first city founded in the centre of the island, a place filled with pre-colonial history, mesmerising nature, architecture and a revolutionary past.

Must-have local experience?
Connect with Puerto Rico's pre-colonial past at the Caguana Indigenous Ceremonial Park, take a dip in Utuado's rivers, and go on a historical walk through downtown. With more time, try camping at a secluded nature spot. Local companies like From Utuado Mountains can help arrange it.

Favourite season?
The dry season (January to May).

FIRST-TIME TIPS

Driving can be challenging. Be ready for steep inclines and <u>upgrade to four-wheel drive</u> if you can afford it.

....

<u>Special dietary requirements</u> can be hard to cater for in Utuado because of its remoteness. If you need particular foods, consider bringing your own supplies – you can stock up at a supermarket like Freshmart in the metro area.

....

Pack sunscreen and bug spray; the tropical mountain vegetation attracts more <u>insect life</u> than the coastal areas.

....

Call or check a business' Facebook page before starting a long drive to reach it. <u>Many places keep erratic hours</u> and some have closed since hurricanes Irma and Maria hit the island.

GETTING THERE

Most visitors to Utuado fly into San Juan International Airport (SJU) but Rafael Hernandez Airport (BQN) in Aguadilla is another viable option. Both are less than 2 hours from Utuado, easily accessed by rental car. There is no public transportation to the area and shared car services can be hard to find.

WHEN TO GO

Mid-Dec—Mar

Avoid hurricane season (June to November) and visit when the weather is cool and dry. This will allow for hiking and nature exploration with less chance of downpours, and maximise the odds of sunshine.

AMAZING CROWD-FREE EXPERIENCES

 Discover petroglyphs at Caguana Indigenous Ceremonial Park. Nearly a millennium old, they're visible on 21 monoliths around an ancient ball court.

 Have a picnic among white boulders at Cañon Blanco. The smooth, water-carved rocks are perfect for sprawling out under the sun.

 Go canyoning, rappelling and tubing down one of the longest underground caves in the world with Tanama River Adventures (tanamariveradventures.com).

 Savour coffee straight from the source at Café Gran Batey, or stay at Hacienda Horizonte (haciendahorizontepr.com) – PR musician Draco Rosa's coffee plantation.

 Take a boat tour to lakeside restaurants on the edges of Lago Dos Bocas and support small businesses while sampling Puerto Rican dishes with a view.

 Try ziplining over treetops in the Puerto Rican mountains on an ecotour with Batey Adventures (bateydelcemi.com). There's also a 150-foot-long suspension bridge to cross.

The Saône riverbank in Lyon at sunset — a French streetscene to rival Paris

Europe

Kufstein

FORGET SALZBURG: THIS TYROL BEAUTY IS THE REAL ALPINE FAIRYTALE

So you like the idea of Salzburg but not its crowds? Cue Kufstein in Tyrol, snuggling up to the Bavarian Alps, just an hour's train ride west of Salzburg. This town is something a child who had been binge-reading too much Brothers Grimm might draw: pastel-painted, gabled houses strung along cobbled lanes; lantern-lit taverns; a cake-topper of a medieval fortress lifting the gaze above the Inn River to fir forests; cow-grazed meadows and jagged, snow-frosted mountains. Resembling a romantic stage set, this town is the Austria of Alpine fantasies.

Kufstein shot momentarily to national glory in the jaunty 1970s folk song *Die Perle Tirols* (The Pearl of Tyrol). And indeed it has views to make you want to yodel out loud, whether you're hiking ever higher into the limestone spires and turrets of the Kaisergebirge, cross-country skiing in quiet exhilaration through the snowy wilds, or lazing on the shores of a jewel-coloured lake. Kufstein delivers an amuse-bouche of culture and a hefty dollop of outdoor adventure.

GO IF YOU LIKE...

- 💚 *Salzburg*
- 💚 *alpine views*
- 💚 *fairytale fortresses*
- 💚 *wild nature*
- 💚 *hiking & skiing*
- 💚 *adventure sports*

Why go to Kufstein?

Kufstein's Altstadt (old town) is like a ready-made Christmas card when the flakes fall softly in winter. The high-on-a-wooded-hill fortress can rival any in Austria, with its turrets, towers and courtyard where the world's largest organ plays. Atmospherically lantern-lit by night, Römerhofgasse presents a romp through the town's medieval past, with overhanging arches and frescoed façades. Flinging you in the rustic deep-end, Auracher Löchl tavern serves *Käsespätzle* (cheese noodles) and schnitzels as big as boots below beams that creak with 600 years of history.

One glance up at the ragged limestone mountains that rise above town like natural ramparts and you'll be itching to head higher. You can almost brush the treetops with your toes on the one-seater Kaiserlift chairlift, which wings you up to 1200m (3937ft) Brentenjoch, the trailhead for hikes in the gnarly peaks of the Kaisergebirge. In winter, try cross-country skiing, tobogganing and snowshoeing through snow-daubed forests.

Right: Kufstein's Altstadt of pastel-hued gabled houses

Below: Kufstein is framed by mountains that locals escape to for both summer and winter activities

© FOOTTOO | SHUTTERSTOCK

FIRST-TIME TIPS

During Advent, Kufstein is full of <u>festive cheer</u>. The Christmas market in the Altstadt is framed by the photogenic fortress.

<u>Visit in the week</u> to give weekend day-trippers the slip.

<u>Pack for the mountains</u>: hiking boots in summer; thermals and ski gear in winter. Although Kufstein is a town, you'll be outdoors a lot.

Spend the night at a remote Austrian Alpine Club hut (June to September) for <u>a true backcountry experience</u> and easy access to trails.

Kufstein's <u>free guest card</u> includes use of local transport, a return ride on the Kaiserlift and fortress entry.

GETTING THERE

Kufstein is roughly an hour away from the major transport hubs of Innsbruck, Munich and Salzburg, all with airports or, if you would prefer not to fly, excellent international rail connections.

WHEN TO GO

Year-round

Go in summer for Alpine hiking in the Kaisergebirge (mountain huts open roughly from June to September) and bracing lake swims, and in winter for snow sports and Christmas markets.

AMAZING CROWD-FREE EXPERIENCES

 Negotiate steep climbs and switchbacks to Tischofer Cave. The heart-pumping hike into a remote, forested valley reveals a cave with evidence of Paleolithic occupation.

 Take the healing sulphurous waters in the neighbouring spa town of Bad Häring, rimmed by forested mountains and splashed by a waterfall.

 Eat fresh mountain cheese at Ackernalm, an Alpine dream of a meadow high above Lake Thiersee.

 Cleanse your chakras at Ayurveda Resort Sonnhof, a loving burst of India tucked into the mountains of Hinterthiersee.

 Witness a fiery dawn on a hut-to-hut hike in the Kaisergebirge, taking you off the beaten track and into the realm of eagles, chamois and ibex.

 Go for a sense-awakening swim in Stimmersee, a bottle-green lake fed by mountain streams and rimmed by thick forest and rugged peaks.

Karpas Peninsula

CYPRUS, BUT NOT AS YOU KNOW IT – TAKE A WALK ON THE WILD SIDE OF THE MED

KARPAS PENINSULA

CYPRUS

Veteran visitors to Cyprus talk nostalgically of the golden age before the beach resorts went up at Agia Napa and Protaras, when this was an island of empty sands, donkey carts and old-timers sipping coffee in the village square. Little known to most, this pristine vision of Cyprus lives on in the undeveloped Karpas Peninsula, where vast unspoilt beaches and half-asleep villages with stone mosques and churches stand as if mass tourism and the 1974 Turkey-led island split never happened.

Jutting east from Cyprus towards the Middle East on the island's Turkish side, the Karpas Peninsula is being nibbled away by development at its edges, but the further you go along what Cypriots call 'the panhandle',

the more life slips back to an earlier, more peaceful time. Instead of sunbathers, you'll find Turkish and Greek Cypriot farmers living a life of gentle calm amid thyme-scented dunes and beaches that see as many sea turtles as people.

GO IF YOU LIKE...

- ♥ *Turkey*
- ♥ *Greece*
- ♥ *Greco-Roman history*
- ♥ *empty beaches*
- ♥ *sea turtles*
- ♥ *wild donkeys*

Why go to the Karpas Peninsula?

By venturing to the Turkish Republic of Northern Cyprus, you've already taken a step off the mainstream tourist circuit, and the Karpas Peninsula takes things a step further. Beyond the village of Yenierenköy, there's little development – just a handful of village guesthouses and the rustic beach cabins at Golden Beach, a strong contender for the Med's best strip of sand.

Ancient history comes with the territory, and there's plenty on the Karpas Peninsula, from the early Christian basilicas at Agia Triada and Afendrika to the time-scarred ruins of Kantara Castle, a one-time haunt of Knights Templar, Byzantine warlords and Ottoman conquerors.

But the best bit is not having to share these wonders with a crowd. This is one of the last parts of the Med where you'll find beaches without a human footprint, and dusty hamlets of stone-built houses where the only sound is Turkish coffee cups chinking in the village square.

Right: Apostolos Andreas monastery, a revered place of worship for local Greek Cypriots

Below: Wild donkeys grazing behind Golden Beach, a contender for best sands in the Med

© CAVAN IMAGES / ALAMY STOCK PHOTO

FIRST-TIME TIPS

Check the latest _immigration rules_ – the south of Cyprus is part of the EU, the north is not, and this means different entry rules. Investigate the latest regulations before crossing the Green Line that divides the island.

....

Know where you're flying – numerous international airlines buzz into the Greek Republic of Cyprus, but all flights to tiny Ercan Airport have to go via mainland Turkey, limiting your choice of airlines.

....

Fuel up before you come – _petrol is hard to find_ on the peninsula, so set off from Famagusta (Gazimağusa) with a full tank, and maybe a filled jerrycan.

GETTING THERE

The nearest airport to the Karpas Peninsula, is Ercan, a tiny hub only served by airlines from Turkey. The alternative is to fly into Larnaka in the south and cross the Green Line that divides the island – this is usually straightforward, but check the situation before crossing. To explore, you'll need wheels – either a rental car, or if you're feeling ambitious, a bike.

WHEN TO GO

Apr–May & Sep–Oct

The peak summer (June to August) brings blinding sunshine and blistering heat, but it's a bit much for some people. Many prefer the late spring or early autumn, for lower daytime temperatures and cooler nights.

AMAZING CROWD-FREE EXPERIENCES

 Bask on Golden Beach, the best sweep of sand in Cyprus. Vast and empty, it's visited by green and loggerhead turtles during the June to September nesting season.

 Climb the ruined battlements of Kantara Castle. On a weekday, you may have this magnificent fortress entirely to yourself.

 Stay in a blissful beach cabin at Golden Beach and other outposts. These basic huts are perfect retreats where the sound of the surf will lull you to sleep, and close to simple kebab and fish restaurants.

 Take a hike along the thyme-scented coastline, prime terrain for walkers, and you're more likely to see wild donkeys than people.

 Drop into the monastery of Apostolos Andreas. Local Greek Cypriots keep the candles burning at this venerable, atmospheric place of worship.

 Sip a coffee with locals in a shady village square. Cypriots avoid the heat of the day in coffee shops along the peninsula and outsiders get a friendly reception.

Tartu

EUROPE'S 2024 CAPITAL OF CULTURE DESERVES TO WOO TOURISTS FROM TALLINN

Tartu will also help alleviate pressure on tourist-stressed Tallinn and its citizens, who find themselves besieged each summer.

Tartu traces its foundations to the 5th century, when Estonia was a pagan wilderness. Serious construction began with wooden fortifications around Toomemägi (Toome Hill) – now the site of Tartu University. Passing though periods of Russian, Swedish, Polish, German and Soviet rule, today it retains a charming heart of 18th-century buildings and cobbled streets. Accessible, reasonably priced and with excellent accommodation and eating options, Tartu deserves more love.

Every visitor to Estonia passes through Tallinn and falls in love, but far fewer push on to the country's true cultural capital — Tartu. This defies logic: it's the oldest city in the Baltics and the country's intellectual centre. In 2024 Tartu will take a well-deserved turn as European Capital of Culture, promising a welcome financial boost for Estonia's second city and providing even more reasons to visit. And those who linger in

GO IF YOU LIKE...

🤍 *Vilnius & Riga*
🤍 *Estonian history*
🤍 *charming streetscapes*
🤍 *museum-hopping*
🤍 *student buzz*
🤍 *cutting-edge culture*

Why go to Tartu?

Now is the time to visit Tartu. It's barely on the tourist trail yet, meaning crowds and prices remain extremely reasonable. And it offers increasing numbers of cultural attractions while remaining committed to preserving its heritage; its election as 2024 European Capital of Culture means a steady build-up of excitement, events and venues in preparation for the big occasion. Newer attractions include the Estonian National Museum, the country's premier cultural venue, which joined the Tartu Art Museum and KGB Museum in 2016.

Tartu is a university town: its iconic eponymous university, on wooded Toome Hill in the very heart of town, is its lifeblood and a fascinating visit in its own right. The reason you'll find so many interesting little bars, so many events, such low prices and such an outgoing, youthful culture in Tartu is largely because of the students. Aparaaditehas, a hub of independent creators and bars in an old factory, exemplifies this.

GETTING THERE

Tartu has excellent transport links with Tallinn, including buses and a regular train that covers the 200km between the two in around two hours. If you've rented a car to tour Estonia, the drive from Tallinn to Tartu through the heart of the country takes around the same time as the train.

WHEN TO GO

Jun–Aug

The Baltics are a byword for freezing winters, but the pay-off for those dark, punishing months is a glorious high summer of seemingly endless daylight, gentle warmth and a spirit of sun-drunk sociability.

AMAZING CROWD-FREE EXPERIENCES

 Stroll wooded Toome Hill – although popular with students and visitors, it's spread-out enough that it's always peaceful.

 Scour Tartu's streets for their renowned sculptures. Look for the one of Oscar Wilde and Estonian writer Eduard Vilde in 'conversation'.

 Ramble Raadi Manor Park, the sad remains of the former home of the von Liphartide family. Passed to the University of Tartu in the 1920s, the Soviets took part of the land to build a WWII airfield.

 Wander Tartu University Botanic Gardens – established in 1803, it now cultivates 6500 plants, including a greenhouse of exotics.

 Scrutinise the antique telescopes and astronomical equipment at Tartu Old Observatory, a puzzlingly under-appreciated attraction.

 Seek out summer swimming spots along Emajõgi River. Tracing the river banks that bisect Tartu will allow you to get the measure of the city as you head north for a dip.

Above: Toome Hill's cathedral, now a ruin, was founded in the 13th century, but the city dates to the 5th century

Utsjoki

GIVE SANTA THE SLIP IN THE PRISTINE WILDERNESS OF FINNISH LAPLAND

There is more to Finnish Lapland than Santa and festive sparkle in Rovaniemi. Give Christmas and the crowds the slip by heading to the country's furthest, most silent reaches, 500km (310 miles) north of the Arctic Circle, where Finland nudges Norway. The Utsjoki region is where Lapland's real enchantment lies and the landscapes of childhood dreams unfold, both when wrapped in its thick blanket of snow in winter, when the Northern Lights flash overhead, and in the never-dying golden days of summer's Midnight Sun.

Remote and sparsely populated, this is one of Finland's true wildernesses: a rolling mass of lichen-draped forests and high fells, three of which are still considered *ailigas* (sacred places) by the indigenous Sámi. Nature takes centre stage here, whether you are huddled up in a log cabin during a blizzard, hooking giant salmon in the fast-flowing Teno River, or dashing through the snow on a reindeer-driven sleigh. It's a place to tiptoe off the map on hiking trails and be awed by the ethereal pink glow of a would-be sunrise during the polar night.

GO IF YOU LIKE...

- 💙 *Arctic beauty*
- 💙 *winter wonderlands*
- 💙 *Northern Lights & Midnight Sun*
- 💙 *remote wilderness*
- 💙 *outdoor activities*
- 💙 *Sámi culture*

Why go to Utsjoki?

Spruce forest, fells, flint-blue lakes and barely a soul in sight bar the odd reindeer... Are you on the road to nowhere? The road to Utsjoki, 70°N of the Arctic Circle, sure feels like it. This region is pure Narnia in winter, when flakes fall thick and fast, temperatures dip below -20°C (-4°F) and the trees are sculpted with hoarfrost. And its remoteness is its saving grace – this alone has kept it so pristine and peaceful.

The Sámi heartbeat is felt keenly here – especially when dashing through newly fallen powder snow on a reindeer-drawn sleigh and listening to haunting Sámi *joik*, the rhythmic poems that evoke the spirit of ancestors, sung around a crackling campfire in a lavvu tent. Foraging, salmon fishing, canoeing and hiking are all summer pursuits, while winter is defined by snowshoeing, ice-fishing, backcountry skiing and watching dumbstruck as the aurora sways in the hush of night. This region and its people bring you that bit closer to nature and a way of life that has been all but forgotten.

GETTING THERE

The most convenient airport is Ivalo, 160km (100 miles) south, which is connected to Helsinki by regular Finnair flights (1hr 40min). From there, you can either drive or take the bus (2hr 20min).

WHEN TO GO

Jun–Sep & Dec–Mar

Summer brings days of saunas, swims and long hikes into the wilds under the Midnight Sun. The darkness of winter is illuminated by snow and frequent Northern Lights shows.

FIRST-TIME TIPS

Pack warm for the Arctic climate. You'll need full-on thermals in winter and mosquito repellent and layers in summer, when evenings can get chilly.

....

Arrange outdoor activities in advance. Many lodges can help organise everything from snowmobiling to Sámi reindeer farm visits and salmon fishing.

....

Here in summer? Go wild camping. Finland has the right to roam, so simply pitch your tent away from civilisation to feel the remote pulse of this region.

....

Strip off and embrace the sauna. Nearly every guesthouse, no matter how simple, has one. A roll in the snow afterwards jumpstarts the immune system.

AMAZING CROWD-FREE EXPERIENCES

 Hike the Utsjoki Trail, a circular 35km (22 mile) trek into the wilderness, knitting together lakes, valleys and fells with arresting views of Norway's peaks.

 Tune into Sámi culture with a visit to a reindeer farm, followed by a ride through the wintry wonderland on a sleigh, and hot drinks and stories around a campfire.

 Crack the art of ice fishing. Dash across the frozen tundra on a snowmobile to a remote lake, then lower your jig-rod to hook Arctic char and trout.

 Fly-fish for salmon on the crystal-clear Teno River as the Midnight Sun burns on above. The river forms a natural border with Norway.

 Slip into snowshoes at twilight to pick your way across the fells in quiet exhilaration, still ruddy-faced from an afternoon sauna.

 Catch the Northern Lights on a dark, clear winter's night. It's as though the Norse gods are drawing across the heavens with invisible ink.

Above: Reindeer are a part of Sámi life in the Arctic Circle – visitors can visit a reindeer farm and even ride a reindeer-pulled sleigh

**Erik Valle**
Sámi reindeer herder

WHY I LOVE UTSJOKI

Because it's home. I have spent my whole life in Utsjoki, growing up in a family of reindeer herders. I love the space, the nature and wildlife.

**Must-have local experience?**
Welcoming guests to my reindeer farm to share a bit of Sámi culture, show them the reindeer and enjoy coffee around an open fire in a lavvu tent.

**Favourite season?**
Every season has its charm here: the fishing and hot days of summer, the hard work of autumn when we gather the reindeer in from the wild and separate them, and winter with reindeer herding and Northern Lights. Here we are so far from any light pollution that the auroras are some of Finland's best.

Hyères

BEYOND PROVENCE'S HONEYPOTS LIES THIS MEDIEVAL TOWN AND MED ISLANDS

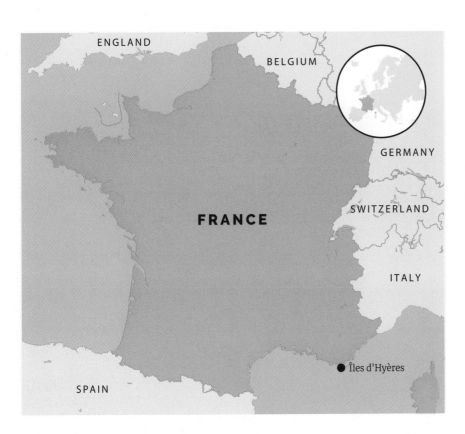

Later it became the property of the Viscount of Marseilles, before the incorporation of Provence into modern France.

Between the medieval centre of Hyères and the sea lie the busy D98 and a modern town dominated by international hotels and casinos. Passers-through run the risk of missing the partially walled Vielle Ville (old town) entirely. The best of Hyères is concentrated in this historic nucleus and the gardens that sprawl above it. But most alluring of all are the Îles d'Hyères, three offshore sirens also known as the Îles d'Or (Islands of Gold).

Visitors to the Provençal coast inevitably make a beeline for glamorous spots such as Cannes, Cap d'Antibes or St Tropez; rarely does Hyères get a look-in. Yet, packed with historic interest and adjacent to some of the loveliest islands in the south of France, a trip to Hyères really pays out. Settlement here dates back to the Phoenicians of 4th-century BCE, who were displaced by the Hellenistic Greeks, then the Romans.

GO IF YOU LIKE...

- 🤍 *Cap d'Antibes*
- 🤍 *gorgeous islands*
- 🤍 *rugged coastal walks*
- 🤍 *isolated calanques*
- 🤍 *Mediterranean beaches*
- 🤍 *literary associations*

Why go to Hyères?

Lovers of French heritage will enjoy the well-preserved medieval layout of Hyères, including the intact 13th-century Porte Massillon and uncovered segments of the Béal – the 15th-century aqueduct that still carries water to the town. Above the cobbled streets and churches lie Parc Bernard and Castel Ste-Claire, a restored 17th-century convent once home to American writer Edith Wharton.

But the most compelling reasons to visit lie offshore: Porquerolles, Île de Port-Cros and Île du Levant, the idyllic triplet of the Îles d'Hyères. Porquerolles, the largest, was bought by the Belgian entrepreneur Francois Fournier in 1907 as a wedding gift for his wife. Covered in vineyards, olive groves and native pine forest, the islands are partially protected within the Parc National de Port-Cros. Come for isolated beaches and waters with wrecks and marine life that beckon kayakers and divers.

Right: Porquerolles is a Mediterranean beauty, though admittedly busy in school holidays

Below: Hyères old town has medieval bones and lively street life worth exploring

FIRST-TIME TIPS

The most atmospheric place to stay is in <u>the heart of the action</u> in the Vielle Ville (Old Town), but you'll find better deals in the more modern streets of Hyères, still close to the centre.

July and August are hot and crowded – <u>hotel prices surge</u> during this period and you'll need to book restaurants in advance.

Consider bringing <u>a picnic and water</u> to the Île de Port-Cros. The island's few bistros only open between April and October and they can get very busy.

If you should stroll into Héliopolis on the Île du Levant, don't be surprised if you see more human flesh than you planned for – it's a <u>nudist colony</u>.

GETTING THERE

Hyères is easily reached by train from Marseilles (about 1hr 35min) or Toulon (20min). Buses take a little longer, but are regular and less expensive. There's really little point in hiring a car to visit Hyères: all the sights are closely grouped, and you can't take vehicles onto the islands.

WHEN TO GO

Mar–May & Sep–Oct

The shoulder seasons give the greatest latitude to explore in peace, and the most temperate weather. Peak season is the summer school holidays (July and August), when Porquerolles feels overcrowded with more than 6000 visitors a day.

AMAZING CROWD-FREE EXPERIENCES

 Take a trail inland from the Port de Porquerolles, through picturesque vineyards to calanques (cove) beaches and pine forests in the centre, north and west.

 Climb steep streets to explore the leafy northern quarters of Hyères, home to the gorgeously landscaped gardens of the Castel Ste-Claire and the less kempt but no less lovely grounds of the Parc St-Bernard.

 Circle the beach-fringed peninsula of Presqu'île de Giens, south of Hyères, where salty lagoons attract flamingos.

 Visit lovely little Île de Port-Cros, epicentre of France's first marine park. Its protected pine and maquis-environment makes for delightful walking.

 Join a catamaran cruise from Port de Porquerolles to explore the marine portion of the Parc National de Port-Cros, try stand-up paddleboarding or go snorkelling.

 Wander the grass-strewn ruins of Olbia, the Greek colony from which modern-day Hyères ultimately descends. Not much drama, but big peaceful vibes.

Lyon

SWAP PARIS FOR FRANCE'S GASTRONOMIC CAPITAL AT THE FOOT OF THE ALPS

Founded by the Romans in 43 BCE, Lyon's Unesco-listed centre has well preserved layers of history in its compact suburbs. Head to the slopes of Fourvière and you'll find medieval thoroughfares, while Vieux-Lyon is a Renaissance jewel and the hilltop suburb of Croix-Rousse is famed for its 19th-century *canuts* (silk workers' houses), built when Lyon was a powerhouse of silk weaving. Today, Lyon's *bouchons* – rustic restaurants serving hearty Lyonnaise dishes – are a legacy of its blue-collar heyday and the city's unique food heritage is one of the reasons why Lyon is often described as France's gastronomic capital.

In the most visited country in the world, the concept of 'underrated' or 'little visited' is all relative. So while Lyon's six million visitors in 2019 might sound like a lot, it's a mere drop in the ocean compared with Paris' average of 30 million overnight stays. And two thirds of Lyon's visitors are business travellers, meaning there are far fewer tourists swanning around its pastel-hued Renaissance streets to hog all the pavement cafe tables.

GO IF YOU LIKE...

- *Paris & Marseille*
- *historic bistros*
- *riverside cities*
- *Beaujolais Nouveau season*
- *film history*
- *Michelin stars*

Why go to Lyon?

Paris may have the Eiffel Tower and Marseille the Med, but Lyon lays claim to the best food scene in France. This was the home of three-Michelin-starred Paul Bocuse, one of France's most celebrated chefs (who died in 2018), but just as important to the city's gastronomic clout are the Mères Lyonnaises – female cooks from humble households who founded the city's *bouchons*. In 2019, Lyon opened the Cité de la Gastronomie, a first-of-its-kind, 4000 sq m (43,055 sq ft) cultural space devoted to food and located inside a 15th-century former hospital.

Lyon has other claims to fame, too. The surrounding region, at the foot of the Alps, is renowned for its Beaujolais- and Côtes du Rhône-producing *terroir*. It's also the home of the Lumière brothers, who played a pivotal role in the dawn of the moving image. Despite being France's third-largest city, Lyon's centre is a cinch to explore by foot and metro. Hop between *bouchons* and wine bars, stroll the redeveloped riverbanks and see history play out in excellent museums. Who needs another trip to Paris when this beauty is waiting?

GETTING THERE

Lyon is well connected to the rest of France by train; the direct TGV from Paris Gare de Lyon to Lyon Part Dieu takes around 2hr. There's also a direct Eurostar train from London (4hr 45min) during the summer months. The city's international Lyons Saint-Exupéry Airport, 25km (15 miles) east of Lyon, also has good links to the rest of Europe.

WHEN TO GO

Jun–Sep

Riverside living makes Lyon the perfect summer city break, but July and August are also the busiest months to visit. July is typically the hottest month, with average highs in the mid-20s°C (mid-70s°F). Come in September to skip the summer crowds.

© VENTDUSUD | SHUTTERSTOCK. © JULIAN ELLIOTT / ALAMY STOCK PHOTO. © RIVER THOMPSON | LONELY PLANET

FIRST-TIME TIPS

Buy the Lyon Card (en. lyoncitycard.com) if you're a museum-hopper. It's available for one to four days and includes entry to 23 museums across the city, as well as unlimited public transport, making city touring hassle-free.

. . . .

Beaujolais Nouveau is released on the third Thursday in November each year and Lyon is one of the best places to celebrate the occasion, with fireworks, music and festivals.

. . . .

Around 80 of Lyon's traboules are open to the public (of more than 400 across the city's most historic districts); download Lyon's official Traboules App to help find the lesser visited alleys.

AMAZING CROWD-FREE EXPERIENCES

 Follow the Paul Bocuse trail — his mini empire includes the Les Halles de Lyon Paul Bocuse, a gourmet food hall stuffed with picnic fodder and five brasseries.

 Visit the birthplace of cinematography at Château Lumière, where two brothers invented a revolutionary camera in 1895 that paved the way for the big screen.

 Explore the Museum of Confluences, a futuristic anthropology collection at the tip of Presqu'île, and a linchpin of long-term plans to redevelop the Saône riverbanks.

 Gorge on rich Lyonnais cuisine, such as creamy *quenelle lyonnaise* or *andouillette* sausage, at a *bouchon* like Le Bouchon des Filles or Daniel et Denise Créqui.

 Scale the slopes of Fourvière via the 1878 funicular to reach the hilltop Basilique Notre Dame de Fourvière — Lyon's version of Paris' Sacre Coeur.

 Duck and weave through Lyon's *traboules* — secret passageways in the historic Vieux-Lyon and Croix-Rousse districts, once used by silk workers to transport textiles.

Clockwise from top left: Inside a *traboule* in Vieux-Lyon; a classic Salade Lyonnaise; the view from Lyon's hilltop suburb of Fourvière

Left: Glacial
Mummelsee lake
viewed from atop
Hornisgrinde

Freiburg &
the Black Forest

AN ECO TRAILBLAZING CITY SWADDLED IN SILENT ALPINE FOREST FANTASIES

The Black Forest? Isn't that Bavaria? Nope, it's right next door. But here you'll find wooded hills and half-timbered towns that hit the same fairytale sweet spot – albeit with a fraction of the crowds. Cuckoo clock and gateau clichés aside, a vast swath of this valley-pleated, fir-cloaked region falls spectacularly under the tourist radar. Feel the magic by diving into its remotest reaches on foot, by bike or road. In the Black Forest National Park, spruce forests bristle above dark-wood-shingle farms and glacial lakes spread out like deep-blue silk sheets. Treading softly through the forest at first light, you'll find the kind of peace that's increasingly rare. Slip on snowshoes or cross-country skis when winter snows fall and the fantasy is complete.

Sustainable? Natürlich. The tree-hugging, nature-loving Schwarzwald is Germany's original green destination and its eco star just keeps rising, with a new Unesco Biosphere Reserve, ultra-green towns like Freiburg shining brightly with solar power, and miles of diligently marked hiking, cycling and e-biking trails.

GO IF YOU LIKE...

- ♥ *Bavaria*
- ♥ *forests*
- ♥ *green travel*
- ♥ *remote farmstays*
- ♥ *road trips*
- ♥ *back-to-nature seclusion*

Why go to Freiburg & the Black Forest?

Vivacious university city Freiburg snuggles close to the French and Swiss borders. It's a historic knockout with a tangle of medieval lanes and Gothic minster, but its gaze is firmly fixed on a green, clean vision of a more sustainable future. Germany's sunniest city, this eco trailblazer has singlehandedly installed more photovoltaic panels than some European countries. And it has gone one step beyond with the Vauban quarter, the world's first plus-energy, carbon-neutral living community.

Being green here comes as second nature. Bavaria has the much-hyped Romantic Road, but the less-travelled Schwarzwald Hochstrasse (Black Forest High Road), which rolls 60km (37 miles) over forest-plaited mountain and moor from Baden-Baden to Freudenstadt, is just as lovely. The route dives deep into the 100-sq-km (38 sq miles) Black Forest National Park. Here you can slip properly back to nature with a night under the stars at one of the designated wilderness camps, with nothing but the woodpeckers and red squirrels for company. Hear that? Silence. Isn't it a beautiful thing?

GETTING THERE

Freiburg has regular train connections from major cities such as Munich, Berlin and Frankfurt, as well as three local airports: EuroAirport Basel-Mulhouse-Freiburg; Stuttgart; Frankfurt. It's also possible to take the Eurostar/TGV to Strasbourg, a quick hop over the French border.

WHEN TO GO

Year-round

Spring brings wildflowers and terrific hiking weather; autumn a colourful riot of foliage and mushroom foraging. Summer is fine (never too hot) for walking, cycling and lake swims. Winters can be beautiful, with snowy days and a flurry of Christmas markets.

AMAZING CROWD-FREE EXPERIENCES

Climb to the top of Hornisgrinde (1164m/3819ft) for an entrancing view of the Mummelsee, a forest-rimmed glacial cirque lake of sapphire blue.

Hike the Westweg trail, stitching together moors, quiet forests and lakes. It kicks off in the northern Black Forest and wends south for 285km (177 miles) to Basel.

Go cross-country skiing in the high woods at Martinskapelle, source of the Danube. Tracks lead to Brend at 1150m (3773ft), where the Alps pop up on clear days.

Discover Black Forest river valleys like Murgtal and Kinzigtal – this is the Black Forest of childhood dreams.

Wander the medieval back alleys of Freiburg, an easy-going, eco-friendly dream of a city, then hitch a cable-car ride to Schauinsland for rippling Black Forest views.

Enjoy a Roman-style steam, scrub and hot-cold dunk in the thermal waters of the palatially domed Friedrichsbad in Baden-Baden, a Unesco Great Spa Town of Europe.

Clockwise from left: Freiburg's old town; the city's open-air market; hiking in the Black Forest on trails from Freiburg's centre

Andrea Philipp
project manager,
Aiforia – Agency
for Sustainability &
partner of Freiburg's
Green City Office

WHY I LOVE
FREIBURG

I love the region's diverse and contrasting mix of landscapes and ecosystems. Freiburg is for nature lovers – Black Forest hiking and mountain biking trails start right in the historic centre, and cyclists and longboarders share 'bike highways'.

Must-have local experience?
With the Green City Map (greencity. freiburg.de), you can easily explore Freiburg's sustainability hotspots, from the model eco district Vauban to the new Town Hall, and the season-driven farmers' market held six days a week on Münsterplatz.

Favourite season?
Late autumn is a wonderful time to enjoy an Indian summer in the Black Forest and the rich harvest of the Rhine Valley. Or come in early December for first snow in the hills.

Andros

A SUN-KISSED GREEK ISLAND BUILDING A NAME FOR HIKING, NOT HOLIDAYS

Andros is a happy anomaly. It's the second-biggest of the Cyclades but, unlike other islands in this holiday-hotspot chain, isn't reliant on tourism. Tourists who do come tend to be Athenian and, historically, shipbuilding has been the main industry here. Ever since the great Greek maritime dynasties opened offices in London in the early 20th century, Andros has had the nickname Micra Anglia (Little England). Today, its sparkling Aegean beaches, archaeological sites and rugged highlands remain pleasingly uncrowded and undeveloped.

Andros is also uncommonly green, blessed with year-round rivers and springs – the Ancient Greeks dubbed it Ydrousa (the 'watery one'). For centuries people here were self-sufficient, cultivating *emasies* (manmade terraces) to produce vegetables, olive oil, wine and herbs. Times have changed, but the notion of self-sufficiency remains – Andros is now home to an inspirational local initiative aiming to revive the island's cultural heritage and support its communities by turning it into one of Greece's best hiking destinations.

GO IF YOU LIKE...

- ♥ *Crete*
- ♥ *Corfu*
- ♥ *the Peloponnese*
- ♥ *hiking*
- ♥ *ancient archaeology*
- ♥ *untouristy tavernas*

Why go to Andros?

Andros has a lot to love. There's its diverse, mountain-rumpled interior, cut with lush valleys and lapped by pellucid-blue waves. There's its elegant capital, Chora, full of Neoclassical mansions built from shipping wealth. There's a smatter of historic sites, including Ancient Greek and 13th-century Venetian ruins and part-restored old watermills. And there are plenty of quiet, shady tavernas that serve cold beer, fresh fish and soft cheese with views out to sea.

But best of all is Andros Routes. Founded in 2010, this volunteer-run project has created a 170km (105 mile)-long network of waymarked trails – including a 100km (60 mile)-long continuous route – utilising old mule tracks, village byways and paved *stenes* (paths lined with Andros' distinctive dry-stone walls). So high is the standard of walks, it's been recognised by the European Ramblers Association as an official Leading Quality Trail. Hiking here not only reveals an undiscovered island, it helps preserve that island for future generations to enjoy.

GETTING THERE

There is no airport on Andros, the northernmost of the Cyclades islands. It's about two hours by ferry from the Greek mainland. Frequent ferries leave from the Port of Rafina (16km/10 miles from Athens Airport, 32km/20 miles from the city centre) for Gavrio on Andros; these services continue to the islands of Tinos (1hr 20min) and Mykonos (2hrs 15min).

WHEN TO GO

Mar–May & Sep–Nov

Summer is really too hot for hiking. Spring and autumn offer manageably warm temperatures and natural delights such as wildflowers and fall colours; mild weather makes hiking possible in winter too.

AMAZING CROWD-FREE EXPERIENCES

 Hike the whole main Andros Route, which extends across the island between Frousei (in the north) and Dipotamata (in the south). Allow 5-10 days.

 Suck lemons in Livadia, where orchards yield much-prized Andros citruses. Eat them as *glyko tou koutaliou* (spoon sweets), a sort of fruit preserve.

 Visit Paleopolis, capital of Andros in the 7th century. Forgotten-feeling and partly excavated, it has a great little archaeological museum and empty beach.

 Explore mill villages like Frousei and Strapouries, or follow Andros Routes' Menites loop via woods and mill ruins — around 200 watermills once dotted Andros.

 Hike to the large monastery of Zoodochos Pigi — the route from the settlement of Ano Agios Petros to this ecclesiastical landmark affords excellent views of the west coast.

 Admire old tower houses in the villages of Kapparia and Aidonia – these stone-made structures once produced highly valued Andros silk.

Olga Karayiannis
founder, Andros
Research Center, &
coordinator, Andros
Routes Project

WHY I LOVE ANDROS

There's a magic on this island I'm
still trying to figure out. Part of
its charm is the amazingly folded
terrain – everything is hidden;
you're constantly discovering
different landscapes.

Must-have local experience?
Walk! The treasure of Andros is
discovering it on foot. And use
your senses: smell the herbs and
flowers; taste the local produce;
feel the temperature changes from
hilltop to valley. In this way, you
really feel Andros is alive.

Favourite season?
In spring the colours are amazing.
In autumn the weather is mild,
the light is soft and you can swim
until December.

Above: Visitors who make it to Andros will find wonderfully
pretty coastal villages and few tourists competing for photos

225

Left: Dettifoss in Vatnajökull National Park is one of Northern Iceland's premier attractions

Northern Iceland

FOLLOW THE ARCTIC COAST WAY ALONG ICELAND'S EMPTY ATLANTIC CROWN

NORTHERN ICELAND

ICELAND

Spectacular as it most certainly is, this Atlantic island has suffered from a serious dose of overexposure (around two million visitors a year pre-pandemic; more than five times Iceland's population). Though that hardly sounds like the definition of offbeat, the fact is that most of Iceland's visitors only explore a small corner of the island. From the capital of Reykjavík, tourists are drawn to big sights like Gullfoss, Geysir and the Blue Lagoon, and perhaps Skaftafell's glaciers or Jökulsárlón's icebergs with time to travel further along the southern Ring Road.

Far fewer venture north – and those that do experience a very different side of Iceland most visitors never see. Coast roads corkscrewing past deserted headlands. End-of-the-world beaches straight out of a Bergman movie. Geothermal hotpots in the middle of nowhere. Peculiar towns, and oddball museums and weird lava caves. Spooky islands where birds outnumber people by 10,000 to one. Sure, it takes a little effort and adventure to escape the crowds, but once you do, you'll experience Iceland at its most raw and empty.

GO IF YOU LIKE…

- 💜 *Iceland's Blue Lagoon*
- 💜 *big waterfalls*
- 💜 *wild Arctic coastline*
- 💜 *seabirds*
- 💜 *black sand*
- 💜 *volcanoes*

Why go to Northern Iceland?

The north has its share of popular sights – particularly the waterfalls of Goðafoss and Dettifoss, and the volcanic craters around Mývatn — so, to get offbeat, you need to stray well away from Highway 1, aka the Ring Road. The best way to do this is along the Arctic Coast Way (arcticcoastway.is), a driving route that opened in 2019 to tackle overtourism on the Ring Road, encompassing 900km (560 miles) of rugged back-roads from Hvammstangi in the west to Bakkafjörður in the east.

This is not a route for the faint-hearted: a third is on gravel trails, and many parts are impassable in winter, so you'll definitely need 4WD. En route, you'll experience some of Iceland's most unexplored landscapes — black sand beaches, rock stacks, glacial deltas and isolated villages that receive only a handful of visitors. Iceland really doesn't get much more off the beaten track than this. Take your time, pack a pair of binoculars and don't be afraid to get a little lost. That's part of the fun.

GETTING THERE

The north coast can be reached in a long day's drive (or bus trip) from Reykjavík. Alternatively you could fly direct to the area's main town of Akureyri and start your trip from there.

WHEN TO GO

May–Oct

Heavy snow and ice close many stretches of the Arctic Coast Way in winter, and there's precious little daylight. Come in summer for long days and (relatively) settled weather.

FIRST-TIME TIPS

Hire a 4WD car. Check the conditions of all the tyres (including the spare) and carry a can of spare fuel, just in case.

....

Take a good road map: phone signal is not guaranteed in Northern Iceland.

....

Check the weather forecast and road conditions before setting out.

....

Remember the midnight sun: pack an eyeshade if you want to have any hope of getting some sleep in midsummer.

AMAZING CROWD-FREE EXPERIENCES

 Walk among the rock formations of Vesturdalur, some of the north's best-kept secrets. Jökulsárgljúfur canyon and Urriðafossar waterfall are highlights.

 Spy all kinds of wildlife on the Rauðanes peninsula. This isolated headland and nature reserve is a prime spot for Icelandic wildlife, including puffins and seals.

 Marvel at the birdlife on Drangey island, ringed by 180m (590ft)-high cliffs and looking like something out of *The Lost World*, with seabirds in their millions.

 Venture under the lava at Lofthellir, a secret lava cave near Mývatn bedecked with dramatic ice formations. You'll need a private guide to visit.

 Edge into the Arctic on Grimsey island, the only part of Iceland inside the Arctic Circle. It's only accessible by tiny plane or a notoriously choppy ferry ride.

 Take a geothermal dip in Hofsós Swimming Pool. Forget the Blue Lagoon – this may be Iceland's most spectacularly sited swimming pool.

Clockwise from top left: Puffins at Rauðanes peninsula; Hofsós pool colliding with the Atlantic; Jökulsárgljúfur's rocky canyon

Copper Coast

PREHISTORY WRIT LARGE ACROSS IRELAND'S OVERLOOKED SOUTHERN GEOPARK

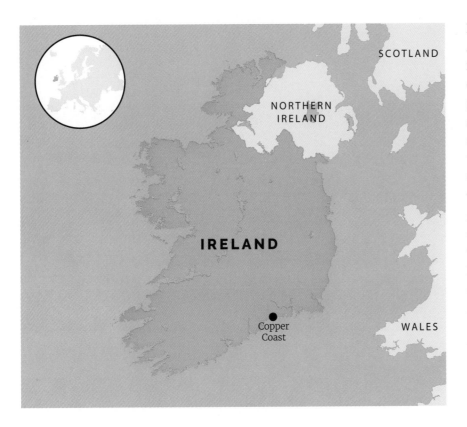

SCOTLAND

NORTHERN IRELAND

IRELAND

Copper Coast

WALES

Formed by volcanic eruptions 460 million years ago, this coast is dawn-of-creation stuff, with every sea stack, buckled rock and glacier-scoured cliff exposing another layer of geological history, and forcing you to contemplate the foundations of the earth itself. On all but the busiest of summer weekends you can expect to have its gorgeously secluded, wave-whipped coves, walking trails and coastal woodlands largely to your lucky self. Beyond the beaches, prehistoric dolmens, promontory forts and ghostly 19th-century copper mining ruins point to an ancient and deeply mysterious past.

The Wild Atlantic Way that skims Ireland's storm-tossed western seaboard gets all the fuss, but southern Ireland's Copper Coast is just as bracingly beautiful. Despite its Unesco Global Geopark status, this 25km (15 mile) stretch of coast, running between Kilfarrasy in the east and Stradbally in the west, remains sorely overlooked — so much so that mention of it often draws blank looks even from the Irish.

GO IF YOU LIKE...

- 🤍 *The Wild Atlantic Way*
- 🤍 *County Kerry coast*
- 🤍 *Giant's Causeway*
- 🤍 *hidden coves*
- 🤍 *prehistoric sites*
- 🤍 *industrial heritage*

231

Why go to the Copper Coast?

Rain or shine, the tug of the thrashing Atlantic is life-affirmingly powerful, whether you're a forager, wild swimmer, surfer, biker, hiker or whale-watcher. You'll want to dally on every rugged cove and gorse-cloaked cliff, but spare time to dive into the region's absorbing history and heritage too: at the Copper Coast Geological Garden, for starters, where you can see Ogham stones inscribed with the early-Christian language used by Celtic saints, and a cursing stone (lore has it your curse will come true if you walk around it anticlockwise).

Prehistory is writ large the length of the coast in dolmens, passage tombs and one of the world's largest concentrations of promontory forts, while the ruined engine house in Tankardstown nods to the coast's 19th-century copper-mining heyday that gives this coastline its name. Don't stop there. The Comeragh Mountains rolling north are wild, lonely and wondrous. Hike along a bracken-tangled trail to the Mahon Falls, which plunge down sheer, moraine-streaked cliffs to a glacier-carved, boulder-speckled plateau.

GETTING THERE

Cork is the closest airport to the Copper Coast. Ferries from Wales dock in Rosslare, around 90km (56 miles) east. There are also quiet, cycle-friendly paths that make the coast a breeze to reach by bike from other parts of Ireland.

WHEN TO GO

Apr–Oct

Ireland's weather is notoriously fickle, but things tend to be driest and warmest from spring to early autumn. Winters can be wet and foggy.

FIRST-TIME TIPS

Visit the Copper Coast Geopark church visitor centre in Bunmahon for a romp through geological history and industrial heritage.

....

Arrange bike hire in advance. The Greenway Man in Dungarvan is excellent for bike hire and cycle tours on the Greenway, a 46km (29 mile) off-road cycle route shadowing old railway lines.

....

Book top tables ahead. At Tannery in Dungarvan, legendary local chef Paul Flynn gets creative with seasonal, regional ingredients in a converted leather factory.

....

The Atlantic coast is wild and very tidal, so make sure you factor in tide times when beach foraging or rambling. A handy resource is Tideschart (tideschart.com).

AMAZING CROWD-FREE EXPERIENCES

 Seek out the Pipes of Baidhb at Knockmahon. These polygonal columns of rhyolite are the Copper Coast's own Giant's Causeway.

 Go for a walk on Stradbally, a pristine scoop of sand where a stream babbles down to the crashing Atlantic and birdsong drifts from ancient sessile oak woods.

 Hunt for edible seaweed with local forager and cookbook writer Marie Power (theseagardener.com) on the craggy wilds of the cliff-clasped beach of Garrarus.

 Drive the Magic Road to Mahon Falls. It whips across remote moors to a fairy tree, where (because of magic or electromagnetic fields), cars roll backwards uphill.

 Take a traditional seaweed bath at Sólás Na Mara, where seawater is pumped directly into cast-iron tubs at high tide at a fish auction house turned intimate spa.

 Add on a side trip to Ardmore, the trailhead for a sublime pilgrims cliff path just west of the Copper Coast. St Declan founded a monastery here in 416.

Above: Hikes around Mahon Falls cut through remote, wild moors backed by views of the Comeragh Mountains

Marie Power
sea gardener, forager, ecologist, cook & author

WHY I LOVE THE COPPER COAST

Whether kayaking around caves and sea stacks, exploring a rock pool or swimming in the crystal-clear waters, the Copper Coast refreshes and relaxes me. It reminds me of happy childhood memories of visiting my grandparents, who lived in Stradbally.

Must-have local experience?
There's wonderful seaweed diversity along the Copper Coast. Foraging is the best way to connect with that food heritage, learning about edible seaweeds and the coastal ecosystem.

Favourite season?
Spring, when young seaweeds are starting to grow and are at their tender best.

Le Marche

ITALY'S PERFECT, QUIET BACKCOUNTRY LYING IN THE SHADOW OF TUSCANY

Le Marche is the Italy you'll wish you'd heard about sooner. Everyone raves about neighbouring Tuscany, but this region is equally enticing. Here, vineyards and olive groves, cypress trees and poppy fields are as soft-edged as a watercolour. Rolling hills are topped by higgledy-piggledy towns, packed with Renaissance art, out-of-tune *campaniles* (bell towers), and piazzas for a lazy *aperitivo*. The coast's limestone cliffs dive to snow-white pebble beaches that fizz into the Adriatic. Swing west and the snow-dusted peaks of the Apennines soar 2000m (6562ft) above wildflower-freckled plains.

Stage your own backcountry road trip, ticking off hill towns like rosary beads and stopping for gloriously drawn-out lunches at family-run trattorias championing regional produce such as truffles, olives, wild boar, salumi and wine. Days wind out to the backbeat of cicadas at starlit *agriturismi*, or in the vaulted splendour of 16th-century palazzi that peer out across some of Italy's loveliest squares. The Italian dream? Most certainly. But whisper it quietly...

GO IF YOU LIKE...

- 🤍 *Tuscany*
- 🤍 *Florence*
- 🤍 *medieval hill towns*
- 🤍 *Renaissance art*
- 🤍 *piazza life*
- 🤍 *remote mountain trails*

Why go to Le Marche?

Tiptoe properly off the map in Parco Nazionale dei Monti Sibillini. Rippling along the Umbrian border and capping out at 2476m (8123ft) Monte Vettore, this under-the-radar, trail-woven corner of the country is extraordinary – whether seen in its winter blanket of snow or with its spring carpet of wildflowers. Wild boar and wolves still roam its remote forests. The mountains give way to the Adriatic coast further east, where Parco del Conero entices with quiet coastal trails twisting to vineyards and wooded cliffs that dip to white-pebble bays.

Le Marche's hill towns are rarely overrun, despite their evident charms. Take Urbino, where Raphael was born, with its feast of Renaissance architecture and art, or medieval, palazzi-lined Macerata of summer opera festival fame. And few Italian cities can rival Ascoli Piceno in the most-beautiful-piazza stakes. Its Piazza del Popolo is a harmonious, colonnaded vision in pale travertine limestone that looks as though it were built by the angels themselves.

GETTING THERE

The main gateway to the region is the airport in Ancona, served by a number of low-cost airlines. The city also has a decent train network linking up to the rest of Italy and, beyond, Europe. Realistically, you'll need a car to reach the remote parts of the region.

WHEN TO GO

Mar–Oct

Coastal resorts aside, you can find peace even in the height of summer, but it can get hot, making late spring (for wildflowers on the Piano Grande) and early autumn (for foliage, truffle hunting and chestnut-driven specialities) preferable.

AMAZING CROWD-FREE EXPERIENCES

 Delve into a forest of stalactites and stalagmites at the Grotte di Frasassi, a karst wonderland and one of Europe's largest cave systems, deep in the hill country.

 Hit the beach in Sirolo, where sublime half-moon bays of gleaming white pebbles and sand are backed by forested cliffs and fragrant *macchia* (Mediterranean shrubs).

 Walk in the silent mountains near Montefortino. One of the most memorable hikes heads through the Gola dell'Infernaccio (Gorge of Hell) canyon.

 Witness the late springtime wildflower eruption on Piano Grande, a 1270m (4167ft) karstic plain in the region's eastern corner. In May and June, poppies, cornflowers, tulips and narcissi paint rainbow hues.

 Get lost in the medieval alleys of Sarnano. Spilling photogenically down a steep hill, this warm-stone town is never more atmospheric than in late-afternoon sun.

 Follow pilgrims to hilltop Loreto, whose bauble-domed basilica shelters a bejewelled black statue of the Virgin.

Above: Le Marche's rolling hills are stitched with classic vineyards, olive groves and flower-filled fields

Left: Treviso
receives as few as
350,000 visitors a
year compared with
Venice's eight million

Treviso

THIS GENUINE SERENISSIMA IS JUST 20 MINUTES FROM CROWDED VENICE

For centuries, Treviso has lived in the shadow of its famous neighbour Venice. But today, while the Serenissima battles with Acqua Alta floods, intrusive cruise ships and over eight million tourists a year, Treviso attracts a mere 350,000 visitors who are delighted to discover this jewel of the rich Veneto region. Wandering on foot from the grand Piazza dei Signori to the ancient city gates, there are grand Renaissance and Baroque palaces, romantic canals and quiet museums hung with masterpieces by Titian, Tintoretto and Tiepolo.

Crucially, there are no crowds to contend with in this friendly, laid-back city – apart from during the early evening *aperitivo*, when everyone heads out for a spritz or a chilled glass of the famed local bubbly, Prosecco. Like Milan, Treviso also has a reputation for Italian fashion, as the home of global brands Benetton, Diesel, Replay and Geox. And it's a jumping off point not just for trips to Venice, but also the seaside resorts of Jesolo and Lignano, the ski slopes of Cortina and the Dolomites, or the idyllic vineyards and villas of Prosecco wine region.

GO IF YOU LIKE...

- ♥ *Venice's canals*
- ♥ *tiramisu*
- ♥ *street markets*
- ♥ *Prosecco*
- ♥ *Italian fashion*
- ♥ *rugby & basketball*

Why go to Treviso?

Irresistible Venice is just a 20-minute train ride away, perfect for a day trip, but then leave the crowds behind and return to one of Treviso's charming B&Bs in a plush Renaissance palace. Enjoy dinner in an authentic trattoria feasting off local specialities like guinea fowl with pomegranate and the ultimate dessert, tiramisu, invented right here. Prices are always reasonable with no rip-off *menu turistico* in sight.

Then concentrate on exploring this historic city, whose roots go back to Roman times. Old Master art exhibitions are displayed at the recently renovated Santa Caterina convent, while Casa dei Carraresi showcases cutting edge modern art. Every morning the outdoor *pescheria* (fish market) is a noisy spectacle, while fashionistas head for Calmaggiore, a vaulted medieval arcade lined with chic Italian boutiques. Sports fans can see top-ranking rugby and basketball matches, and while Venice tends to go to sleep early, there is a vibrant nightlife scene here.

GETTING THERE

Treviso has its own small airport, popular with European low-cost airlines, while Venice's Marco Polo international airport hub is a 30min bus ride away. Treviso is also well connected by train for those travelling from other parts of Italy.

WHEN TO GO

Year-round

Treviso is a genuine all-year destination; it's especially good as a base for the Venice carnival in February, as staying in Treviso and visiting as a day-trip will avoid excessive hotel rates in the Serenissima.

AMAZING CROWD-FREE EXPERIENCES

 Mount the 500-year-old fortified city walls for a stroll right around the heart of historic Treviso, traversing a grassy promenade beside the city's moat.

 Pack a picnic to eat waterside on a lazy cycle ride along the scenic Sile river, taking advantage of the fact Treviso is a genuine bike city.

 Plan a side-trip to magical Villa di Maser, a sumptuous Palladian villa with interiors decorated with astonishing 16th-century trompe l'oeil frescoes by Paolo Veronese.

 Track down the little-known Museo Collezione Salce, with its dazzling collection of vintage ad posters for brands like Martini, Campari, Vespa and Ferrari.

 Admire 14th-century frescoes in the secluded seminary of Chiesa San Nicolò, painted by Tommaso da Modena — a contemporary of Giotto.

 Rise early to walk the romantic Buranelli Canal. You'll travel along an arched medieval arcade lined by Renaissance palaces and crisscrossed by ornate bridges.

Above: Like Venice, Treviso is a city framed by water and spanned by many pretty bridges, but with fewer tourists competing for space

Alfredo Sturlese
owner of Treviso's legendary 1930s trattoria Toni del Spin

WHY I LOVE TREVISO

This is a small, human city – no need for a car as you can walk or cycle everywhere. But, like a big city, we also have great museums, green spaces and chic shopping. Just none of the stress.

Must-have local experience?
Stop off at a traditional osteria, mix with friendly locals at the bar, sip a glass of our sparkling Prosecco and try a traditional snack like polenta with creamy baccala (cod).

Favourite season?
Autumn through to the end of the year, when we have our famous radicchio festival (usually around November) and the three-week Christmas market, where the whole town comes out every evening.

Moselle Wine Route

COULD GERMAN MOSELLE'S LITTLE SISTER BE WEST EUROPE'S LAST WINE SECRET?

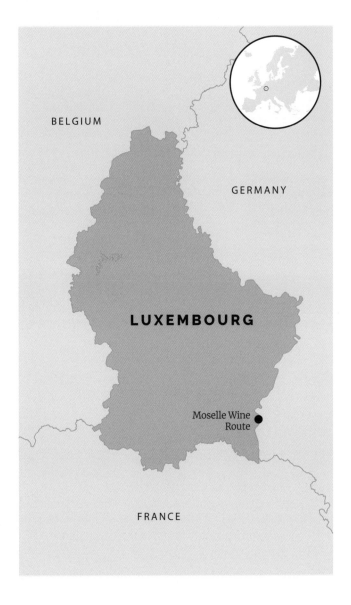

Wine and Luxembourg may not sound quite right together, but grapes have been cultivated on the Grand Duchy's side of the Moselle since Roman times. Today, along a scenic 40km (25 mile) stretch, some 55 independent *vignerons* are producing quality vintages. Vineyard owners have discovered wine tourism, and many are genuinely eco-minded, persevering with organic and biodynamic cultivation. Between wine tastings you can jump on an old-fashioned steamer chugging the river, visit the quirky wine museum of the Wäistuff Tavern in Possen or try lethal fruit schnapps in artisan distilleries along the Moselle. All without the tour buses you'll find on the German side.

Luxembourg is so small geographically that there are many easy detours too. The medieval town of Echternach is gateway to the Mullerthal Trail, where locals go rambling and rock climbing in what they call their 'Little Switzerland'. Even Luxembourg City is an eye-opener, an impregnable castle-fortress sitting atop a towering rocky outcrop.

GO IF YOU LIKE...

- 💜 *winery touring*
- 💜 *river cruises*
- 💜 *gourmet picnics*
- 💜 *nature hiking*
- 💜 *artisan liqueurs*
- 💜 *German Moselle wine*

Why go to the Moselle Wine Route?

While Germany's Moselle wines are renowned the world over, their sister wines in Luxembourg are little known, and offer remarkable quality and value for money. Here, the steep valley slopes rise up almost perpendicular from the river, covered in graphic terraces of vines. And Luxembourg's *vignerons* could not be more welcoming of visitors. Highlights include Domaine Kox in Remich, Caves Saint-Martin and its underground galleries of ageing bubbly, and family-run Maison Schmitt-Fohl. The region's wineries offer cellar door tastings and quaint winemaker villages provide cosy inns and B&B accommodation.

During the day, you can head for the river, hike or bike through vineyards and unspoilt forests, then dine in a snug rural *bistrot*. Discover speciality dishes like *knippelen* (dumplings with creamy wild mushrooms or smoked pork) – the perfect match for Luxembourg's aromatic Müller-Thurgau grape variety, elegant Pinot Noir or luscious Gewürztraminer. And forget Prosecco for a sunset aperitif — the delicious local bubbly here is Crémant.

GETTING THERE

Luxembourg City has an international airport and direct high-speed train links to Paris, Brussels, Amsterdam and Frankfurt. Within Luxembourg, all public transport is free. From Luxembourg City's central terminal it's 50 minutes by bus to Remich, Luxembourg's unofficial Moselle wine capital. Or you could rent a bike for the whole trip and cycle the 25km (15 miles) to Remich.

WHEN TO GO

Apr–Oct

The region is perfect for visiting any time from the first buds of spring to the lush summer when the vines hang heavy with bunches of grapes, until the golden colours of autumn take hold.

© SABINO PARENTE / ALAMY STOCK PHOTO. © HALIT OLMEZ / ALAMY STOCK PHOTO. © SABINO PARENTE / ALAMY STOCK PHOTO

FIRST-TIME TIPS

Plan a trip in October post-harvest to visit winemakers when they finally relax.

....

Never turn up for a tasting at a wine cellar without calling ahead. And greet locals with moien – *'hello' in the regional dialect.*

....

A solo hike through the vineyards can be unforgettable, but be sure to download a proper map as GPS is not always reliable here. The Pocketguides, available from local tourist offices or online at visitmoselle.lu/de/shop, include QR codes for digital GPX files.

....

As an alternative to the classic river cruise, try La Péniche Vintage *departing from Remich, a retro barge that provides tastings and the chance to buy vintage wares.*

AMAZING CROWD-FREE EXPERIENCES

 Follow the waterside Trois Rivières Path (PC3) bike track hugging the Moselle for some 40km (25 miles) from Schengen to Wasserbillig, stopping off at wine cellars, country *bistrots* and villages above the river.

 Indulge in a fabulous wellness stay at Mondorf-les-Bains, a quaint 19th-century spa that offers hot thermal baths, hammam and massages.

 Navigate the Moselle piloting your own electric boat from Remich – no licence necessary. The rental company also has stand-up paddleboards to really escape the crowds (wateradventures.lu).

 Hike the Wine & Nature Path Palmberg Ahn, a looping trail beginning at the winemaker's village of Ahn, then heading into the Palmberg nature reserve for wooded gorges, waterfalls and cliffs.

 Take a detour to Château de Clervaux in the Luxembourg Ardennes for a moment of reflection at its moving exhibition dedicated to the devastating Battle of the Bulge, the final campaign of WWII.

Clockwise from top left: Aerial view of the Moselle river; heavy grapes at October harvest; vineyard-cloaked hills around Remich

Delft

THE LOW-KEY ALTERNATIVE TO AMSTERDAM WITH MORE CANALS THAN CROWDS

Delft

NETHERLANDS

GERMANY

BELGIUM

thanks to the general absence of the raucous party crowds often found in Amsterdam. As a busy university town, Delft isn't a quiet backwater by any means, but it's undeniably more peaceful than the Netherlands' major tourism hubs.

To express that in numbers, Delft sees just 5% of the tourists of Amsterdam, while serving up a much more charming, unadulterated version of Dutch life. Canals line streets wrapped around a central, town-hall-dominated market square, and the nightlife scene is focused on coffee shops that prioritise coffee and hearty, homey *bruin cafes* (brown cafes, the traditional Dutch pub) without a pink cowboy hat in sight.

Sure, the historic Netherlands city of Delft attracts its share of day trippers, but most retreat to Rotterdam and Den Haag for the night, leaving the most atmospheric hours of the day – early morning and evening – to those who stay overnight. At the right time of day, the hometown of Johannes Vermeer and the birthplace of Delftware pottery can still feel a bit like stepping into a Golden Age painting,

GO IF YOU LIKE…

💜 *Amsterdam, Netherlands*
💜 *Bruges, Belgium*
💜 *canals*
💜 *pubs*
💜 *cafe culture*
💜 *architecture and history*

247

Why go to Delft?

Broadly, the drawcards of Delft are the drawcards of Amsterdam – canal-lined streets, iconic Dutch architecture, interesting museums, lively cafe culture and a rich history – but without the crowds. You can browse museum displays on Vermeer, Delftware and Dutch history without being swept away by a human tide, and you won't have to run a gauntlet of drunken soon-to-be-weds to get back to your hotel after a relaxing evening meal.

Historically, Delft has strong ties to the noble House of Orange-Nassau. This is where William of Orange became the first political leader to be assassinated with a handgun in 1584, and many of his successors lie interred in the handsome Nieuwe Kerk. But Delft was eclipsed by Amsterdam, Rotterdam and Den Haag, which explains its unspoilt atmosphere today.

GETTING THERE

The nearest international airport to Delft is in Rotterdam, but the airport is actually in between the two cities, less than 12km (7.5 miles) from Delft. Getting to Delft from larger Dutch cities like Rotterdam, as well as Amsterdam and Den Haag, is super easy thanks to efficient train services. Den Haag also runs frequent trams to Delft.

WHEN TO GO

Mar–May

Summer brings the best weather for outdoor drinking and dining, but Delft gets fewer day-tripping visitors in the spring, meaning more breathing space. Reduced rainfall and spring flowers make April to May a particularly appealing time to visit.

FIRST-TIME TIPS

Visit during the week; weekends are always busier, and there's also more visitors in school holidays.

. . . .

Make sure you're here on a Thursday, the big market day – Delft has the Dutch market holy trinity: an antique market; a flower market; and a food market.

. . . .

Leave your car behind. The city authorities charge a minimum of €29.50 per day for the few parking spaces located in the historic centre, and parking is not available by the hour.

. . . .

Consider the low carbon route to Delft – bike trails run from Den Haag (11km/7 miles northwest) and Rotterdam (28km/17 miles southeast), connecting with international ferries and trains.

AMAZING CROWD-FREE EXPERIENCES

 Go out early to wander along Delft's townhouse-lined canals before stopping in for morning coffee at a backstreet cafe.

 Drop into a historic Delft bakery to charge up on *oliebol* (Dutch donuts), *boterkoek* (butter cake) and tasty *broodje* (sandwiches).

 Climb the tower of the Nieuwe Kerk just before closing time for dizzying afternoon views over the city rooftops.

 Discover what inspired *Girl with the Pearl Earring* **painter** Johannes Vermeer, and other artists from the Delft school, by walking the streets, before visiting the Vermeer Centrum Delft, which covers the artist's life and works in detail.

 Rent a bike and cycle into the countryside southwest of Delft, through a landscape that has changed only superficially from the scenes depicted on Delftware pottery.

Above: Delft has the same canals, classic Dutch architecture and cafe culture as Amsterdam — but none of the rowdy party tourists

North Macedonia

EUROPE'S LAST FRONTIER IS THIS ANCIENT BEAUTY IN THE BALKANS

Against Croatia's 60 million annual visitors and even Albania's six million, North Macedonia looks like a Balkan no-man's land. Less than 800,000 international tourists made it here in 2019. Undoubtedly, its landlocked status lessens the mass-market appeal, though visitors will certainly feel like they're gazing out to sea from medieval Ohrid's lovely lakeside shingle beach. Between huge Lake Ohrid and Lake Prespa, North Macedonia has more waterside tourism than you might think. Yet there's so much more to this friendly country.

Great swaths of it are dramatically defined by canyons and mountains, including a string of little-developed national parks where quiet hiking trails spin a web between Ottoman-era villages with pencil-thin minarets, slow food producers and community tourism initiatives. And North Macedonia's complex past, with Greek, Roman, Ottoman and Yugoslav heritage, creates a rich historical backdrop. These deep roots can be explored in the museums of Skopje, one of Europe's most bonkers, unique capital cities.

GO IF YOU LIKE...

💜 *Montenegro & Croatia*
💜 *medieval churches*
💜 *Ottoman architecture*
💜 *European Muslim heritage*
💜 *quirky capitals*
💜 *slow food*

Why go to North Macedonia?

Picture a lunch of delicious fried freshwater fish with your toes in the water, and boat trips around shores flanked by frescoed Byzantine churches. Here on Lake Ohrid, the ancient town of the same name is a waterside beauty and its clifftop Church of Sveti Jovan the country's most photographed monument. This is the North Macedonia that savvy tourists know but, even here, outside of July and August it feels untrammelled.

The further you retreat from Ohrid, the less developed the tourist infrastructure becomes. Tiny family-run guesthouses dot the hillside villages of the Bab and Shar mountains close to the borders of Albania, Kosovo and Greece – all at bargain prices for Europe. Many are championing local producers, eager to ply visitors with traditional recipes, homemade fruit *rakija* and breads slathered in local cheese and honey. In the centre of the country, little-known grapes flourish on 19th-century vines in the small Tikveš Wine Region. And then there's North Macedonia's eastern lands to get lost in, where tourism fizzles into the unknown.

GETTING THERE

A handful of budget airlines fly directly into Ohrid from European cities, but the main international airport (especially for long haul) is in the capital, Skopje. Border crossings from North Macedonia's Balkan neighbours are relatively hassle-free, but historic tensions with Greece make the southern route more tricky – check ahead before attempting to cross from Greece.

WHEN TO GO

May–Sep

Late spring and summer bring the best weather; lowland temperatures can reach highs of around 40°c (104°F) in July/August. The country's mountain areas climb to more than 2500m (8202ft), meaning there's likely to be a night-time chill in the air year-round.

AMAZING CROWD-FREE EXPERIENCES

 Explore the quirky capital of Skopje, where an Ottoman-era Old Town rubs shoulders with huge warrior statues, fountains and giant new Neoclassical museums.

 Stroll the beach boardwalk around Ohrid to the 13th-century clifftop Church of Sveti Jovan at Kaneo, pausing for a lakefront fish fry before hopping on a boat back.

 Stay the night at lofty Sveti Jovan Bigorski Monastery in Mavrovo National Park. Founded in 1020, this Byzantine complex is still very much a working institution.

 Hike or kayak the glorious folds of Matka Canyon, 40-minute drive from Skopje. Overnight at Canyon Matka Hotel and you'll get it all to yourself at first light.

 Taste local produce in Dihovo village, a pretty hive of community tourism at the base of Pelister National Park, with mountain trails leading from the front door.

 Pay your respects at Tetovo's painted mosque — an exquisitely decorated reminder of Europe's Muslim past, in a town that tourists rarely visit.

Above: The red-roofed town of Ohrid, with Roman ruins and Byzantine churches, is North Macedonia's tourism pin-up

Senja

CLOSER TO THE ARCTIC AND JUST AS SPECTACULAR AS THE LOFOTEN ISLANDS

Senja is where God threw away the rule book and went a bit wild. Granite mountains whoosh above white-sand beaches and a sea fading from turquoise to sapphire blue. Rocks resemble great sea creatures leaping from the deep. The forests are thick and ancient – primordial almost. Spectacular? Beyond belief. So why haven't you heard of this slice of Norway? Probably because the Lofoten Islands, immediately south, have stolen Senja's thunder.

This is one Arctic fantasy island you'll want to whisper quietly about; a place of raw, brutal beauty that's not quite of this world, where glacier-eroded peaks thrust with all their might above scoops of creamy sand and the Atlantic is often in a rage. Come to hike along cliffs that nosedive to the sea, kayak beneath a rave of Northern Lights, or hunker down in a clapboard cottage in a fishing village as the whales come out to play and the winter snows drift in, painting the landscape pearl-white.

GO IF YOU LIKE...

- ♥ *the Lofoten Islands*
- ♥ *Arctic wilderness*
- ♥ *Northern Lights & Midnight Sun*
- ♥ *just-caught seafood*
- ♥ *dramatic rockscapes*
- ♥ *charismatic fishing villages*

Why go to Senja?

Nature runs riot on Norway's second largest island, where silence still reigns and life moves to long-forgotten rhythms in tune with the pristine Arctic environment. It's because of this that the island is set to become a Nordic-certified 'sustainable destination', where you'll soon be able to travel with a clean, green conscious.

Far north of the Arctic Circle, Senja is at the mercy of the elements – whether seen in the never-dying light of the Midnight Sun or in winter snow. The sharply defined seasons dictate how days are spent. Choose summer to hike along the astonishingly rugged coastline, rip across the sea on a RIB to sight puffins, porpoises and white-tailed eagles, fish for giant cod and strike out into the gnarled, 600-year-old pine forests of Ånderdalen National Park. Winter has a different and, some say, more magical vibe. Paddle around islets as the aurora flashes above, go ski touring or dogsledding and watch orcas and humpbacks breach and lobtail as they flock here for the seasonal cod-spawning feast.

GETTING THERE

The nearest international airport is in Tromsø, served by Norwegian Airlines and with direct flights to a number of European cities. Or you can travel by train to Narvik and onwards to Senja by bus (there's a road link to the mainland from Finnsnes). Ferries link Finnsnes to Tromsø and Harstad.

WHEN TO GO

Jun–Sep & Dec–Apr

Go in summer for long summer nights, camping, kayaking and hiking. Winters bring snow, subzero temperatures, regular shows of Northern Lights and great conditions for skiing and dogsledding.

AMAZING CROWD-FREE EXPERIENCES

 Discover Ånderdalen National Park – Norway in microcosm. Its virgin forests and granite heights are a haven for elk, reindeer and birds like the black-throated loon.

 Go on an expedition. Basecamp Senja (basecampsenja.no) throws you into the wilds with multiday whale and Northern Lights safaris, and dogsledding fjord trips.

 See the island from on high by hiking to the knife-edge peak of Segla, a 640m (2100ft) fist of rock punching above the deep-blue Mefjord.

 Hit the beach at Ersfjord, a sensationally lovely arc with a backdrop of shaggy green mountains; or Bøvær, overlooking the 98 islets speckling Bergsfjorden.

 Be blown away by the view at Okshornan, wholly deserving of its 'Devil's Jaw' name, with mountains like broken teeth thrusting up above Ersfjord and the crashing ocean.

 Road trip or cycle the Norwegian Scenic Route Senja – a coast-hugging, 102km (63 mile)-long ride between Gryllefjord and Botnhamn. The views are out of this world.

Above: Arctic sunset brings an otherworldly palette to the snow-flanked fjords of Senja

Left: Dog-sledding is just one of the snowy pursuits visitors can try in Poland's mountains

Tatra Mountains

QUIET PISTES AND HIGHLANDER CULTURE IN POLAND'S BARGAIN WINTER PEAKS

likely to spot a marmot or chamois. The population of the latter – a short-horned goat-antelope – has increased substantially since 2000, thanks to the efforts of a local rescue project.

Tatra National Park gets very few overseas visitors, and Poles tend to prefer it in summer months. Walk, snowshoe or cross-country ski the 274km (170 miles) of trails in winter and you'll barely encounter anyone. In the mountains' foothills is the main resort town Zakopane, which can get busy in ski season – but it's worth visiting for the cheerful bars and restaurants, all an absolute bargain. Book your bed out of town and you'll have a cosy bolthole to return to after the day's adventures.

Poland's winter playground is virtually unheard of outside the country, but offers a good-value alternative to Europe's Alpine resorts. Situated in the far south, the mountains are shared with neighbouring Slovakia – each has designated their side a national park, and together they constitute a Unesco-protected Biosphere Reserve. Hidden among the rocky peaks are brown bears, lynxes and wolves, although you're more

GO IF YOU LIKE...

💜 *skiing & snowboarding*
💜 *alpine resorts*
💜 *folk culture*
💜 *winter walking*
💜 *epic mountain views*
💜 *hearty cuisine*

Why go to the Tatra Mountains?

Winter holidays in Alpine Europe are expensive, but Poland remains enduringly good value. Day passes cost a fraction of what they would in France or Switzerland, and après-ski and accommodation are also keenly priced. New hotels are popping up in Zakopane, but the best options are the more authentic chalets at places like Tatra Wood House and Villa Dorota, both in comparatively secluded locations out of town, or Hotel Bukovina, surrounded by forest.

This area is home to Poland's Górale people, also known as 'Highlanders', an ethnic group with a unique culture still very much alive today. Willa Koliba is a fine example of their distinctive architecture and houses the Museum of Zakopane Style, recently refurbished and a great place to see their extraordinary folk art. Local operator BazaTatry (bazatatry.com) offers tours to learn more about the Highlander life, plus winter activities including ski lessons, sleigh rides and snowshoeing.

GETTING THERE

Zakopane – the gateway to the area – is a two-hour drive from Kraków Balice, the nearest international airport. It's also entirely possible to reach Kraków by train from many European capitals (London to Kraków, for example, takes 22 hours), then transfer onto one of the regular local buses or trains to Zakopane.

WHEN TO GO

Dec–Mar

There is generally snow in the Tatras all winter, but visit in February to experience the Highlander Carnival, or March to avoid the peak of the ski season – Polish school holidays usually fall during the months of January and February.

FIRST-TIME TIPS

Even if you don't plan on hiking, winter visitors will benefit from mini-crampons, breathable thermal layers and waterproof boots, jacket and trousers.

....

It's relatively straightforward to explore this region car-free as there are a multitude of city buses, private mini buses and taxis servicing the area.

....

For knockout views over Poland and Slovakia, take the cable car from Kuźnice to the summit of Kasprowy Wierch (1987m/6519ft). Get up early for the 20-minute ascent – after 9am there can be long queues. You can buy advance tickets online to avoid the wait, but they sell out early (pkl.pl).

AMAZING CROWD-FREE EXPERIENCES

 Hitch a ride with some huskies. Fun Dog (fundog.pl) offer solo sled excursions and cuddle time with their friendly pack of Siberian Huskies and Alaskan Malamutes.

 Hike in Tatra National Park. The hour-long walk through the forested valley of Dolina Strążyska is a gentle introduction.

 Book a Highlander banquet. Several local restaurants offer traditional dishes — like smoked cheese or potato pancakes — served by staff wearing the beautifully embroidered clothing of the Górale.

 Attend Bukowina Tatrzańska's little-known Highlander Carnival. Every February, the village celebrates its unique culture with singing, dancing and sleigh-racing.

 Get an uninterrupted panorama over the mountains. One of the best Tatra views is at Polana Głodówka, an open glade that's also ideal for making snow angels.

 Pay an early visit to Jaszczurówka Chapel. Inspired by the dwellings of the Górale, this wooden church looks magical freshly dusted with morning snow.

Clockwise from top left: Tatras meadows in winter; a finely embroidered Górale jacket; the Jaszczurówka Chapel

Left: Ribeira D'Ilhas
has one of the most
challenging surf breaks
in the country

Ericeira

THE SURFER SECRET THAT STANDS POLES APART FROM PORTUGAL'S BUSY ALGARVE

PORTUGAL

SPAIN

● Ericeira

MOROCCO

Unmatched Atlantic swells beat upon a multitude of bronzed beaches. Neat rows of white-and-blue heritage houses line rocky clifftops. And fresh shellfish is caught daily from the coastline's nurseries. Understated Ericeira boasts an extensive appeal of world-class surf, sand and seafood. It might just be the perfect laid-back alternative to the Algarve which, in 2019, was the only region in Portugal to hit the 20 million-mark for overnight stays three years in a row.

Easily accessible by road from Lisbon, Ericeira is home to the only World Surfing Reserve in Europe, and a multitude of exceptional surf schools and retreats. An international reputation as a surfing destination has put this location on the map, but ample stretches of sand and efforts to remain sustainable mean it's still largely intact as a peaceful Portuguese fishing village. And there's more than just surf here. Visitors can explore local vineyards in the Lizandro Valley and the Baroque-style Mafra Palace, and while away evenings in boho bars gazing out over the glorious sunset-lit Atlantic.

GO IF YOU LIKE...

- 💜 *surfing*
- 💜 *seafood*
- 💜 *sand between your toes*
- 💜 *laid-back vibes*
- 💜 *Mundaka, Spain*
- 💜 *Baja California, USA*

Why go to Ericeira?

With a dozen surfing beaches all within an 8km (5 mile) stretch, you won't have to battle for space in the water around Ericeira. Each beach has individual characteristics – from vast, paddle-friendly beginners' Foz do Lizandro to the epic fast-barrelling Coxos waves. The shoreline is also renowned for its consistency: when other Portuguese surf spots go flat, Ericeira stays remarkably steady, with unwavering temperatures to match. But, above all, the area's appeal lies in efforts to retain its old-world charm, support local businesses and keep natural resources intact.

With a name deriving from the Portuguese for sea urchin, Ericeira – once a small harbour – is now a major fishing hub, but it's gone to great lengths to support the local fishing communities and promote local markets. In the village's old town, visitors will find a lack of commercial shops and fast food. And in 2021 the Ericeira World Surfing Reserve began drafting a Sustainability Plan to help turn the area into a key sustainable tourist destination in Portugal.

GETTING THERE

Ericeira is located approximately 50km (31 miles) northwest of Lisbon. Fly into Lisbon Portela Airport and either rent a car or book a taxi for a picturesque 40-minute drive. Buses are also available but take a little longer. Ericeira itself is small enough to get around on foot or by bicycle.

WHEN TO GO

Year-round

Ericeira is a year-round destination, with many sunny days even in winter. For beginner surfers, the best waves are May to early September. From September to November, the swells become increasingly powerful — best suited to those with more experience.

AMAZING CROWD-FREE EXPERIENCES

 Sample fresher-than-fresh shellfish at seafront Mar à Vista. This seemingly humble restaurant specialises in dishes such as spider crab, goose barnacles and *arroz de marisco* (mixed seafood rice).

 Salute the sun at a holistic hilltop yoga and surf retreat. Rustic Casa Paço D'Ilhas (casapacodilhas.com) has pools, outdoor yoga decks and activities.

 Tackle the barrelling breaks at Ribeira D'Ilhas, one of the most challenging surf breaks in Portugal. Not for the faint-hearted.

 Explore the decadent halls and library of Mafra Palace, a fine example of Portuguese Baroque and Neoclassical architecture, 10 minutes from Ericeira.

 Cycle the vineyards of the Lizandro Valley, exploring off-road tracks on a boutique winery tour, followed by tasting local varieties.

 Skate with a backdrop of the sea at Praia do Matadouro. Ericeira Boardriders skate park is a fine spot at sunset – rent skateboards from the adjoining Quiksilver shop.

Above: Ericeira has a dozen surf beaches and is home to Europe's only World Surfing Reserve

Braga

PORTUGAL'S OTHER CITY BREAK, FOR HISTORY AND CROWD-FREE HIGH JINKS

City-breaking in Portugal has become quite the done thing: pre-pandemic, Lisbon and Porto were attracting even more tourists per capita than famously overrun Barcelona. But the masses haven't made it to Braga. Not yet. Portugal's third-largest city, in the vineyard-swathed northern Minho region, is the country's oldest, founded by the Romans as Bracara Augusta in 20 BCE. As the main hub of Christianity in Iberia during the reconquest and the seat of Portugal's archbishops, it's also the country's religious capital – every corner reveals another fine old church, tiled chapel, station of the cross or shop selling spiritual knick-knacks.

Yet there's energy and innovation here too. Braga has a large, flourishing university and a young population (one of the youngest in Europe). Investors are reviving dishevelled buildings in the historic centre. And in 2021, the city was named top place to visit by independent tourism association European Best Destinations. Old at heart, young in spirit, Braga is abuzz.

GO IF YOU LIKE…

- ♥ *Lisbon, Portugal*
- ♥ *Porto, Portugal*
- ♥ *Salamanca, Spain*
- ♥ *churches*
- ♥ *Baroque architecture*
- ♥ *student nightlife*

Why go to Braga?

Not too big, not too small, Braga is just right for a couple of days' easy exploration. It also feels like a lived-in city, not a sell-out to tourism. Perhaps that's why its residents rank as Portugal's happiest. The centre comprises traffic-free streets, wide avenues and 35 churches – including the Sé, Portugal's oldest cathedral. While there are a few Roman relics (including excavated baths), the dominant architectural style is flamboyant Baroque, on display everywhere from the Arco da Porta Nova gate to the azulejo-tiled Palácio do Raio and, just outside the city, the Unesco-listed basilica of Bom Jesus do Monte.

The profusion of students – who you might spot wandering around in their black capes and tricorn hats – ensures there are plenty of cool bars, too. The area behind the Sé offers especially rich pickings; pause at any of them for a cheap glass of refreshing *vinho verde* (locally made wine).

GETTING THERE

Around 50km (31 miles) from the Spanish border, Braga is the same distance north of Porto. Direct buses connect Braga to Porto Francisco Sá Carneiro International (50min), the closest airport. The two city centres are also linked by direct trains (from 1hr) and buses (1hr). Trains from Lisbon to Braga take from around 3hr 30min.

WHEN TO GO

Apr–May & Sep–Oct

Spring and autumn offer pleasant weather and quieter streets; also, students will be around, adding youthful energy. Holy Week (pre-Easter) is the city's biggest event.

FIRST-TIME TIPS

Plan your church-hopping – most, including the Sé, close for an hour or longer in the middle of the day; also note times of services so you don't disturb worshippers.

....

Seek out excellent-value *lunchtime menus* – these can include two or three courses and a drink for as little as €10.

....

Try some local specialities, such as frigideiras *(meat-filled pastries),* bacalhau à Braga *(salt cod, peppers, onions and sliced potatoes)* and pudim Abade de Priscos *(a crème caramel dessert).*

....

Combine Braga with Guimarães – this gorgeous medieval city, considered the birthplace of Portugal, is a 25-minute bus ride away.

AMAZING CROWD-FREE EXPERIENCES

 Browse the merchant's residence of Casa Rolão. This handsome, 18th-century house now includes a bookshop, vintage boutiques and a quiet garden cafe.

 See inside the Sé, Portugal's oldest cathedral. It has an exquisite choir and a naturally mummified archbishop, as well as a museum full of ecclesiastical treasures.

 Shop at the Mercado Municipal – this market *is* crowded, but with locals buying fresh produce. Renovated in 2020, it's now topped with a timber-and-glass roof.

 Admire Braga's award-winning Estádio A Pedreira. Tickets to see Sporting Braga play are cheap (from €10) but to see the stadium crowd-free, join a guided tour (€6).

 Explore the landscaped park of Bom Jesus – a 20-minute bus ride from Braga, this basilica is popular but sits within a lovely green space where you can escape people.

 Make an alternative pilgrimage along the little-known Caminho da Geira e dos Arrieiros — a 239km (148 mile) trail from Braga to Santiago de Compostela.

Above: Braga's handsome city centre is a lively hub with churches and flamboyant Baroque architecture

Kamchatka

RUSSIA'S FAR EASTERN LAND OF FIRE AND ICE IS BONE-TINGLING DRAMA

A place of primal volcanic beauty, Kamchatka is one of the world's last bastions of pristine nature. There are no railways or roads connecting it to the rest of the country, and it is closer to Alaska than to the nearest Russian Far East city of Vladivostok. The 1250km (777 mile)-long peninsula's remoteness, coupled with the bureaucratic difficulties and the not inconsiderable costs of travelling to this Russian border zone, means that Kamchatka's status as an offbeat destination is golden.

Comparable to Iceland in terms of fire-and-ice drama, Kamchatka welcomed some 240,000 tourists in 2019 compared with Iceland's two million. At 270,000 sq km (104,247 sq miles), Kamchatcha is more than double the size of its Nordic counterpart, yet has a smaller population. Those that do live here – a mix of hardy Russian settlers and native Koryaks, Chukchi and Itelmeni people – are a friendly and adventurous community who think nothing of trekking up an active volcano, through forests where 30,000 brown bears live, and surfing in the bone-chilling waters of the Bering Sea.

GO IF YOU LIKE...

- 💜 *Iceland*
- 💜 *Alaska*
- 💜 *volcanoes*
- 💜 *wildlife*
- 💜 *fishing*
- 💜 *hot springs*

Why go to Kamchatka?

Unesco World Heritage-listed for its outstanding volcanic landscape, Kamchatka also offers one bear to every 30 human inhabitants, hundreds of thermal springs, 100,000 lakes and rivers, abundant reindeer and moose, and rare birdlife. Eco-tourism is a big draw here. Over the last decade, Kamchatka has also become an unlikely hot spot for extreme surfing. From the black sands of Khalaktyrsky beach, the pioneering surfers at Snowave Kamchatka (snowave-kamchatka.com) have been leading the way — and you can join them for surf lessons (winter gear rental included).

Interactive exhibits at the Vulcanariam Museum in Petropavlovsk-Kamchatsky provide fascinating background details on the local volcanoes and their awesome thermal powers. And set to be completed in the next few years is the Three Volcanoes resort (3vpark.ru), a massively ambitious project that will include new hotels, restaurants, a spa, ski slopes and hiking trails.

Right: There's one bear to every 30 human inhabitants in Kamchatka

Below: The Valley of the Geysers in the protected Kronotsky Biosphere State Reserve

Daria Gremitskikh
guide,
Kamchatintour

WHY I LOVE KAMCHATKA

I love it for its incredible natural beauty, different seasons and kind people.

Must-have local experience?
Climbing an active volcano, such as Avachinsky. It's a good chance to test your endurance and enjoy nice landscapes.

Favourite season?
Summer (early June to end of August), because it's not very hot. It's possible to climb volcanoes and mountain ranges, and go fishing and rafting during this season. It's also a good time for boat trips in the Pacific Ocean — we have a good chance of seeing huge whales and big families of orcas in summer.

FIRST-TIME TIPS

Check you have the correct permits — Kamchatka is a border region and highly militarised zone. Arranging your visit via a local tour company will ensure your necessary paperwork is in order.

Basing yourself at Yelizovo has the advantage of being right next to both the airport and the helipad, saving hours of transit time if you plan to make multiple forays into Kamchatka's wilderness.

Take warning flares with you on any forest hikes, particularly between June and September, as you might encounter bears.

Be prepared for your plans to change – Kamchatka's weather is volatile, which can affect flight schedules to star attractions such as the Valley of the Geysers.

GETTING THERE

The only way to arrive in Kamchatka is by air or to sail in on a cruise, such as those offered by Hapag Lloyd or National Geographic. Daily direct flights depart from Moscow (9hr), Khabarovsk (2hr, 45min) and Vladivostok (3hr 20min) — all go to Yelizovo Airport, Kamchatka's main air hub.

WHEN TO GO

May–Sep

July and August offer largely warm, clear days of extended sunlight; it's the prime season for hiking and fishing. May to early June is peak bird-watching season and the best time to kayak the shoreline. September offers spectacular autumn colours.

AMAZING CROWD-FREE EXPERIENCES

 Fly in a helicopter to Valley of the Geysers, one of Kamchatka's natural star attractions. It's part of the protected Kronotsky Biosphere State Reserve.

 Climb to the active 4km (2.5 mile)-wide cone of Mt Mutnovskaya, pockmarked with boiling mud pools and ice crevices cut by the hot vapours of volcanic fumes.

 Trek to hidden hot springs in Nalychevo Nature Park covering the lovely Nalychevo Valley and the dozen volcanoes (four active) that surround it.

 Cruise out into Avacha Bay for a view of Petropavlovsk's stunningly beautiful waterside setting, with volcanic Mt Vilyuchinsky in the distance, and to reach Starichkov Island, a haven for birdlife.

 Go for a dip at leafy Paratunka, a quiet place where locals come to relax in hot-spring-fed swimming pools.

 Track down reindeer herds near Esso managed by nomadic Evens, reachable by helicopter in the warm months and by snowmobile during winter.

Left: Hiking through the dramatic Garganta del Cares, a trail chiselled out of limestone rock

Asturias

SPAIN'S GOURMET BACKCOUNTRY OF WHITE-SAND BEACHES AND QUIET TRAILS

'Asturiano: loco, vano y mal Cristiano!' goes the centuries-old saying, proclaiming the inhabitants of one of Spain's least-visited regions to be crazy, vain, and poor Christians. Asturias and its denizens have long been unfairly maligned and overlooked in favour of more famous neighbours, but travellers who skip this part of coastal northwest Spain are truly missing out. Squeezed between the fishing villages of Galicia, the fertile pastures of Cantabria and the medieval towns of Castilla y León, Asturias is both beautiful and wild. Inland, it bristles with mountain ranges, while the coastline is as dramatic as they come. Here, wave-battered cliffs lead to pristine, white-sand beaches and colourful fishing villages.

Across rustic, timeless villages and historic cities with centuries-old architecture, locals are fiercely proud of the fact that Covadonga in Asturias was the only part of Spain to hold out against the Moors. And the region's simple, solid cuisine – hearty stews, cider, super-fresh seafood and pungent cheeses – are finally being recognised as a gourmet's delight.

GO IF YOU LIKE...

- ♥ *the Pyrenees*
- ♥ *architecture & history*
- ♥ *dramatic coastlines*
- ♥ *Galicia*
- ♥ *seafood*
- ♥ *pubs*

Why go to Asturias?

Broadly speaking, Asturias is in many ways Spain in microcosm: its attractions are the country's attractions, only minus the crowds that descend on the likes of Barcelona, Madrid and the Costa del Sol. Though the villages in the pine-fringed valleys of the interior may be all cobblestoned timelessness, with granaries on stilts and red-roofed stone houses, the two main cities are anything but provincial. Conservative Oviedo features some of the finest pre-Romanesque buildings in the country, while the brash port of Gijón hosts avant-garde festivals.

Asturians are serious foodies, too: they manage to coax myriad flavours out of local ingredients, without a hint of an English tourist menu in sight. Signature dishes – like sea urchins with ham – are the edible embodiment of this region's peaks and coastline. And Asturias wears its changeable weather well, like Scotland or San Francisco. Even drizzle can't dampen the spirits of hikers who take to the trails in the Picos de Europa mountain range.

GETTING THERE

Asturias' main cities of Gijón and Oviedo are connected to nearby international gateways of Bilbao, Santiago de Compostela, Santander and San Sebastián by frequent and reliable train services. Another great way to arrive is by bicycle, either along Spain's north coast or by taking the cycle lanes along the classic Camino de Santiago and then crossing the Picos de Europa near León.

WHEN TO GO

May–Jun & Sep

No crowds, less rain and more sunny, warm days, in spite of the cool and often damp weather influenced by the proximity of the Atlantic Ocean. These months are also the best time for hiking in the Picos de Europa.

FIRST-TIME TIPS

Try to avoid travelling in November, the rainiest month and one of the coldest, and also in August, when the hiking trails in the Picos de Europa teem with trekkers and accommodation is priciest.

If trekking during July and August, plan your routes well ahead of time and book accommodation weeks in advance. This applies particularly to mountain refuges in the Picos de Europa, and to lodgings in the main access towns: Cangas de Onís, Arenas de Cabrales, Potes and Posada de Valdeón.

Food and drink fans should hit festivals like the Villaviciosa apple/cider festival in October, the Langreo fiesta dedicated to fabada (a rich bean stew), or the August festival of cabrales cheese in Arenas de Cabrales.

AMAZING CROWD-FREE EXPERIENCES

 Hike the Ruta del Cares, a trail carved into rock above the dramatic limestone canyon of Garganta del Cares, connecting Poncebos in Asturias with Caín in Castilla y León.

 Stroll along Playa de la Franca, Playa de Borizo, Playa de Torimbia and other deserted crescents of sand that dot the Asturian coastline, or hit the seven surfing beaches surrounding Gijón.

 Knock back a fizzing *culín* of cider inside the village taverna in Espinaredo, one of Asturias' traditional villages that time forgot.

 Marvel over Unesco-listed rock art at the Cueva de Tito Bustillo, near the fishing town of Ribadesella. Dating back to 15,000-10,000 BCE, the well-preserved paintings include some fine images of horses.

 Sample cabrales – a strong blue cheese made from blending cow's milk with goat's and sheep's milk, and matured in caves in the foothills of the Picos de Europa. Don't miss a trip to the cave museum depicting the cheese-making process in Arenas de Cabrales.

Clockwise from top left: Oviedo's delightful old town; Asturian cider; deserted Playa del Silencio; salty-fresh seafood

277

Cáceres

A BEWITCHING BEACON OF SPANISH CULTURE IN THE WILDS OF EXTREMADURA

Crammed with architectural riches spinning back to Roman times, Cáceres' Unesco-listed Ciudad Monumental is one of Spain's most bewitching historic centres. Yet, hidden away in land-locked Extremadura — one of the country's least-visited corners — and partly due to the lack of a local airport, Cáceres and its surrounding region remain overlooked by most of Spain's international visitors. Extremadura receives just under two million tourists a year, compared with 30 million in neighbouring Andalucía — and less than 300,000 make it to Cáceres.

Surrounded by 16th-century walls, this seductive cobbled city unravels in a swirl of ancient spire-topped churches, somnolent labyrinthine alleys and luxurious mansions, some now historical hotels. In recent years, Cáceres has grown into an under-the-radar gastronomic destination, home to fabulous cheeses, a thriving tapas scene and some of Spain's finest *jamón ibérico*. Now with an arty edge, too, it doubles as an urban base for exploring the rest of endlessly beautiful Extremadura — and savvy Spaniards are starting to visit.

GO IF YOU LIKE...

- 💜 *Madrid's art galleries*
- 💜 *awe-inspiring spaces*
- 💜 *Andalucía's food scene*
- 💜 *historical hotels*
- 💜 *Málaga, Barcelona & Valencia*
- 💜 *Spanish gastronomy*

Why go to Cáceres?

The 2021 arrival of the major Museo Helga de Alvear art gallery is the latest in a string of exciting reasons to explore beautiful Cáceres. The city was named Spain's Gastronomic Capital in 2015 and has since quietly put itself on the map for travellers keen to experience a slice of culture-rich inland Spain, with a food-loving twist and a distinctive artistic flair. Throw in a raft of tempting, original hotels (a handful of creative recent openings now mingle with the luxurious Parador de Cáceres) and one of Spain's most sought-after fine-dining restaurants, pioneering Atrio (also a luxe design hotel), and Cáceres's many charms easily rival those of Spain's better-known cities.

Once here, you'll inevitably be tempted by the region's immense natural beauty and Extremadura continues to push forward with renewable energy and responsible tourism projects. The bird-filled Parque Nacional de Monfragüe, the rolling valleys of the northeast and the remote Las Hurdes hills are just a few wild *extremeño* highlights on Cáceres' doorstep.

GETTING THERE

With no airport of its own, reaching Extremadura in the first place is part of the adventure. The nearest airports are in Seville and Madrid, which both have good train connections to Cáceres in around 4hr; book through Renfe (renfe.com). To explore beyond the city, it's best to hire your own wheels, as public transport is limited.

WHEN TO GO

Sep–Oct

The weather is warm but not overwhelmingly hot in early autumn (typically around 15°C to 25°C/60°F to 77°F) and there are fewer visitors; Extremadura's surrounding landscapes begin to burst into autumn colours during these months.

FIRST-TIME TIPS

The best bird-watching season in the Parque Nacional de Monfragüe is March to October, when migrating species return from Africa. Day trips from Cáceres can be arranged through Birding Extremadura (www.birdingextremadura.com).

....

If you're keen to dine at two-Michelin-star Atrio, book at least a month ahead – more for weekends and bank holidays. There are sometimes last-minute cancellations so it's worth calling to try your luck, and for the busiest times of year there's usually a waiting list you can join.

....

Don't miss the Museo de Cáceres, which occupies part of the city's ancient Moorish castle and hosts a terrific fine arts gallery with pieces by Joan Miró, Pablo Picasso and other Spanish greats.

AMAZING CROWD-FREE EXPERIENCES

 Wander Cáceres' sparkling Ciudad Monumental, perhaps on a theatrical after-dark guided tour with Cuentatrovas de Cordel (cuentatrovas.com).

 Dive into the *extremeño* food scene, with the old town's lively tapas bars serving some of Spain's best *jamón*, gooey Torta del Casar cheese, La Vera paprika and other delights.

 Explore the 2021-launched Museo Helga de Alvear; this important contemporary art collection includes Pablo Picasso, Doris Salcedo, Tacita Dean and more.

 Hike in the Parque Nacional de Monfragüe, an hour's drive northeast of Cáceres, where Spanish imperial eagles, black vultures and other birds soar above Río Tajo.

 Day-trip to Extremadura's capital Mérida for some of the country's most important Roman remains, and Trujillo, made rich by Spain's conquistadores.

 Head off the beaten track into the beautiful, remote valleys of northeastern Extremadura: La Vera, Jerte and Ambroz — all within 90 minutes' drive of Cáceres.

Toño Pérez, *chef & owner, Atrio hotel & restaurant*

WHY I LOVE CÁCERES

We have one of the most incredible pantries in Spain, best represented by the dehesa (local meadows where Iberian pigs graze) – a prime example of sustainability.

Must-have local experience?
Cáceres has a rich collection of cultural attractions, including the Museo Helga de Alvear. The natural environment of Extremadura is another key draw — particularly Sierra de Gata, Las Hurdes and the Jerte, Ambroz and La Vera valleys.

Favourite season?
Any time of year. We have wonderfully bright summers, ochre-tinged autumns, distinct winters and springs that burst into natural beauty.

Above: Around Cáceres lie rural boltholes like Parque Nacional de Monfragüe

281

Swiss National Park

SWITZERLAND'S ONLY NATIONAL PARK IS AS PRISTINE AS YOU'D EXPECT

In the mad dash to popular Alpine peaks, the Swiss National Park barely gets a look in. Secreted away in the country's southeast, where snow-frosted mountains ripple across to Italy, the park's under-the-radar location is its saving grace. Here the landscapes have been shaped by giant forces; human intervention is kept to a leave-no-trace, conservation-driven minimum and nature is left utterly to its own devices. The result is a glimpse of the Alps before the dawn of tourism.

You can give civilisation the slip on trails where yours are the only footsteps. You can find silence, seclusion and summit after ravishing summit. When an environmentally on-the-ball country like Switzerland has just one national park, you can bet it's a knockout.

And, indeed, this 172 sq km (66 sq mile) park is a spectacle of razor-edge mountains punching high above 3000m (9840ft), quiet moors, forests, wildflower-spattered meadows, waterfalls and startling blue lakes. The park is so untouched, ancient and unaltered that dinosaur tracks are still regularly found in its heights.

GO IF YOU LIKE...

- *the French Alps*
- *Canada*
- *wildlife-spotting*
- *peaceful hiking trails*
- *pristine Alpine landscapes*
- *back-to-nature seclusion*

Why go to the Swiss National Park?

Sustainability wise, the Swiss National Park gets a gold star. Established in 1914, this was the first national park in the Alps and its original conservation ethos lives on today. Since its early beginnings, no trees have been felled, no meadows cut and no animals hunted. As such, the park is a safe haven for classic Alpine wildlife: marmots, chamois, deer and, at higher elevations, ibex can be spotted with luck, patience and binoculars. And there are also plenty of feathered friends: golden eagles, bearded vultures and Alpine choughs wheel in these big skies.

The only way to get a grip on this isolated, wildly mountainous national park is to hit the hiking trails dipping into its heart. It will be the little things that touch you: edelweiss quivering in the breeze; the first sun creeping over the summits; the piercing whistle of a golden eagle as you crest a rise. Some call the park a 'Canada in miniature', but why imagine yourself anywhere else?

Right: Chamois is just one classic Alpine species that can be spotted in the park

Below: The high plateaus of the Swiss National Park feed into dozens of dazzling sapphire lakes

Hans Lozza
Swiss National Park communications director

WHY I LOVE THE SWISS NATIONAL PARK

I love the forests, where dead trees are simply left, providing a habitat for many animals. And it's special that hiking trails are the only infrastructure here.

Must-have local experience?
A trip to Val Trupchun for its rich wildlife. There are many marmots and, with luck, the bearded vulture can be seen. In summer, around 450 red deer and 100 ibex roam.

Favourite season?
June, when the mountain pastures are in bloom and the young chamois, ibex and deer can be easily observed. Early October is also beautiful, when the larches change colour.

FIRST-TIME TIPS

Rise early for terrific wildlife spotting ops and to experience the trails at their peaceful dawn best.

....

Stay overnight in the park. Wild camping is off-limits, so bed down at the rustic Chamanna Cluozza, which fulfils every off-grid log hut fantasy with uplifting views and hearty food. Bring your own sleeping bag.

....

Join a guided ranger tour to maximise chances of glimpsing the park's rarest, shyest inhabitants. Expert guides lead insightful half- and full-day walks mid-June to mid-October.

....

Stop by the visitor centre in Zernez for info on the park's wildlife, geology, topographic maps and guides.

GETTING THERE

Zürich is the closest airport to the Swiss National Park. Or take a train to one of the major Swiss cities, then connect to the excellent SBB public transport network. Regular buses and trains serve the Engadine villages on the park's fringes, including Zernez, Scuol, Lavin, Zuoz and S-chanf.

WHEN TO GO

Jun–Oct

The hiking season in the Swiss National Park is roughly from mid-June to mid-October. Many trails close in winter to give wildlife all-important breathing space.

AMAZING CROWD-FREE EXPERIENCES

 Hike to the Lakes of Macun, a high-Alpine plateau with 23 lakes of sapphire, azure and turquoise blue. This 21km (12 mile) trek from Zernez is challenging but unforgettable.

 Clamber up the summit of Munt La Schera, heading through one-of-a-kind steppe landscapes, for views into the snow-dusted peaks of Italy's Stelvio National Park.

 Go off piste in the thrillingly remote Val Mingèr. Look out for chamois, red deer and weirdly eroded rock formations on the 5.5km (3.5 mile) hike to Sur il Foss.

 Spot wildlife in the Val Cluozza. Marmots, chamois, deer, golden eagles and ibex can be seen in the gloriously unspoilt valley, reached via an 8km uphill ramble through larch and pinewoods from Zernez.

 Dive into the park at Val Trupchun. A flat, gentle family-friendly hike leads from S-chanf to this sublime mountain valley. The stag rutting is spectacular in autumn.

 Hunt for fossilised coral and dinosaur tracks on the 15.5km (9 mile) trek over the Murter saddle (2547m/8356ft) to Spöltal.

Left: Crags atop
Ragleth Hill

Shropshire Hills

OVERLOOKED UPLANDS OF FASCINATING ROCKS AND QUIET WALKING POTENTIAL

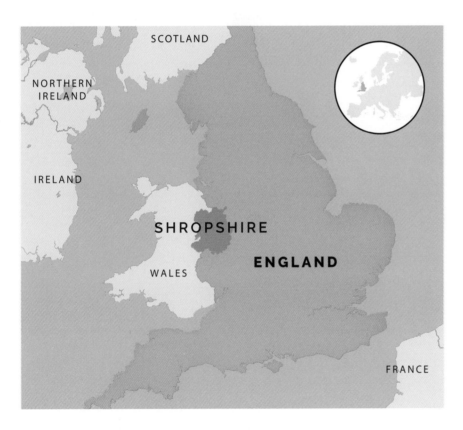

The most famous line penned about Shropshire is by poet AE Housman, who writes of its 'blue remembered hills'. Funny, then, that this landlocked Midlands county feels long forgotten. Despite being the birthplace of industry – coke-smelting and iron-founding in the 18th century – rural Shropshire remains largely unscarred. Its rolling downs, medieval towns and pastoral sensibilities hark back to a simpler age.

Nowhere is this more true than in its southwestern quarter, designated as the Shropshire Hills Area of Outstanding Natural Beauty (AONB). Stretching from the Welsh border towards the town of Telford, the AONB encompasses a wealth of upland icons and unusually complex geology, including the Long Mynd plateau, the quartzite Stiperstones ridge, the limestone escarpment of Wenlock Edge, the lofty Clee Hills (including county high-point 540m Brown Clee) and the Wrekin, a distinctive summit comprising eight different types of rock. It's excellent hiking country. But, although the footpaths are there and the beauty guaranteed, many people simply race through the region without stopping, on their way elsewhere.

GO IF YOU LIKE...

- ♥ *Wales*
- ♥ *Yorkshire Moors*
- ♥ *Yorkshire Dales*
- ♥ *castles*
- ♥ *hiking*
- ♥ *geology*

Why go to the Shropshire Hills?

The Victorians dubbed this area Little Switzerland. The craggy Stiperstones are a bit Dartmoor. There are parts that look like the Yorkshire Moors and Dales. But ultimately Shropshire has its own identity, encompassing gorgeous countryside, varied walking and good eating – medieval Ludlow, just south of the AONB, was the UK's first Cittaslow, a 'slow town' focused on promoting local produce.

As this is Welsh Borders country, there are also castles and defences aplenty, from handsome Stokesay, the best-preserved fortified medieval manor in England, to the dramatic ruins of 13th-century Clun Castle. The Shropshire Hills is also a living landscape. New initiatives such as the National Trust-led Stepping Stones Project and the government's Farming in Protected Landscapes are aiming to conserve the AONB by connecting wildlife habitats and helping farmers and communities work in ways that benefit nature. Visitors are also encouraged to respect the environment, to ensure it remains 'outstanding' for years to come.

GETTING THERE

The AONB's main town is Church Stretton, which is connect by train to Shrewsbury (15min north) and Ludlow (15min south). Shrewsbury is served by direct trains from cities such as Birmingham (1hr), Manchester (1hr 10min) and Cardiff (2hr). The nearest airport is Birmingham (1hr 20min drive).

WHEN TO GO

Apr–Jun & Sep–Oct

Shropshire is never overcrowded and hiking is possible year-round, but the spring and autumn months offer mild temperatures and even quieter trails.

© EDDIECLOUD | SHUTTERSTOCK. © JOHN EVESON / ALAMY STOCK PHOTO. © NEIL MCALLISTER / ALAMY STOCK PHOTO

FIRST-TIME TIPS

Visit the Shropshire Hills Discovery Centre in Craven Arms – pick up maps, books and advice before exploring further afield, and visit its award-winning cafe.

Make use of the summer shuttle buses. Operating at weekends from early July to late September, buses run between Church Stretton and Stiperstones via the Long Mynd.

Plan your lunch – this is a rural area; if you're out walking, you may not find an open pub or shop en route, so be prepared.

Don't sweat the pronunciation – even residents remain divided on the correct way to say the county town's name: Shroosbury or Shrowsbury?

AMAZING CROWD-FREE EXPERIENCES

 Hike the southern loop of the 290km (180 mile) Shropshire Way, meandering around the Area of Outstanding Natural Beauty; follow the orange buzzard waymarks.

 Trot along the Blue Remembered Hills Bridleway by horse. This 61km (38 mile) circular travels around Clun via Bury Ditches hill fort, the River Teme and Offa's Dyke.

 Descend into well-preserved Snailbeach mine, which closed in 1955 but is now open to visitors. The surface buildings are free to roam, or book a tour into the tunnels.

 Lose the crowds on the Long Mynd plateau — the 16km (10 mile) Ratlinghope Ramble takes in the quieter, western side.

 Raise a glass in Bishop's Castle, a sleepy little market town that's home to two breweries, including the Three Tuns (established 1642) – the oldest working brewery in Britain.

 Climb the Ercall, part of the Wrekin reserve – this small hill is less-visited but no less fascinating, with exposed rocks dating from the beginnings of life on earth.

Clockwise from top left: Rainbow streets in Bishop's Castle; the town's Three Tuns brewery; hike the Long Mynd via the 16km (10 mile) Ratlinghope Ramble

The Torridon Hills

THE STUFF OF DREAMS FOR MUNRO-BAGGERS AND MIDDLE-OF-NOWHERE LOVERS

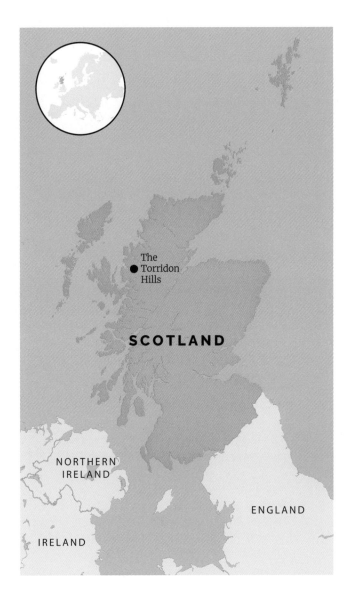

The Torridon Hills

SCOTLAND

NORTHERN
IRELAND

ENGLAND

IRELAND

No one is calling the 500-mile North Coast 500 road undiscovered – but it sure still seems quiet compared with Scotland's Southern Highlands. And the Torridon region, centred on the charming loch-side Torridon village, is far enough off the tourist loop to draw only a select band of travellers. You only really wind up here if you have a deep-seated passion for the outdoors — not in a climb-Ben-Nevis-for-the-bragging-rights kind of way, but more because of a long-term infatuation with mountains (or munros, as they're known in these parts) at their most aesthetic, where raw coastlines and wild serrated headlands shelve into silent inlets.

Torridon village, with its whitewashed cottages mirrored in the bruise-coloured waters of Upper Loch Torridon, is only the beginning of the adventure. Beyond are the Torridon Hills, looming close enough that it feels they're threatening to shunt the place into the sea. This is where hill walkers, climbers, wildlife-watchers and middle-of-nowhere-lovers start to believe they have passed into paradise. The beauty is that it's all very real.

GO IF YOU LIKE...

- 💚 *Scottish Highlands*
- 💚 *cute coastal villages*
- 💚 *magical middle-of-nowhere restaurants*
- 💚 *wildlife-watching*
- 💚 *wilderness hiking*
- 💚 *Munro-bagging*

Why go to the Torridon Hills?

The Torridon Hills possess special qualities that make many of Scotland's outdoor adventurers wax lyrical about them, over and above all other mountains. Comprised of some of Britain's oldest sandstone, a sort so spectacularly showcased throughout this range that it is known as Torridonian Sandstone, the rock here has ruptured into particularly postcard-perfect peaks. Crested with dramatically broken pinnacles and riven by deep gullies that give their sides the look of piped icing, they are some of Scotland's most handsome summits.

There are three Munros (Scottish summits over 914m/3000ft) for the Munro-baggers. Mountaineers can tackle glorious climbs, such as the tantalising triple buttress of Beinn Eighe's Coire Mhic Fhearchair. Hikers have myriad mountain and coastal traverses, with ancient woods and lonely glens in between. And hunkering beneath all this is Torridon village, so unassumingly lovely that you could end up prolonging your stay to enjoy its cute coastal restaurants, seaweedy shores, deer, waterbirds and sea otters.

GETTING THERE

From Glasgow, home to Scotland's main international airport, Torridon lies roughly 350km (217 miles) north, which is a 4.5hr to 6hr drive, depending on if you go the pretty way via Inverness or the absolutely stunning way via Fort William. The nearest train station to Torridon is Achnasheen, 5hr from Glasgow and 32km (20 miles) from Torridon; buses run from the station to the village.

WHEN TO GO

Apr–Sep

The driest part of the year in a notoriously soggy part of the world is peak time to hit Torridon and hike up its mountains. Outside this period, many facilities close.

FIRST-TIME TIPS

Take care on the area's <u>single-track roads</u>. Use passing places to let oncoming traffic or faster vehicles behind you pass by.

....

Treat the mountains with respect: these are among Scotland's wildest uplands. Notify your accommodation where you intend to explore and <u>bring everything you need with you</u> (full tank of petrol, full kit for whatever outdoor activity you are up here for) – otherwise it's a 1.5-hour trip into Inverness for supplies.

....

<u>Accommodation in Torridon is limited</u>: book ahead.

....

Those here for a multiday outdoors adventure can shelter in <u>wilderness refuges</u> called bothies if necessary.

AMAZING CROWD-FREE EXPERIENCES

 Cosy up for a pre- or post-hike bite of fabled carrot cake at the Torridon Café, huddling right under the peaks or eat at the Torridon Hotel, a turreted Victorian mansion with a roaring log fire and loch views.

 Climb Beinn Alligin, one of Scotland's most beautiful mountains, offering humbling views of the Torridon Range and the loch-bedaubed wilderness below.

 Try hardcore rock-climbing in Beinn Eighe's westernmost flanks, at the triple buttress of Coire Mhic Fhearchair.

 Explore the rarely traipsed coastline of Loch Torridon on coast paths between Inveralligin and Red Point.

 Have a wildlife-watching field day, spotting sea otters and pine martens by Loch Torridon, roe deer in the woods and red deer and golden eagles in the mountains.

 Scale the mountain road to Lower Diabaig for an unforgettable meal at Gille Brighde among a smattering of whitewashed seaside cottages, where local seafood is crafted into flavour-packed dishes.

Above: Hiker on the ridge of Beinn Alligin, a Torridon highlight and one of Scotland's most beautiful peaks

Taranaki Maunga's (Mt Taranaki) cone, framed by Egmont National Park in New Zealand's North Island

Oceania

Palm Island

AN ABORIGINAL ENCLAVE SEEING THE FIRST GREEN SHOOTS OF TOURISM

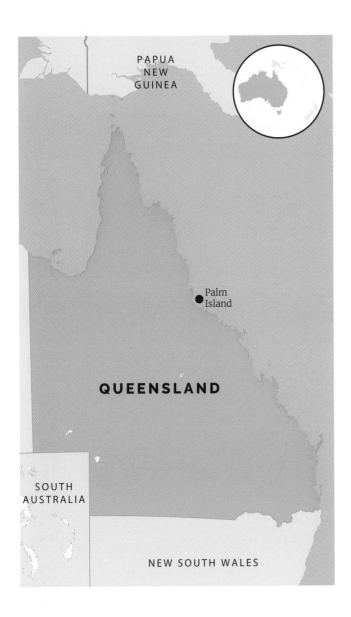

Palm Island isn't your typical Great Barrier Reef hideaway. There are no luxe resorts and no hip restaurants or bars. The traditional home of the Manbarra Aboriginal people, this rainforest-covered hunk of granite – the largest of 16 isles in the Greater Palm group north of Townsville – is better known for its troubled past than its tourism potential.

Between 1918 and 1975, Palm Island was Queensland's largest and most punitive Aboriginal Reserve, where Aboriginal and Torres Strait Islander people from across northeastern Australia were confined, forced to work for little or no pay and forbidden from speaking their own languages. Social problems have lingered on the island also known as Bwgcolman, which means 'many tribes – one people', yet visitors who make the effort to come here will find that Palm Island is as friendly as it is beautiful, with gorgeous bays to swim and snorkel in, small rainforest-clad mountains to climb, and a unique opportunity to connect with Indigenous Australian culture and understand its complex history.

GO IF YOU LIKE...

- 💜 *the Great Barrier Reef*
- 💜 *Aboriginal & Torres Strait culture*
- 💜 *emerging destinations*
- 💜 *snorkelling & scuba diving*
- 💜 *tropical islands*
- 💜 *rainforest hiking*

Why go to Palm Island?

Palm Island is often described as the island that tourism forgot. Or was, until it was earmarked for an instalment of the Museum of Underwater Art (MOUA) in 2022. Designed to inspire ocean conservation, the series of spectacular underwater sculptures dotted around the Townsville region invites snorkellers and divers to experience the Great Barrier Marine Park – which Palm Island forms part of – in a whole new way. A local Indigenous guides training programme launched in 2021 also means that you might be lucky enough to explore MOUA (and other local sights) with a knowledgeable Traditional Custodian of this rustic escape.

Day trips from Townsville with SeaLink ferries launched in 2022, and there's talk of a dive centre opening on the island. With few other tourism facilities on Palm Island beyond a council-run hotel and a seaside pub, it's not a place you come for a resort-style holiday. But that's all part of its charm.

GETTING THERE

The easiest way to get to Palm Island is by ferry from Townsville, which runs Wednesday to Monday (1hr 45min). There are also regular scheduled small-plane flights from Townsville to Palm Island with Hinterland Aviation (20min), which also offers charter flights.

WHEN TO GO

May–Sep

The days are warm and the weather is (relatively) dry on Palm Island during the winter months.

FIRST-TIME TIPS

Before you visit, check in with the local council. It can connect you with local guides and <u>advise on sacred sites</u> and events with restricted access.

* * *

Reading up on Palm Island's difficult history provides valuable <u>insights into local culture.</u> Tracking down a copy of Palm Island: Through a Long Lens, *by Dr Joanne Watson (2010) is a great place to start.*

* * *

If you're planning to do some hiking, <u>bring snacks</u> as there's nowhere to buy food beyond the town centre.

* * *

No glass bottles can be carried onto the ferry, and any <u>alcohol brought to the island</u> must have an abv of less than 4%.

AMAZING CROWD-FREE EXPERIENCES

 Explore Palm Island's instalment of MOUA, ideally with an Indigenous guide if the option is available.

 Hire a local Indigenous guide to take you to remote beaches and snorkelling spots, or to take you to cultural sites in the most respectful way.

 Take a stroll south of the jetty to the lookout at Casement Bay. It's a 30-minute walk, and another 30 minutes if you'd like to carry on to secluded Pencil Bay.

 Summit Mt Bentley (548m/1798ft) for fantastic views across the Palm Island group, and Hinchinbrook Island beyond. From the jetty, it takes two to three hours to hike along the road (which becomes a track) to get to the top. It's a great sunset spot.

 Enjoy a freshwater swim in the small waterfall at the end of Palm Valley Rd.

 Take in a Palm Island sunset with a cold drink in-hand at the Coolgaree Bay Sports Bar & Bistro, the island's only pub.

Above: Once a punitive Aboriginal Reserve, Palm Island and its residents are now looking to a brighter future

Vicki Saylor
*Manbarra
Traditional Owner
& cultural adviser*

WHY I LOVE
PALM ISLAND

You immediately feel your body relax when you arrive on Palm Island. It's a beautiful place, but it's the culture that I really love, and want to know more about. There is always something new to learn.

Must-have local experience?
Start your visit at the Bwgcolman Indigenous Knowledge Centre, where you can learn about local history and culture before you head out and explore the island.

Favourite season?
In July and August, you can often spot migrating humpback whales on the boat trip from Townsville. We also have lots of cultural celebrations in July's NAIDOC Week (naidoc.org.au).

Cobourg Peninsula

ONLY INTREPID ADVENTURERS NEED APPLY FOR ACCESS TO THIS WILD LAND

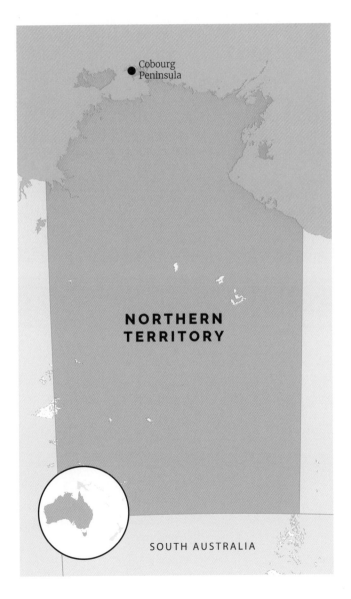

Dangling off the northwestern tip of Arnhem Land, the Cobourg Peninsula brings new meaning to the term 'wild place'. Protected by 4500 sq km (1737 sq miles) Garig Gunak Barlu National Park, the peninsula is a spectacular mosaic of sandy beaches lapped by sparkling water and fringed by burnt-orange bauxite cliffs and open eucalyptus woodland. While birdwatchers may be aware that the park encompasses the world's first Ramsar Wetland of International Importance, and anglers may know that some of the nation's best fishing can be enjoyed here, even most Aussies won't have heard of this corner of Australia, which is also home to the eerie ruins of the Victoria Settlement, one of two failed British settlements on the peninsula.

With a permit required to enter the region, which has few facilities beyond a basic national park campsite, a Cobourg trip requires a high degree of planning, which helps to explain why only a handful of travellers make the effort each year. But this has all helped to preserve its wild, rugged beauty.

GO IF YOU LIKE...

💙 *off-grid adventure*
💙 *saltwater crocodiles*
💙 *fishing*
💙 *birdwatching*
💙 *wild coastal landscapes*
💙 *roughing it*

Why go to the Cobourg Peninsula?

In an era where wild, crowd-free places have never been more desirable, the Cobourg delivers. While there's only one public campground, it's rare you'll share it with more than a few other carloads of travellers. The national park ranger stationed at Black Point could possibly be the only person you meet.

Many visitors to the Cobourg bring a boat. But you can also book fishing and Victoria Settlement tours with Venture North Safaris (venturenorth.com.au), which operates from Algarlarlgarl (Black Point). Visitors keen to get a more comfortable taste of the Cobourg can also sign up for a guided 4- or 5-day 4WD adventure from Darwin with Venture North Safaris, which has an atmospheric private coastal camp with glamping tents. With only six guests per tour, it's an intimate experience that also takes in Kakadu National Park and includes an Aboriginal-guided tour of Injalak Hill, one of Australia's richest rock art sites.

GETTING THERE
The Coburg Peninsula is approximately 500km (310 miles) northeast of Darwin, with a 4WD required to navigate the mostly unsealed roads. The last place to buy fuel and other provisions is in Jabiru, around 270km (168km) south of the peninsula. Charter flights land at the small airstrip at Algarlarlgarl (Black Point).

WHEN TO GO

May–Oct

Roads are typically open during the entire dry season, but check with Northern Territory Parks and Wildlife (nt.gov.au) before setting out.

FIRST-TIME TIPS

Apply for *a permit to visit the region* via the Northern Territory Parks and Wildlife office six weeks in advance.

....

Visitors must be self-sufficient. Bring all food, water, fuel, first-aid kit, tool kit and spare tyres.

....

Swimming is off-limits. There are saltwater crocodiles on the beaches and sharks, box jellyfish, blue-ringed octopus, stonefish and sea snakes in the waters.

....

Study the state's *Be Crocwise guidelines* (becrocwise.nt.gov.au) before you go.

....

There's *no mobile reception* in the national park; you'll need a Telstra phone card for the public phone.

AMAZING CROWD-FREE EXPERIENCES

Explore the ruins of the 19th-century Victoria Settlement, one of two failed colonial settlements established on the peninsula, which is only accessible by boat.

Visit the Cultural Centre at Algarlarlgarl (Black Point) to see displays of Aboriginal, Macassan and European histories of the area, and spot birds on the 1.5km (1 mile) Wetland Walk.

Set up camp at Smith Point, where you'll probably spot more saltwater crocs than you will people.

Gaze across the Arafura Sea from Smith Point Beacon, built on the peninsula's northern tip in 1845 to assist navigation around the Orontes shoal.

Fish off wild beaches (or from a boat), use hand spears to catch mud crabs in seaside mangroves, and pry succulent oysters from the rocks.

Go for a night walk with a powerful torch to spot nocturnal wildlife including savannah gliders, agile wallabies, brush-tailed rabbit rats and more.

Clockwise from top left: Arnhem Land Aboriginal craft; the peninsula's birdlife is a big attraction; miles of sandy beach fringe Cobourg

Stewart Island/ Rakiura

KIWI BIRDS AND OUTDOOR EXPERIENCES DEFINE THIS END-OF-THE-WORLD ISLAND

Anchoring the country at a latitude of 47° S, New Zealand's often-overlooked 'third island' is a forested destination of primordial wilderness, featuring a verdant coastline of coves and bays, and native birdlife largely unencumbered by predators. The independent and resourceful human population numbers just 400. Sea birds patrol the ocean, boisterous kākā (native parrots) enliven the sole settlement of Oban and the island's bush trails and remote beaches offer the rare opportunity to see New Zealand's kiwi bird in the wild.

Rakiura National Park encompasses around 85% of Stewart Island/Rakiura, and the Rakiura Track, one of New Zealand's Great Walks, provides a 39km (24 miles) two- to three-day walking adventure through some of the island's untouched landscapes. Equally spectacular are celestial displays of the Southern Lights (Aurora Australis), occasionally brightening long winter nights. These dancing illuminations give Stewart Island its traditional Māori name: Rakiura (Glowing Skies).

GO IF YOU LIKE...

🩶 *remote islands*
🩶 *unique birdlife*
🩶 *dark-sky experiences*
🩶 *hiking*
🩶 *fishing and kayaking*
🩶 *low-impact travel*

Why go to Stewart Island/Rakiura?

The island's pin-up is the endemic and endangered tokoeka kiwi, which can often be seen snuffling along remote stretches of Rakiura's coastline, and are sometimes sighted crossing forested trails on the Rakiura Track. Hiring a local guide is one of the best ways to explore Stewart Island's fauna and the nearby bird sanctuary of Ulva Island/Te Wharawhara.

Across on Ulva Island, a diverse avian chorus is underpinned by the rare tieke (South Island saddleback). Snorkelling in the Ulva Island-Te Wharawhara Marine Reserve is another highlight, and kayaking and fishing are other ways to experience the island's cool, clear waters. Minimal ambient light and light-pollution-free skies cleansed by southern breezes have also made Stewart Island a destination for stargazers. In 2019, it was designated the world's southernmost International Dark Sky Sanctuary. Stewart Island's newest attraction is the rehoused Rakiura Museum/Te Puka o Te Waka, which opened in December 2020 in a swanky facility with exhibitions exploring the fascinating natural and cultural history of the island.

GETTING THERE

Departing from Bluff on the southern tip of New Zealand's South Island, ferries cross the occasionally rough waters of Foveaux Strait to Stewart Island (1hr). There are also short 15-minute flights from Invercargill airport, 28km (17 miles) north of Bluff, and Invercargill is linked by domestic flights to New Zealand's main regional cities of Auckland, Wellington and Christchurch.

WHEN TO GO

Dec–Mar

Stewart Island's changeable weather means visitors can experience all four seasons year-round, but the best chance for settled weather is during New Zealand's summer (Dec-Feb). Prime Aurora Australis viewing season is April to September.

FIRST-TIME TIPS

Campsites and huts on the Rakiura Track must be booked ahead online with New Zealand's Department of Conservation (doc.govt.nz)

....

Free shuttle bus transfers are provided from Invercargill to the Bluff ferry terminal for ferry passengers

....

Stock up on camping supplies at Invercargill supermarkets and outdoor shops before travelling to the island.

....

Schedule your visit so you can attend Sunday night's pub quiz at the South Seas Hotel. Even Prince Harry took part when he was on Stewart Island.

AMAZING CROWD-FREE EXPERIENCES

 Negotiate subtropical rainforest and coastal coves on the Rakiura Track, or take on the more challenging North West Circuit trail – both island highlights.

 Stargaze after dark and admire the shimmering spectacle of the Aurora Australis amid Stewart Island's International Dark Sky Sanctuary, on a tour with Ruggedy Range (ruggedyrange.com).

 Take an easygoing birdwatching stroll around Ulva Island wildlife sanctuary, home to forested and meandering trails.

 Take an overnight adventure to see kiwi and other endemic birds in the verdant Freshwater Valley and on the isolated beaches of remote Mason Bay.

 Depart from the sheltered waters of Paterson Inlet for fishing and kayaking adventures around Stewart Island's serrated coastline of bays and coves.

 Set out on spectacular short walks, including day hikes to Port William or Māori Beach, before returning to cosy beds around Oban and Half Moon Bay.

Clockwise from top left: The main town of Oban; beautiful beaches encircle the island; the Rakiura Track; an endangered kākā parrot

Furhana Ahmad
Owner & nature guide, Ruggedy Range Wilderness Experience

WHY I LOVE STEWART ISLAND/RAKIURA

I'm in awe of the islands' natural beauty and the daily thrill of seeing native birds and surprising marine life.

Must-have local experience?
Predator-free Ulva Island is simply beautiful, with a primeval forest of towering trees, ferns and mosses, lovely beaches, and native and endangered birds that can be observed close-up.

Favourite season?
Land birds can be seen year-round, but around February some species are moulting and may be hidden. Seabirds are best seen from January to September, while orchids and native flowers bloom from October to March. My favourite time to hike is definitely during the longer days of summer.

Taranaki

SUBALPINE HIKING TO RIVAL TONGARIRO, BUT WITH ADDED CULTURE BENEFITS

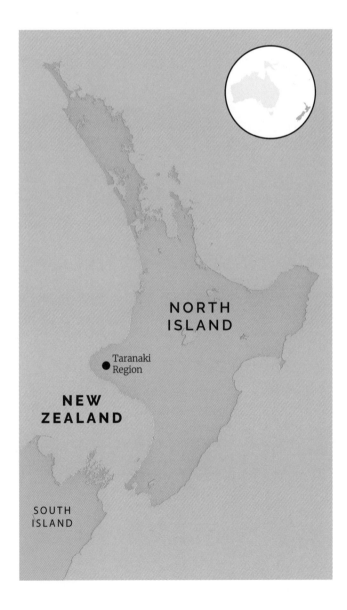

NORTH
ISLAND

● Taranaki
Region

NEW
ZEALAND

SOUTH
ISLAND

Usually overlooked by travellers heading south through Tongariro National Park, the Taranaki region combines verdant dairy farming country, rugged and exciting surf beaches, and the soaring conical profile of Taranaki Maunga (Mt Taranaki). Framed by Egmont National Park, the mountain is a consistent and comforting presence on the near horizon for visitors to the area, and is also the location for a challenging summit hike and the exciting Pouakai Crossing, the latter gaining a reputation as one of the world's best one-day outdoor adventures to rival Tongariro.

Taranaki's vibrant urban hub is New Plymouth, emerging as a gourmet hotspot with excellent cafes and restaurants. Here you'll find a new breed of chefs, brewers and distillers all inspired by Taranaki's edge-of-the-map isolation. Equally innovative is the Taranaki culture scene, with the groundbreaking architecture and contemporary art of New Plymouth's Govett-Brewster Art Gallery/Len Lye Centre and the eclectic annual WOMAD Festival of world music.

GO IF YOU LIKE...

- 💜 *Tongariro Crossing*
- 💜 *climbing Mt Fuji*
- 💜 *driving California's Hwy 1*
- 💜 *contemporary art*
- 💜 *grassroots food scenes*
- 💜 *alternative music festivals*

Why go to Taranaki?

The Taranaki region is fast developing a reputation for quality cuisine, and main city New Plymouth is no longer in the culinary shadow of bigger NZ siblings such as Christchurch and Auckland. New Plymouth's West End Precinct is paricularly exciting. Standout addresses here include the Social Kitchen, Monica's Eatery and Ms White. Nearby, the Shining Peak Brewery and Three Sisters Brewery both serve up excellent craft beers. Fenton St Gin at Stratford's Fenton Street Arts Collective and the Little Liberty Creamery in Inglewood, serving plant-based ice cream, are two other regional artisan producers reinforcing Taranaki's culinary revolution.

After the flavour-packed hedonism of New Plymouth, embark on a leisurely road trip around Taranaki's SH45 – the renowned 'Surf Highway' detours through coastal hamlets and down unsealed rural roads to rugged surf beaches and an historic lighthouse. Then strap on your hiking boots for the Pouakai Crossing, the longer two-day Pouakai Circuit or the considerable challenge of ascending the summit of the region's beloved mountain.

GETTING THERE

On the central west coast of New Zealand's North Island, Taranaki's regional hub of New Plymouth is around a 5hr drive south of Auckland. Including a transfer in Hamilton, InterCity buses make the journey in around 7hr. Air New Zealand has direct flights from Auckland, Wellington and Christchurch.

WHEN TO GO

Dec–Mar

The best time to hike in Egmont National Park is during New Zealand's summer, from December to March. Note that Taranaki Maunga's altitude means weather can be changeable year-round, so warm clothing and rainwear is essential, even in summer.

FIRST-TIME TIPS

When hiking the two-day Pouakai Circuit, overnight accommodation at the Pouakai Hut must be booked in advance online with New Zealand's Department of Conservation (doc.govt.nz).

If you're travelling with your own vehicle, a convenient option for the Pouakai Crossing is to leave it at the trail-end car park and book a one-way shuttle from there to the track's start point.

Plan ahead for WOMAD Festival (womad.co.nz); tickets and your New Plymouth accommodation need to be booked in advance.

AMAZING CROWD-FREE EXPERIENCES

 Hike the one-day adventure of the Pouakai Crossing with its combination of waterfalls, cliffs and mountain reflections in the region's alpine tarns.

 Ascend the classically symmetrical volcanic summit of Taranaki Maunga for well-earned views of the coastal and rural landscapes framing Egmont National Park.

 Road-trip along Taranaki's SH45 – New Zealand's 'Surf Highway' – detouring to Tasman Sea beaches, Cape Egmont Lighthouse and sleepy coastal settlements.

 Visit New Plymouth's Govett-Brewster Art Gallery/Len Lye Centre for a world-class collection of contemporary art focused on NZ-born kinetic artist, the late Len Lye.

 Walk or bike New Plymouth's 12.7km (8 mile) Coastal Walkway, with city beaches and Len Lye's *Wind Wand* installation, ending at skeletal-looking Te Rewa Rewa Bridge.

 Negotiate short walks on Taranaki Maunga's eastern slopes including the moss-cloaked rainforest trail of the Kamahi Loop Track.

Above: Fitzroy Beach in Taranaki's vibrant urban hub, New Plymouth

Papua New Guinea

BARRIERS TO TRAVEL KEEP THIS ASTONISHING COUNTRY OFF THE TOURIST TRAIL

INDONESIA

PAPUA NEW GUINEA

SOLOMON ISLANDS

AUSTRALIA

A land of sheer mist-covered peaks, wild rivers and vast swaths of rainforest untouched by modern civilisation, Papua New Guinea is one of the world's great biological frontiers. Travelling here guarantees unforgettable experiences, from watching the magnificent displays of birds of paradise to feeling the first rays of dawn atop a 4000m (13,123ft) summit deep in the jungle. The diving is world-class, with WWII wrecks and colourful reefs, and as with terrestrial adventures, crowds are nonexistent. The nation's indigenous heritage encompasses astonishingly diverse cultures. Highland festivals are big sources of local pride, with singing and dancing, elaborate feather headdresses and face and body painting. Papua New Guinea's flourishing tribal art traditions date back centuries.

Despite its extraordinary treasures, Papua New Guinea receives barely 200,000 visitors a year. The country's remoteness, lack of infrastructure and the high cost of travel keep many people away. Concern about safety also deters visitors, but with sensible precautions the chance of running into trouble is small.

GO IF YOU LIKE...

- 💚 *the Great Barrier Reef*
- 💚 *birdwatching*
- 💚 *rainforests*
- 💚 *craft markets*
- 💚 *islands*
- 💚 *trekking*

Why go to Papua New Guinea?

If you've ever wondered whether tourism can be a force for good in the world, then now is the time to go to Papua New Guinea. Travelling sustainably here can help support struggling guesthouse owners, specialist guides, artisans and countless others whose livelihoods depend on foreign visitors. PNG embraces eco-tourism. Local guides can help you experience the country's wildlife wonders, arrange for visits to remote communities and share cultural insights about this vastly complicated and oft-misunderstood place.

Travel here is difficult: small planes access some places, but in many other areas the only way of getting around is by foot or motorised canoe. With slow travel becoming more popular, Papua New Guinea should rise up adventurous travellers' bucketlists, as journeying at a snail's pace is practically obligatory in this nation of mountain-covered wilderness. It's also the best way to get beneath the surface, catching local festivals, visiting markets and seeing other authentic facets of this land of over 800 languages.

Right: Marine diversity is huge in PNG, but the rainforest-fringed beaches see few visitors

Below, clockwise from left: Landing in the highlands; Swathed in forest, the Highlands region hosts many local festivals; diving at Milne Bay

© CHRIS TAYLOR | 500PX

FIRST-TIME TIPS

Visas are required, though these are available upon arrival for many nationalities (including the USA, UK, EU, Australia and New Zealand). Make sure your passport is valid for at least six months after you land.

Take sensible precautions to _minimise the risk of robbery_. Wear unremarkable clothes and keep pricey electronics hidden. Carry a small amount of local currency, aka 'raskol money', in your pocket to appease any would-be thief and hide other cash in a money belt or your shoe.

When arranging tours, the _phone is the best first point of contact_; responses on email or via websites can be very slow.

GETTING THERE

All international flights come through Port Moresby, PNG's capital city on the south coast. From there, you'll have to catch a plane onwards, unless travelling in the region surrounding the capital, which includes Owers Corner, the start of the Kokoda Trek. Many PNG flights originate in Australia (Cairns, Brisbane), making PNG a good add-on to an Australia trip.

WHEN TO GO

Jun–Sep

The dry season has cooler temperatures and fewer showers, making for excellent trekking, wildlife watching and other outdoor adventures. Some big-name festivals happen at this time, including the magnificent Goroka Show.

AMAZING CROWD-FREE EXPERIENCES

 Look for birds of paradise in the Tari Basin, a world-renowned spot for seeing avian wildlife. Several eco-friendly lodges put you close to the action.

 Walk the Kokoda Track, a challenging six-day journey up mountains and across rushing rivers that passes WWII battlefields.

 Explore the palm-fringed beaches and volcanic islands of Milne Bay. From the gateway town of Alotau, you can head off on adventures to see wildlife, pristine waterfalls and mountains.

 Take a boat tour along the Sepik River, visiting carved _haus tambarans_ (spirit houses), learning about traditional customs and overnighting in waterfront stilt villages.

 Make the ascent up Mt Wilhelm, Papua New Guinea's highest peak at 4509m (14,793ft). On clear days you can see both coasts from the summit.

 Dive over sunken ships and colourful coral reefs in the Coral Triangle, an epicentre of marine biodiversity on this planet.

And there's more...

25 OTHER OFFBEAT DESTINATIONS TO PUT ON YOUR RADAR

Malawi

This lakeside nation's national parks and wildlife reserves, resurrected by trailblazing NGO African Parks, are an uplifting conservation story. The laid-back beach towns, mountaintop former mission stations and biodiverse Lake Malawi add further dimensions to 'the warm heart of Africa'. From diving among tropical fish to hiking through mountainside tea plantations, Malawi offers a diverse range of experiences in an area smaller than most American states.

Odense, Denmark

Despite being the birthplace of Hans Christian Andersen, Odense gets very little international recognition compared with Copenhagen, just 1hr east by fast train. But the 2021 opening of Odense's striking HC Andersen Hus museum could change that. And there's lots more besides fairytales: Odense's historic harbour has been revamped with a free swimming pool and the Storms Pakhus food market; and the island of Funen beyond — Denmark's green heart — is home to castles, pretty villages and foraging beaches.

Gujarat, India

Neighbouring Rajasthan and Mumbai often steal the limelight, yet Gujarat has much to offer. Marvel over the remarkable, centuries-old temples and mosques of the capital, Ahmedabad; wander the labyrinthine streets of Diu, a former Portuguese enclave; or join pilgrims at the extraordinary hilltop sites of Shatrunjaya and Junagadh. Further out, there are tribal villages to explore, intricate textiles in Kachchh and the salt plains of Little Rann, where wild asses, hyenas and wolves roam.

Mungo National Park, Australia

Nearly 1000km (621 miles) west of Sydney, spectacular Mungo is as remote as it is culturally significant. The world's oldest ritual burials were performed in this otherworldly corner of New South Wales 42,000 years ago. Along with 20,000-year-old human footprints, they tell the incredible story of the long history of Australia's first people. Excellent visitor facilities make Mungo feel surprisingly accessible, despite its location.

Tunis, Tunisia

This ancient North African city is by-passed by most tourists heading for Tunisia's beach resorts or to the more famous medinas of nearby Morocco. Yet Tunis has just as much atmosphere as Marrakesh: a medieval medina and maze of souks in the kasbah, and restaurants where you can feast on tajines while being serenaded by haunting Malouf music. The city's Bardo Museum also houses one of the world's largest mosaic collections, while the Roman ruins of Carthage lie around 20km (12 miles) away.

Gargano Peninsula, Italy

From the raffish port city of Bari, winding roads lead north to the serrated coastline of Gargano, an alternative to the hugely popular — and very pricey — Amalfi Coast. Boat trips from the whitewashed promontory towns of Vieste and Peschici explore sea caves and isolated beaches, while the nearby Foresta Umbra (Forest of Shadows) is popular for hiking and mountain-biking. There's even a hint of Capri in a day-trip to the offshore Isole Tremiti.

Cockpit Country, Jamaica

One of the few true wildernesses in the Caribbean, Cockpit Country is a crinkled web of hummocks, ravines and karst formations covered by jungle-like vegetation. You can undertake a 16km (10 mile) bushwhack across it on the Troy–Windsor Trail, visit bat-infested caves with spelunkers, or enjoy an authentic slice of Jamaican village life on its fringes. Not to be missed is Accompong, a historic Maroon colony founded by indigenous Taíno and free Black people.

Banda Islands, Indonesia

The polar opposite of Bali's tourist-focused excess, the Banda Islands in Indonesia's eastern Maluku province are fascinating. Though obscure now, they were disputed by all the great European seafaring powers centuries ago, when they were the only viable sources of nutmeg and cloves — spices on which fortunes could be made. Charming and secluded, they're now best known for snorkelling and scuba-diving, and accessible by ferry or small plane from Ambon.

South Luangwa National Park, Zambia

Kruger, Chobe, Etosha, the Serengeti – Africa's most famous national parks are also among the continent's most crowded. Known for its wildlife and unspoilt vegetation, 9050 sq km (3495 sq miles) South Luangwa NP is a fantastic alternative, with atmospheric campsites and stylish safari lodges alongside the majestic Luangwa River, brimming with burping hippos.

Uruguay

This small South American country is completely different to its two noisy neighbours, Argentina and Brazil. It's easy to get around, with welcoming locals, fabulous beaches and vineyards producing terrific wines. The capital Montevideo is safe and friendly, with fine art deco architecture and a 24km (15 mile) promenade along the ocean-like Río de la Plata delta. The steaks and tango are as good as in Buenos Aires and this progressive, LGBT-friendly nation has press freedom, legalised cannabis and renewable energy.

Abruzzo, Italy

Located in the centre of one of the world's most touristed countries, less than two hours from Rome, Abruzzo is strangely underappreciated by non-Italians. Welcome to a throwback Italy of wheezing Fiats, flat-capped farmers, semi-abandoned hilltop towns and lonely mountain trails once used as WWII escape routes. The region, which has more national parks than anywhere else in Italy, is home to one of Europe's most southerly glaciers and the rare Marsican bear.

Niue, South Pacific

As the world's first country designated a Dark Sky Place, the far-flung nation of Niue offers not only stellar stargazing, but also dazzling coral reefs, tropical rainforest trails, Niuean art and culture galore, and a deliciously slow pace. Reachable only via a 3hr flight from Auckland, this small South Pacific island receives just 11,000 visitors each year. And when you're out exploring its secluded coves, caves and pools, you'll feel like you are the first to discover them.

Bardia National Park, Nepal

In Nepal's remote northwest, Bardia is little-known compared with Chitwan National Park, which means fewer crowds to see its one-horned rhinos and elephants — and you're also more likely to spot an elusive Bengal tiger here. The sustainable Bardia Ecolodge (bardiaecolodge.com) is a real find too.

Baltimore, USA

A scant 64km (40 miles) up the road from Washington, DC, Baltimore feels a world away from the marble-filled corridors of power, with brick-lane dive bars, quirky galleries and hometown heroes like rebel filmmaker John Waters. 'Charm City' lives up to its moniker with authentic old-school spots —Faidley's has been serving up delectable crabcakes since the 1880s — while the American Visionary Art Museum features ingenious works created by outsider artists.

Virginia, USA

American schoolchildren well know the sights of Virginia, a place of colonial lore (Jamestown, Williamsburg), presidential estates (Mt Vernon, Monticello) and battlefields (Yorktown, Antietam). History aside, many surprises lurk in this southeastern state. Wild ponies thunder along the shores of Chincoteague Island, while cloggers pound the floorboards in the bluegrass-loving western valleys. And the Appalachian peaks make a memorable backdrop for hiking in Shenandoah National Park or scenic drives on the Blue Ridge Parkway.

Mid-Wales, UK

Sandwiched between the better-known mountains of Snowdonia and the Brecon Beacons, Mid-Wales is a big green gap in most people's geographical knowledge. It's cartographically empty, too: this area has mainland Britain's lowest population density and greatest unbroken wilderness outside the Scottish Highlands — its nickname is the 'Desert of Wales'. But if you truly love the outdoor life, come. These bulky, boggy hills, giant lakes and spruce forests offer adventures without another soul.

Vitoria-Gasteiz, Spain

Bilbao and San Sebastián may hog the spotlight, but the capital city of Spain's Basque Country is actually Vitoria-Gasteiz. Food plays no less of an important role here, with award-winning *pintxos* bars hidden along the town's narrow pedestrianised lanes. The city is also a green haven, ringed by the Anillo Verde — a series of interconnecting parks, ponds and marshes linked by cycling paths. Other surprises include the astonishing collection of building-size murals hidden in the old quarter.

Elk Island National Park, Canada

While Elk Island is one of Canada's smallest national parks, this Alberta bolthole has plenty of big animals. The hard-to-spot elk give the park its name, but the 1000-plus bison that roam the protected prairies are the bigger draw for visitors. Located 40km (25 miles) east of Edmonton, Alberta's capital, the park has played a major role in bringing back the once-endangered bison. Staff educate visitors about both the animals' habits and the park's conservation programmes.

Annecy, France

Nothing dials up the romance like a city of canals, but nothing dials it down like streets crammed shoulder-to-shoulder with tipsy soon-to-be-weds and day-trippers. In lieu of Amsterdam and Venice, try the cathedral city of Annecy, where charming lake-fed canals meander through 16th- and 17th-century streets that you haven't seen a thousand times on Instagram. It's a place to wander on foot, visiting historic churches, Haute-Savoie food markets and lakeshore beaches on Lac d'Annecy.

Sapporo, Japan

Sapporo is Japan's fifth-largest city and the largest in Hokkaidō, the country's northernmost major island. It's famous for ramen, its winter Snow Festival, and for easy access to mountains and hot springs. Yet, often overlooked as just a transit stop, Sapporo itself has much to offer. It has everything you could want of a Japanese city — vibrant nightlife and colourful nightscapes, as well as myriad dining and shopping options — and its compact grid layout means it's easy and quick to navigate.

Wat Phu, Laos

This 1000-year-old temple near Pakse was built by the same culture as Angkor. At one time, the Khmers even had an imperial road connecting the two sites. Though it lacks the scale of Angkor, its dramatic location above a bend in the Mekong and its relative obscurity, with access via a crumbling staircase cut into the hillside, make it special. Covered by strangler figs and gnarled roots, it's dedicated to Shiva and awash with carvings depicting mythological figures, legends and gods.

Route of Parks, Chile

Imagine a road trip encompassing 17 national parks, knitted together by a pioneering plan to give 60 local communities ownership over the biodiversity in their backyards. This is Ruta de los Parques de la Patagonia, conceived by legendary conservationist Kristine Tompkins. Covering 2735km (1700 miles) from Puerto Montt to Cape Horn, the term epic doesn't do justice to its itinerary of rainforests, fjords, wetlands and ice fields. It's Torres del Paine, but much else besides.

Dominica

Despite being a vision of gobsmacking primordial loveliness, Dominica consistently ranks as one of the least-visited islands in the Caribbean. Difficult flight connections don't help its plight. Nor do its black-sand beaches, which defy the Caribbean fly-and-flop image. What visitors get instead is a paradise that looks little changed since Christopher Columbus dropped anchor here in 1493 — one where steaming pools, secret waterfalls and excellent Waitukubuli Trail hikes rule.

Curonian Spit, Lithuania

According to legend, this pine-forested, sandy sliver of sand jutting out into the waters of the Baltic Sea was created by the sea giantess Neringa. Stretching from Lithuania towards Kaliningrad in Russia, it's Unesco-listed and nicknamed the 'Sahara of Lithuania' thanks to the Parnidis sand dune that towers above Nida village. Draws include cycling between picturesque villages with wood-carved weathervanes, dining on smoked fish and spotting elk and wild boar.

Corn Islands, Nicaragua

These two tiny drops of tranquility, 70km (43 miles) off Nicaragua's shores, are a far cry from the beach parties and dive-site gridlock found in other Central American islands. There are some fine places to stay and eat (try the local lobster), but nothing too ostentatious, so you can focus on the beaches, shoreline snorkelling, and diving with schooling hammerhead sharks.

Index

Offbeat
September 2022
Published by Lonely Planet Global Limited
CRN 554153
www.lonelyplanet.com
10 9 8 7 6 5 4 3 2 1

Printed in Malaysia
ISBN 978 18386 9430 2
© Lonely Planet 2022
© photographers as indicated 2022

General Manager, Publishing Piers Pickard
Associate Publisher Robin Barton
Commissioning Editor Lorna Parkes
Designer Daniel di Paolo
Editors Clifton Wilkinson, Polly Thomas
Print Production Nigel Longuet

Lonely Planet Global Limited
Digital Depot, Roe Lane (off Thomas St),
Digital Hub, Dublin 8,
D08 TCV4
Ireland

STAY IN TOUCH lonelyplanet.com/contact
Authors Anna Kaminski; Brendan Sainsbury; Brett Atkinson; Carolyn Heller; Christina Webb; Harmony Difo;
Helen Ranger; Hugh McNaughtan; Isabella Noble; James Bainbridge; Jen Ruiz; Jessica Lee; Joe Bindloss; John
Brunton; Karla Zimmerman; Kerry Walker; Lorna Parkes; Luke Waterson; Nora Rawn; Oliver Berry; Orla Thomas;
Rebecca Milner; Regis St Louis; Sarah Baxter; Sarah Reid; Simon Richmond; Stephen Lioy; Trent Holden.

Cover photograph of Patagonia by Jonathan Gregson